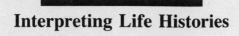

Interpreting Life Histories

Interpreting Life Histories

An Anthropological Inquiry

Lawrence C. Watson
Maria-Barbara Watson-Franke

Rutgers University Press

New Brunswick, New Jersey

Library of Congress Cataloging in Publication Data

Watson, Lawrence Craig, 1936–

Interpreting life histories.

Bibliography: p.

Includes index.

1. Ethnology—Biographical methods.

2. Personality and culture. I. Watson-Franke,

Maria-Barbara, 1938–   . II. Title.

GN346.6.W37   1985   920'.001'8   84–22332

ISBN 0–8135–1090–2

The dialectic of experience has its own fulfillment not in definitive knowledge, but in that openness to experience that is encouraged by experience itself.

Hans-Georg Gadamer,
Truth and Method

Contents

Preface

This essay is an attempt to question traditional interpretations of the life history and to offer an alternative approach that does justice to the individuality and subjectivity of lives in cultural context. It is not a detailed review of the literature or an exhaustive survey of historical developments in this field. We have drawn on hermeneutics, a philosophical discipline having to do with the theory of interpretation, as well as phenomenology and existentialism, in our search for a starting point to reexamine the life history.

We feel that an understanding of the "insider" (emic) viewpoint is particularly important in the analysis of the life history and a much needed corrective to such uncompromisingly "outsider" (etic) approaches as psychoanalytic theory and behaviorism, to mention only a few. We believe the individual is becoming lost in the present emphasis on models, experimentation, and quantification so prevalent in anthropology and the other social sciences. If we accomplish anything in this essay, we hope to restore some lost integrity and dignity to the individual in the face of the scientific onslaught that threatens to reduce him to an increasingly insignificant role in human affairs. As we see it, a return to the life history is really a return to the individual in the fullness of his social and unique humanness.

We wish to thank the following people for their contributions to this project: Molly Gardner, for helping us with some of the research; Kenji Ima, for his thoughtful comments on the manuscript; and Barbara Schloss, for generously typing the manuscript for us.

Chapter 3 is based on a revised, expanded version of Lawrence C. Watson's article "Understanding a Life History As a Subjective Document: Hermeneutical and Phenomenological Perspectives," originally copyrighted by the American Anthropological Association and published in Ethos 4(1)(1976):95–131.

All quotations from the German have been translated by the authors.

We must add a note on our use of language. Certain portions of the book address the individual explicitly and therefore create the danger of using sexist language, since the use of plurals would not be appropriate.

For stylistic reasons only and to enhance readability, we have in those instances chosen to use the pronoun "he." We would like to lessen the sexist impact of such language use by stating here that this pronoun usually refers to both female and male individuals.

Chapter 1
Life History Research in Anthropology

Although the life history has been used as a source of information about the human condition in social scientific research for more than sixty years, it has nearly always occupied a marginal role in comparison with such techniques as structured observation, interviewing, and testing procedures designed generally for experimentation and hypothesis testing. As an unwanted stepchild, the life history did not benefit from any consistent point of view defining its objectives in the larger context of the social sciences and in anthropology in particular. Moreover, there has been little agreement regarding a valid frame of reference for actually interpreting life history data as such. As a result, studies utilizing life history materials and other personal documents are difficult to appraise, for their objectives and methods have been almost as diverse as the personalities, interests, and motivations of the investigators themselves. More or less comprehensive summaries of the status of life history by such writers as Allport (1942), Kluckhohn (1945), Dollard (1949), Langness (1965), and Langness and Frank (1981) make clear that the potentialities of the life history are great in aiding our understanding of human behavior.[1] We agree that the potential is there, but sadly we find little in the way of clearly reasoned theory or methodology concerning the inherent attributes of personally recounted lives, namely, their individuality and subjectivity.

Until recently those who have collected life histories have not really studied the life history in any fundamental sense. Whatever such a document is potentially capable of telling us about an individual life or the texture of individual experience, the fact remains that the researcher has frequently collected and then utilized it merely as a supplementary source of data that enables him to pursue other interests, such as testing theories or implementing methodologies.

1. Two recent general surveys—one from a sociological perspective (Plummer 1983), the other a psychologically oriented study (Runyan 1982)—are available; both books do address humanistic concerns, along with methodological, historical, and theoretical issues.

The study of the life history, as customarily approached, paradoxically deflects attention away from the very object of its intrinsic concern: the human being himself. To compound the problem, where interest in the individual's narrative *is primary*, the life history has often not been interpreted at all, the investigator simply allowing it to "speak for itself" (see Lewis 1961). This is not enough. The life history requires additional interpretive elucidation. In this book we will propose an interpretive ground plan for a fuller understanding of life histories as unique subjective expressions, as articulated through the subject's culturally defined world. To this we will join an essential discussion of the implicative role of the interpreter's own larger and often unstated experience in the interpretive rendering of the other's life.

What Is the Life History?

The life history is one distinctive type of personal document. Personal documents as a generic category include any expressive production of the individual that can be used to throw light on his view of himself, his life situation, or the state of the world as he understands it, at some particular point in time or over the passage of time (see Allport 1942). The following productions are definable subspecies of personal documents: life histories, autobiographies, dream reports, diaries, letters, various kinds of test performance, and forms of artistic expression such as written fiction and painting.

What, then, is distinctive about the life history as a personal document? As we see it, the "life history" is any retrospective account by the individual of his life in whole or part, in written or oral form, *that has been elicited or prompted by another person*. The life history account may close at an earlier point of time or at the moment the subject is relating or writing it down. We use the term "autobiography," by contrast, to refer to a person's *self-initiated* retrospective account of his life, which is usually but not always in written form.

The life history is ordinarily written by the subject or recorded in a sequence of occasions or sessions, especially if it aims to be fairly detailed or complete. This recording occurs, as a rule, within a limited time span so that the individual reviews his life from a more or less consistent perspective. We must recognize, however, that during the time he is committing his life to record, a person may experience some change of outlook or character that makes him start reassessing his life in a way that was impossible when he started. Sometimes the very act of recalling one's life can bring unexpected insights that change the view of past experiences, particularly under the promptings of the one who does the eliciting. Since the subject is recalling his life for the benefit of another person, to a greater or lesser degree, changes in his relationship to that person will seriously affect what he says about himself. Indeed, because of the very intervention of the "other" in the elicitation of life histories, we must consider the issue of the constructive nature of the life history text itself within the encounter situation, involving the informant and his interlocutor.

Sometimes it is difficult to differentiate between the life history as authentic subjective report and the "biography," where the recorder tampers with and rearranges the material to such an extent that the result ends up being the recorder's report of the subject's life. What makes this problem so very insidious is that the recorder may completely rewrite the account in the first person without indicating that he has done so. In any event, because of the uncertain boundary lines, we will be considering personal documents that could be either life histories, autobiographies, or biographies, depending on how one applies the criteria of inclusion into these categories.

The life history obviously must be differentiated in a technical as well as existential sense from a diary, where events of the life are recorded daily from an immediate perspective that is constantly changing. Thus, in a diary the life of a boy is seen through a boy's eyes; the life of the man through the man's eyes. In the life history, by contrast, the whole life course is seen from the point of view of the person as he is currently trying to make sense of his relationship to past events, and he may not remember or choose to emphasize the things that were once important. Even a diary, however, can in its own way be retrospective if the subject in recording the events of the day refers back to earlier experiences, or reinterprets the past, after some delay in writing it down, in terms of what he is presently experiencing. Some published life histories, in fact, are an amalgamation of true retrospective recall and events set forth in diaries. Don Talayesva's autobiography in *Sun Chief* (Simmons 1942) is a good example.

Before approaching the main task of this essay, we will trace the historical and theoretical development of the life history in anthropology, to provide a context for our thesis. Though the three schematic phases given below cannot possibly encompass all life history work in anthropology, let alone in the social sciences, we hope the arrangement offers a general foundation for understanding the rest of the volume.

The Life History and the Study of Culture

Anthropologists, from the beginning of the discipline, collected personal histories from the individuals in the cultures they studied. Eliciting accounts of individual experiences to obtain information about general practices was in the very nature of ethnographic fieldwork. Individual accounts were checked against other individual accounts, synthesized, and supplemented by the fieldworker's own observations to form the basis of the ethnographic monograph. But, also from the beginning, the personal accounts themselves were lost in the monograph—summarized and dissected into the conventional cultural categories—often with no reference to the actual persons who contributed information.

Kroeber, in his introduction to a collection of fictionalized personal accounts, described the frustration of the ethnologist bound by the requirements of a formal scientific monograph. Monographs, he wrote, stick closely to the objective facts recorded. The mental workings of the people whose customs are described "are subjective, and therefore much more charily put into print" (Kroeber 1922:12–13).

Added to the anthropologist's reluctance to depart from the formal ethnographic framework was the perplexing problem of what to *do* with unaltered personal histories. To satisfy the need to go beyond the monograph, portions of life histories were published, but with no stated purpose other than to "illustrate" objective facts about a culture. Kroeber, for example, published personal accounts of the war experiences of three Plains Indians, "obtained for the picture they give" of the war-life described in his ethnography of the Gros Ventre (Kroeber 1908:197).

More subjective materials, dealing with the perceptions and feelings of informants, were relegated to fictionalized accounts, such as those compiled by Elsie Clews Parsons (1922) in her anthology, *American Indian Life*. Parsons invited anthropologists to create life histories of individuals, based on their field experiences. Sapir contributed to the collection the life story of Tom, a fictional Nootka trader. The two great forces in Nootka life, Sapir wrote, were privilege and the network of descent and kinship relations. He traced the evolution of Tom's understanding of these forces: "In such a house Tom early learned his exact relationship to all his kinsmen. He soon learned also the degree of his relationship to neighboring house groups" (Sapir 1922:307). Sapir, through Tom, made explicit many elements of the Nootka life cycle, and carried the story even beyond Tom's death to illustrate recent changes in burial customs. In these and other early works, the personal narratives, whether actual or fictional, were viewed as picturesque supplements to dry ethnographic reports, rather than as whole and valuable texts in their own right.

Paul Radin was the first to use the life history as a major source of information about a culture, first in his "Personal Reminiscences of a Winnebago Indian" (1913), and then in longer autobiographies. His aim was to obtain an "inside view" of another culture, told in the words of an insider, so as not to destroy all the subjective value associated with the events related (Radin 1920:383). Radin discovered that the personal histories he gathered "threw more light on the real Indian than any of the more elaborate things I had collected in the usual external fashion which is the pride of scientific procedure among ethnologists" (Radin 1926:x).

Crashing Thunder (1926), was a full and detailed life history of a Winnebago man, heavily annotated with cultural context supplied by Radin. Though *Crashing Thunder* was the history of a single person, Radin denied that his purpose was to show a specific individual. Rather, he wished to have a "representative middle-aged individual of moderate ability" describe his life in relation to the social group (Radin 1920:384). It was the social group, not the individual himself, that Radin most wanted to understand (but see Little 1980 for a correction of this traditional view of Radin). And yet, Radin insisted that the only reasonable way to understand a culture was by understanding that a society is composed of "specific, not generalized men and women." In examining cultural patterns, we should know that "it is not, for instance, a Crow Indian who had made such and such a statement, uttered such and such a prayer, but a particular Crow Indian," Radin (1933:184) wrote in an essay on method and theory in anthropology.

Though Radin said that it was culture that he wanted to understand through individual experience, Marett, in a review of Radin's essay, took exception to Radin's emphasis on the individual. It was with the larger issues of religion, morals, and law that anthropology should concern itself, not "the private life of that 'well-known Winnebago named Dog-Head' or that 'even more famous Winnebago named Large-Walker'" (Marett 1934:117).

Though Radin opposed the imposition of massive theoretical

constructs to explain individual lives, work in other fields, especially sociology and psychology, was beginning to affect the treatment of individuals in anthropological publications. Thomas and Znaniecki's use of personal documents in a sociological work, *The Polish Peasant in Europe and America* (1927), first published in 1920, had a significant influence on all the social sciences. Studies using personal documents become widespread in sociology after the appearance of *The Polish Peasant*, and George Murdock (in Blumer 1939:135–136) attributed anthropology's increased interest in personal narratives in large measure to this monumental publication.

Thomas and Znaniecki saw life histories as "the perfect type of sociological material" to characterize the life of a social group (1927: 1832–1833). Personal documents, they argued, should be the primary basis upon which to formulate abstract social laws:

> Whether we draw our materials for sociological analysis from detailed life-records of concrete individuals or from the observation of mass-phenomena, the problems of sociological analysis are the same. But even when we are searching for abstract laws life-records of concrete personalities have a marked superiority over any other kind of materials. (Ibid.:1832)

The life history text in *The Polish Peasant* was supplemented by copious footnotes explaining the cultural context of incidents in the narrator's life. But more influential were interpretations of the account grounded in the authors' own theory of personality development. Again, a life record was used as an illustrative device, not to portray so much the cultural context, as in anthropological studies, but to prove, point by point, that a specific psychological theory had merit.

Workers in all the social sciences began to be concerned with making their disciplines more "scientific" and so directed their attentions to methods that were likely to lead to the establishment of laws of social behavior. Partly as a result of the ideas expressed in *The Polish Peasant*, anthropologists started collecting life histories with an eye toward their utility as elements in the creation of a social science more attuned to generalization and comparison.

The Psychocultural Phase

Along with the great emphasis on scientific methodology, the 1930s saw the emergence of a field of study within anthropology that was to have a significant impact on the way life histories were viewed. The alliance of psychology and anthropology, to form what would become known as the culture and personality school, was proposed most prominently by Edward Sapir, who advocated that cultural anthropology and psychology "join hands in a highly significant way" (1932:233). Considering culture as a superorganic, impersonal whole was a useful enough principle to start with, Sapir wrote, but had become a deterrent to the study of the individual and his relationships with other individuals. Furthermore, the more fully one tries to understand culture, "the more it seems to take on the characteristics of a personality organization" (1934:412).

Kluckhohn noted that anthropologists had rarely given systematic attention to the problem of how specific bits of culture were transmitted from individual to individual. To remedy the deficiency, we should not be satisfied with information that described skill acquisitions and the like in neutral tones. We must have the sort of data that reflect "the affect dimension and bear upon the emotional structure of the transmission of culture" (Kluckhohn 1939:98–99). Life history documents, he concluded, would prove invaluable in illuminating the problem of culture transmission. A volume of life histories of Ojibwa women appeared about this time (Landes 1938), with special attention to child-rearing practices and sex role learning.

DuBois observed that the more culturally minded anthropologists were beginning to drift toward psychology, in which one could study the least common denominator, or what she called "the ultimate reality in the realm of culture" (1937:285–286)—the individual. They borrowed the concepts and methods that were prevalent at the time. Psychoanalytic principles still held dominion but were just beginning to waver under pressure from behaviorists with experimental methods. Anthropology, therefore, was to be the recipient of often conflicting psychological perspectives.

Sapir (1938a) did not counsel a certain kind of psychology for anthropology to incorporate, saying that none had yet evolved that could do more than ask intelligent questions. But Dollard did not question the merit of a psychoanalytic approach to achieve a science of life history analysis. His *Criteria for the Life History* (1949), first published in 1935, offered a blend of principles from cultural study and psychoanalysis and was designed to reduce "confusion" in the life history field.

Dollard's criteria, in retrospect, seem highly arbitrary and deeply colored by his Freudian theoretical perspective. He wrote that Radin's *Crashing Thunder*, for example, did not even warrant an examination because Radin's comments upon the text were "characterized by a literary and impressionistic admiration rather than by a laborious theoretical construction of Crashing Thunder's life experience" (Dollard 1949:260). Nonetheless, despite reservations we may now have about Dollard's preoccupation with the imposition of theoretical constructs, it must be allowed that he directed attention to life study, and Langness and Frank (1981:20–21) further credit his work as bringing genuine improvement in fieldwork methodology.

Within a few years of Dollard's publication, two highly influential life histories appeared, Dyk's *Son of Old Man Hat* (1938) and *Sun Chief*, collected and analyzed by Simmons (1942). *Son of Old Man Hat* is the personal history of a Navaho man, recorded through his twentieth year of life (and extended three more years in Dyk and Dyk 1980). It is in no way a theoretical document and contains no interpretation by Dyk. In fact, as Sapir (Dyk's teacher) wrote in his introduction to the book, nowhere is even the concept of "personality" in evidence. Rather,

> We are in constant rapport with an intelligence in which all experiences, remote and proximate, "trivial" and "important," are held like waving reeds in the sensitive transparency of a brook. Such concepts as "ego" or "frustration" seem heated and out of place when we try to feel with this intelligence. (Sapir 1938b:viii)

In *Sun Chief*, Simmons (1942) did employ the concept of personality in relation to culture in his analysis of the life history of Don Talayesva, a Hopi Indian. The idea of "adjustments" an individual makes to the limitations imposed by his biological capabilities, physical environment, society, and culture plays a crucial role in Simmons's analytical scheme. Realizing that an analysis of an entire personality with his formula might prove superficial, he attempted an in-depth "situational analysis" using this concept of adjustment. A detailed, reasoned analysis of one incident in Don Talayesva's life was presented, bringing into play all four variables. *Sun Chief* was recognized as a major contribution to the growing interest in the life history, both for its thoughtful analysis and because Simmons provided the immediate context of the document, including a description of the relationship between the narrator and the ethnographer (Kluckhohn 1943).

DuBois (1944) and the psychoanalyst Abram Kardiner (Kardiner 1945) used life history material to develop and test Kardiner's assumptions about basic personality structure as it cohered in individual character adaptation. Kardiner (1939, 1945) defined basic personality structure as the "effective adaptive tools" an individual shares with other members of his culture as a result of similar childhood experiences that were frustrating or conflict producing. During her fieldwork in the Dutch East Indies, DuBois collected life histories and dream reports and administered various psychological tests to her informants. The results were interpreted by Kardiner and other specialists in *The People of Alor* (DuBois 1944) and were deemed to be supportive of Kardiner's contention that each society creates a type of personality in its members that in turn contributes to the formation of institutions in that society. Kardiner (1945:37) emphasized the importance of obtaining a fair sample of life histories for comparison, both within and between cultures, and it was this sort of methodological issue that came to occupy a prominent place in discussions of the value of the life history.

Between 1939 and 1945, the Social Science Research Council supported the publication of three works (Blumer 1939; Allport 1942; Gottschalk, Kluckhohn, and Angell 1945) to appraise the actual and potential contribution of personal documents to a science of social behavior.

Blumer's work evaluated the techniques used by Thomas and Znaniecki in *The Polish Peasant* and concluded that the study fell far short of achieving scientific worth. The transcript of the conference that met to discuss Blumer's critique revealed the skepticism with which personal documents were beginning to be viewed by social scientists attempting to transform their fields into rigorous scientific disciplines, noted Thomas (1978:124). Thomas wrote that the conference marked the end of personal narrative study in sociology.

The tone of Allport's study of personal documents in psychology was not nearly so pessimistic, though he too suggested that those who use personal documents should do so much more critically; students of the life history should adhere more closely to scientific standards of sampling, validity, reliability, and objectivity.

Kluckhohn (1949) echoed Allport's sentiments in his contribution to the 1945 work. He included lengthy and detailed instructions to anthropologists regarding appropriate methods of life history collecting and analysis, again paying special attention to the necessity of representative samples and so forth. But Kluckhohn was confident that if anthropologists improved their methods and applied themselves to better analysis and interpretation, the life history would prove worthwhile in culture and personality research. Anthropology, Kluckhohn (1945:163) wrote, "stands on the threshold of an epoch when the coarseness and crudeness of its work requires the refinement which can only be brought by a partially experimental approach."

By the 1950s the culture and personality school, with which life history study was then firmly associated, began to wane. Life histories did not disappear from scholarly consideration, but the development of the field lacked cohesion. Life history material was used in the service of many research areas, including individual adjustment to culture conflict (Spradley 1969), role analysis (Hughes 1965, 1974), identity conflict and self-appraisal (Watson 1970), and individual adaptation within a sociocultural system (Aberle 1967). White (1973), for example, studied the human life in progress, using autobiographical materials in conjunction with other measures. Theoretically eclectic, White drew on Freudian theory, self theory, and other models to build up a holistic interpretation to account for continuities and adaptive changes in the lives of persons at different times.

Erik Erikson (1958, 1969, 1975) popularized the psychohistorical technique, in which the lives of historical persons were reconstructed and analyzed from the standpoint of identity development in a larger sociohistorical context. But perhaps the best-known personal documents of this era were the almost literary works of Oscar Lewis (1959, 1961, 1964, 1966, 1970), who attempted to portray the subjective side of family dynamics, with a focus on Latin America. Lewis, however, did not provide a detailed methodology for his family autobiographical approach, nor did he attempt to tie it into any particular theoretical perspective (see Watson 1982, 1983).

Lewis's family autobiographies underscored the aesthetic and literary qualities of subjective accounts. But outside the framework of the psychocultural approach of the preceding years, the question of their utility remained. "At their best," remarked Barnouw (1963:198), "life histories are fascinating documents. The main difficulty lies in knowing what to do with them."

Toward an Interpretive Approach

Twenty years after Kluckhohn (1945) observed that the largest deficiency in life history study was the near absence of analysis and interpretation, Langness, in his comprehensive survey of the field, confirmed that life history materials remained impoverished in this respect. "Kluckhohn did set very high standards it is true," wrote Langness (1965:20), "but even when measured against lesser ones the available published materials are sadly inadequate when it comes to interpretation and analysis." Langness, however, was little more forthcoming with recommendations for analysis and interpretation of life histories than others in the field, although he did indicate various research problems, such as role conflict, deviance, and culture change, that could be studied through personal documents.

Another to note the lack of a coherent frame of reference was Mandelbaum (1973), who wanted to contribute to the life history field the beginnings of a general body of concepts. Mandelbaum reconstructed and analyzed the life of Gandhi by applying a set of three concepts: the dimensions, turnings, and adaptations of an individual life. He defined dimensions as categories for understanding the main forces at work in lives, and he distinguished four—biological, cultural, social, and psychosocial. Turnings demarcated periods in an individual's life as a result of major changes, and adaptation encompassed both changes and continuities chosen throughout the life course to adjust to new conditions.

It is important to realize that Mandelbaum did not intend his categories to be more than preliminary in establishing a framework for life study. Mandelbaum wished only to open discussion of interesting leads. He granted that perhaps "the fresh angle of approach provided by almost any coherent and cogent study of life history gives rise to such leads more than does any special potency of these particular suggestions" (ibid.:193). M. Brewster Smith, in his comments on Mandelbaum's paper, questioned, though, whether any etic analysis "is feasible for something as inherently 'emic' as human lives" (in Mandelbaum 1973:204).

Both Schwartz (1977) and Freeman (1979) subsequently used Mandelbaum's scheme with some success. Freeman, however, went beyond the formula to discuss the influence of the investigator and field situation in structuring the outcome of the life history—its form, content, and meaning—an issue that had been long neglected. His *Untouchable: An Indian Life History* (1979) is an engrossing story of one person in the social milieu of the lowest caste of Indian society.

Freeman, using Mandelbaum's analytic scheme, found four major turnings in Muli's life: his decision to become a pimp, his marriage, his entry into the business world, and his subsequent failure at business.

Mandelbaum's concept of adaptation was used to show that Muli became a pimp to cope with poverty, discrimination, and his own physical limitations as a farm laborer.

Freeman reveals, though, not only the cultural and immediate context of Muli's history, but also aspects of his own history that contributed to the product. He tells us, for example, that because he had grown up in a family that was discriminated against as members of a minority religious group, he was motivated to seek an oppressed person for his study and to portray his sufferings. Freeman's own life experiences undoubtedly directed his choice to highlight the psychological effects of discrimination in Muli's life (Freeman 1979:395). A life history is a joint production, he wrote, and the role of the observer in understanding a life history is crucial:

> No comparison of life histories is possible without knowledge of the editor's perspectives and values that influenced the final form of the history. Failure to assess or at least recognize the observer's or editor's role leads to an image of a life history that is distorted and incomplete, since each editor, though not consciously, is necessarily influenced by his own perspectives. (Ibid.:393)

Simple assumptions of the past began to be scrutinized and discarded in the 1970s. Crapanzano (1977) and Frank (1979) even deliberated the legitimacy of using life histories to study cultures that may have distinctly different ideas of the "self" than our own. Autobiography is itself a mode of expression that is derived from a specific world view. Questions the investigator poses to the subject, Crapanzano wrote, reflect certain expectations within the investigator's culture, and "the very question of life history itself may be an alien construct for the subject" (1977:4). Frank argued that the life history could even be considered a double autobiography, as it is the result of a process "that blends together the consciousness of the investigator and the subject, perhaps to the point where it is not possible to disentangle them" (1979:85).

Earlier efforts at objectivity and neutrality in the collection and presentation of life histories came to seem naive. Mintz (1979:19), writing about the life history interview, rejected the idea of a verifiable truth in an informant's words and spoke of "the illusiveness, the many-sidedness of truth." In his volume on life history in the social sciences the sociologist Bertaux declared that "the scientificity of sociology is a *myth*," and its aim should be to acquire knowledge, not to produce scientific results (1981:30). And Freeman noted that criteria such as representativeness and generalizability, previously used to evaluate life histories, were, if not wrong criteria, then misleading ones (1979:399).

The specter of repeated attempts in the past to find some use for materials that investigators intuitively understood to be valuable indicated that something very fundamental about life histories needed to be reassessed. Imposing constructs external to the subjective experience of persons, especially those in other cultures, had yielded only limited benefit to the life history field. If we were to exploit fully the potential contribution of life history documents to anthropology, the essential subjective nature of the documents must be not only acknowledged but adopted as a major element in the interpretive process.

Methods grounded in phenomenology, which takes account of subjective experience as a phenomenon in its own right, seemed especially well suited and were examined in a series of works dealing with life histories (Watson 1976a, 1978, 1983; Frank 1979; Miller and Stephenson 1980; Crapanzano 1980). Since the phenomenological approach refuses to enforce constructs alien to the individual life as it is related, this approach brings closer an understanding of subjective experience in a culturally defined experiential context.

Watson (1976a) further advocated the union of the phenomenological perspective with the hermeneutical position. In hermeneutics, a philosophical discipline concerned with the nature and activity of interpretation, the gap between investigator and subject is overarched by questioning cultural preunderstandings, which are pregiven assumptions about the world, and establishing a dialectic with the phenomenon we hope to understand. By bridging back and forth between the different contexts, understanding and interpretation are made possible. Frank (1979) and Agar (1980) investigated the possibilities a hermeneutical approach offered to anthropological research, and Little (1980) reassessed the work of Radin from a hermeneutical perspective. Little suggested that Radin, in stressing internal evidence, providing contextual aspects, and adhering closely to experiences in his subject's life, was doing sound hermeneutics in *Crashing Thunder*.

Miller and Stephenson (1980) and Little stressed that the object of an application of hermeneutics to life study is not explanation, as in previous approaches, but *understanding*. Miller and Stephenson took the hermeneutical position in their study of the life of Jakob Hutter, a sixteenth-century millenarian movement leader and showed it superior in understanding Hutter's life in its social context than alternative methodologies.

Tuhami: Portrait of a Moroccan (Crapanzano 1980), which we critically examine later in this essay, was another attempt to understand a life from the hermeneutical position. In it Crapanzano elucidates the issues raised by such an approach, especially those of the changing perspectives, negotiations, and renegotiations the investigator made in the process of eliciting the history from Tuhami; he further illustrates the mediations Tuhami himself made with his life as a result of the encounter. Crapanzano makes clear that Tuhami's life, controlled as it was by saints, she-demons, and what we would consider fantasy, could not be understood if the investigator did not allow for another's rendition of "reality." Hermeneutical procedures require that the investigator "make room" for a frame of reference that is foreign to him, and Crapanzano demonstrates in *Tuhami* the advantage of this approach in life history study.

Whether implicit, or made explicit in the hermeneutical perspective, a recurrent idea expressed in recent works is that self-reflexivity is required of the anthropologist. According to Myerhoff and Ruby, in their introduction to a volume on reflexive perspectives in anthropology, being reflexive means that

> the producer deliberately, intentionally reveals to an audience the underlying epistemological assumptions that caused the formulation of a set of questions in a particular way, the seeking of answers to those questions in a particular way, and finally the presentation of the findings in a particular way. (Myerhoff and Ruby 1982:6)

The stance advocated by writers on reflexivity is a logical extension of the scientific requirement that researchers be explicit about their methods (ibid.:17–18). In life history study, the implication of such a requirement is that the investigator disclose not just the story of a person's life as it was related, but also his own epistemological assumptions, his own world view, which contributed so significantly to the final construction. The hermeneutical perspective incorporates reflexivity as an essential element in an interpretive framework.

Myerhoff (1982) further noted that life histories enhance reflexive consciousness in the narrators as they tell their stories, which may be essential work for very old persons. Myerhoff eloquently depicts the reflexive and integrative process of life-telling in a group of elderly Jewish immigrants who were members of a senior citizens' center (Myerhoff 1978, 1982).

Works on the life history in recent years have not, of course, been restricted to those employing a phenomenological, hermeneutical, or reflexive orientation. Angrosino (1976), for example, offered the life history of a political leader in Trinidad to illustrate important features of the West Indian personality in its postcolonial environment. Sexton (1981) analyzed the life history of a Mayan man, based on five major themes he drew from the history (family and community solidarity, grinding poverty, reliance on alcohol, recurrent illness, and sensitivity to agents of change). And Brandes (1982) treated methodological issues in the collection and presentation of life history materials, such as choosing an informant, eliciting the autobiography, and editing the resultant transcript.

A significant contribution to the field was the publication of *Lives: An Anthropological Approach to Biography*, by Langness and Frank (1981). The work is an expansion of Langness's book of 1965 and extends his survey to include developments in the subsequent years. The later book deals extensively with issues of methodology that have preoccupied life historians since the inception of serious study—establishing rapport with an informant, interviewing skills, sampling. The section on methods, along with one addressing ethical concerns, provides a useful guide for those contemplating a life history study.

Langness and Frank also trace the history and theoretical development of life study, giving special attention to the recent emphasis on analysis and interpretation, an emphasis they feel is long overdue: "Only insofar as you can understand all of the steps in your analysis, and communicate them to others can you be said to have completed a useful or meaningful life history" (1981:86). They observe that too many life histories subsume the analytic scheme and assumptions in the biographical materials themselves (ibid.:78).

Langness and Frank discuss two rather novel and intriguing suggestions for interpretation. One has its basis in Sartre's idea of a "fundamental project," or "the organizing principle or nexus of meanings and values that inform a person's choices" (ibid.: 109), and the other the observation that the manner in which death is conceived in a culture affects the life history an individual tells (ibid.:115). The authors do not directly advise the use of such concepts in interpreting life histories, but they do open up interesting possibilities.

Eckhardt and Schwartz, in a review of *Lives*, wrote that Langness and Frank "speak of the future contributions of the life history method more so than they do of its current accomplishments" and note that the "omni-use" of the life history accounts for its lack of focus (1983:75–76). This review also suggests that there has been little common thread running through the historical development of life history in anthropology, save perhaps for the last few years. The life history has meant entirely different things to its various proponents. In the past, investigators used life histories for any purpose that suited their individual research needs or the requirements of a theory subscribed to at the time, with little thought to the integrity of the subjective life history or to consolidating previous research. Unfortunately, the result is that the usefulness of life history analysis is difficult to see from either a scientific or a humanistic perspective. If the scientific viewpoint had been regularly applied, life history data at least would have been analyzed, evaluated, and tested according to larger, agreed-upon theoretical and methodological structures, making standardization and strict comparisons in life history research possible. On the other hand, if a humanistic strategy, emphasizing the specific and unique, had been more consistently adopted, we would now have at our disposal a series of revealing statements, relatively unencumbered by the filtering effects of theoretical constructs, about the characteristics of subjective individuals.

The Circumstances of Data Gathering

Because of the intensely subjective (as opposed to objective, impersonal) nature of the life history, it is important to identify the specific and immediate conditions under which it was written or related that influenced its meaning for the subject and for the person who elicited it as discourse and recorded it. As we have seen, this theme has just recently been taken up by anthropologists working in the life history field. In no true sense can the life history be divorced from the subjective mental sets or orientations that produced it in the encounter, for it is through those meanings that it is mediated to us in textual form and poses its special interpretive challenges.

Since interpretation is frequently what we are concerned with in approaching the life history, we must know something about the context in which the text was evoked before we can begin to make any sense of it. This fundamental consideration, it seems to us, is always an essential aspect of all life history research, but until recently it had often been neglected. All too often, the relationship of the final life history product to the subject himself, to the social context in which the subject wrote or related it, and/or to the investigator, recorder, or catalyst whose operations have helped bring it into being is not in the least bit clear. Yet we must take all these factors into consideration in life history research, if we are in a position to do so, for obviously all of them in their various ways have played a part in determining the eventual form of the finished product, that is, the life history as it appears to us as text.

The anthropologist who wishes to make sense out of the life history data he himself has collected in the field is in a special position for he has elicited the material from a native informant with whom he has entered into some kind of face-to-face relationship. Since the informant is often illiterate, he must talk directly to the anthropologist about himself over a more or less extended period of time. This human encounter structures what is related, and so the anthropologist, in order to interpret his own data, must find out something about the dynamics of the situation, including the motivations, understandings, defenses, and situational constraints that influenced the data-collecting setting, the results, and the very process of interpretation itself.

If the reader, the potential analyst of the life history, is removed from all immediate control over the situation, it is helpful for him to have some information from the original investigator about the original context out of which the life history emerged. If such information is provided (and it is often not) it is usually found in the preface, analysis, or annotations that accompany the life history. We have tried to delineate some of the critical questions that should be answered, theoretically, before an interpretation of the life history is attempted.

1. How well did the investigator know the subject and what was their relationship? Ideally, the circumstances of their relationship should be spelled out in as much detail and depth as possible, including the development of the relationship over time, the present social context in which the relationship is embedded, and the emotional dynamics of the relationship at the time the data were being recorded. The anthropologist, let us not forget, is involved in the data-gathering situation no less than his informant. He occupies no privileged position, even though he may think his scientific status as an "objective" observer exempts him from any necessity for self-appraisal. We

should keep in mind that he is the one doing the interpreting and making sense of the situation in his full individuality.

The informant orients his account to the anthropologist as another person with a particular set of perceived characteristics. Understanding the nature of the relationship makes clear what meaning it had in personal and interpersonal terms, thus giving us an idea of the motivating human circumstances of the life history.

2. What were the circumstances in which the subject related his life history? What was the form in which it was recorded? Did he write it alone? Did he dictate it to the ethnographer? If so, where and how did this happen? Knowing what the subject had to contend with in his immediate environment when he recalled his life would have a great deal to do, we suspect, with what was recalled and what was modified or suppressed. The original situation could have been conducive to openness or it could have been stressful and threatening. And whether it was one or the other, or something different, would of course depend on how cultural factors and definitions entered into the data-collecting situation. We noticed in our fieldwork, for example, that Guajiro children would not volunteer much personal data in the presence of adults, although they would do so when they were alone. This situation can be interpreted as a response conditioned by the child's attitude of fear and respect toward adults, who are perceived as harsh, demanding, and critical in this culture.

3. What inducements, persuasions, arguments, and reasons did the ethnographer use to motivate the subject to relate his life? An investigator's honest assessment helps to clarify the reasons why the informant is doing what he is doing. These reasons, in turn, may shed some light on the meaning of the informant's statements about his life in the context of his relationship to the ethnographer. It is also helpful when the investigator can indicate the impact of his inducements on the psychology of the informant. Presumably his knowledge of native character in general and his understanding of the specific informant would enable him to do this.

4. What, if anything, did the subject have to say about the data-collecting situation and its requirements, and in what way did he think it influenced his recollection of his life? Sometimes such observations are volunteered freely by the informant; sometimes the investigator elicits them. In any case, this valuable source of insight into the native view of the situation is all too often neglected. Obviously, unconscious factors in the subject's motivations would have to be inferred.

5. What were the investigator's own preconceptions about the culture, the subject, and the data-collecting situation, and what self-perceived theoretical commitments did he have that might have influenced how he collected, arranged, and interpreted the material? Since social scientists usually do not discuss their biases, we are left with little insight into their activity as analysts or interpreters. We can only guess the specific ways in which they influenced the form, content, and meaning of the life history.

6. To what extent were questions used to elicit autobiographical data? What particular questions were used? How did the use of certain questions influence specific aspects of the recollected life history? It is important to know what material was volunteered and what material was given under questioning or extraordinary inducements. A piece of autobiographical data means quite a special thing when it is recalled spontaneously, repeated, and elaborated. It says something about what that person values and the way he naturally thinks of himself and his life. When an item is a response to a question, it is oriented to a set of external expectations, and the problems of maintaining interpersonal adequacy or winning friendship or approval are likely to be important considerations.

The frequent failure of the anthropologist to mention the questions he asked to elicit and direct the flow of the life history is at first glance puzzling, but is really quite understandable. In the field we are acutely aware of how important questions are in obtaining information. We think in terms of right and wrong questions, good and bad questions. But once we return from the field with reams of field notes and all the "important" questions answered, the sheer bulk of the data seizes us in its forceful immediacy, and we turn to problems of organizing it and putting it to the test of our theories. In the process the importance of the questions that got us the data recedes into the background. Yet these questions still retain a crucial significance; only when we understand them can we properly identify the meaning of the data-collecting setting for the informant as well as for the ethnographer.

7. To what extent was a native interpreter used to translate the life history from the original recitation, and what was his role in the process of data gathering? If the life history was recorded verbatim by the anthropologist, without a translator, what language was used and what facility did the informant and/or recorder have in it? The one who reengages the life history must be aware of the distorting effects of the translation process: not only may meanings be changed as a result, but

a native interpreter fundamentally changes the social stimulus situation for the informant, and adds the distorting effects of his own personality, interests, and attitudes to the act of translating what the informant says. The role of the translator in DuBois's (1944) collection of Alorese life histories is a case in point.

8. What techniques were used to record the life history? The completeness of the life history may ultimately rest on whether the investigator tape-recorded everything and could go back to the original data, or whether he used an effective shorthand, tried to record it longhand, or simply wrote down later in the day what he recalled from memory, if, let us say, the subject objected to having his life history recorded directly. Moreover, the mode of data collecting may influence the meaning of the situation from the subject's standpoint.

9. To what extent, if at all, has the original life history material, as dictated or written down, been edited in the final presentation as text? What has been eliminated from the native informant's original account? To what degree has the recorder and/or editor rearranged the life history to conform to a logical chronological sequence? These questions focus attention on the issue of whether or not the original chains of thinking and conceptions of chronology have been retained. There is a difference between native categories, standards, and thought processes, which may seem incomprehensible or illogical to us, and the anthropologist's notions of how the data ought to be ordered for scientific or aesthetic purposes.

Even in a life history as excellent as *Sun Chief*, Simmons (1942) tells us that he eliminated two-thirds of the original material because it was "repetitious" and rearranged the material into a more orderly chronological sequence to enhance readability. We do not, however, know precisely what was eliminated or the standards Simmons used to make these decisions. If we had all the original material and some idea of its original order, we might find that the life history had an entirely different flavor.

Unfortunately, meaningful answers to the various questions we have posed here are rarely provided, and thus we are deprived of potential sources of insight and understanding, which, if available, would enable us more easily and effectively to determine the meaning of the life history in its finished textual form as it has moved through different contexts of "becoming" what it is. Without this knowledge we have little or no way of knowing, for example, what the subject had in mind when he related his life and what went on in the mind of the anthropologist at the various stages of data gathering and interpretation.

It is clear that the final, published text of any life history we wish to interpret takes on a complex set of meanings in the process of its construction that defines its *meaning as text*. These meanings have come into being as part of a long sequence of explicit and implicit negotiations between and among the parties to the life history endeavor (Crapanzano 1977, 1980; Frank 1979). If we want to understand what the text is all about, we must include as part of our interpretive efforts the goal of reconstructing, as much as we can, the constructive process itself. This reconstructing, of course, must also include the self-construction of the anthropologist through the text, as he projects an image of himself for the benefit of the particular audience he is addressing in his work.

Interpreting and Understanding the Life History

Upon the scaffolding of our understanding of the anthropological life history as discourse translated interpretively into text, we must now consider our own interpretive reencounter with the "finished" product: the written or published document itself.

As we shall attempt to demonstrate in detail in later chapters, interpretation is a subjective activity, subsuming many complex operations, which requires the interpreter to bridge the gap that separates him and the context of his thought from the object of interpretation, in this case, the life history text. In the view of hermeneutics, the interpreter must be willing to broaden and modify his own taken-for-granted preunderstandings as he enters into a dialogue with another's life, which is embedded in its own (but for us, foreign) meaning-horizon. Through a dialectic in which we pose questions appropriate to the meaning-context of the world of the life history, we receive back answers that raise new questions, allowing us to correct the direction of interpretation. This dialectic initiates an open and unfettered dialogue that eventuates in some merging of our context of thought with that of the text in question. This dialectically produced synthesis or integration defines "understanding" in the hermeneutical sense.

Understanding is obviously limited if the one who interprets an object in a context far removed from himself does so strictly within his own frame of reference; on the other hand, it is impossible completely to leave one's own familiar horizon and enter into another world entirely on its own terms. The would-be interpreter can never fully eliminate his own biases even if he is aware of and reflective about some of his own starting points. The very language a person uses, for instance, provides a ready-made description of the world; he cannot thoroughly foresee and understand its effects on his thinking.

In life history research the interpreter's ordering and making sense of the life history are considered meaningless or unimportant. It is as though the events described and the conclusions to be drawn from them were self-evident empirical realities or objective modes of thought having no connection to the intentions, hidden meanings, and values of the people involved in the whole enterprise. It is important for us to be self-reflective about our own interpretive activity, therefore, in order to clarify how "meaning" is mediated precisely through our own particular dialectical engagement with the thing we are trying to understand.

We shall take up some of the problems raised by hermeneutics in regard to interpretations in the next chapters, and we shall return to them in our critique of various interpretive strategies in life history research.

Basic Approaches to Studying the Life History

Phenomenological and existential hermeneutics provide a challenge and a much needed alternative to the limited understanding of the informant's subjective world that other interpretive approaches offer. The two most important of these other strategies that we shall consider are (1) the study of personality, both structural and developmental, primarily through psychoanalytic theory, and (2) the study of the individual–culture/society relationship from structural-functional perspectives. We shall touch only briefly on the main issues at this time, leaving the remainder of the essay to develop them more fully.

The Study of Personality

The life history has not infrequently been used to study or test theories about individual or group personality and aspects of personality functioning. The life history, from this perspective, is believed to shed light on or reveal certain aspects of the person's intrapsychic structure through his self-reported behavior, provided that the interpreter has the theory and the correct tools of analysis at his disposal.

The study of personality is one variant of *etic-nomothetic* inquiry. In the etic-nomothetic approach a phenomenon is understood in terms of an external set of standards or categories used by the investigator to make sense of it (Berry 1969; Price-Williams 1974, 1975). Furthermore, these categories take their meanings from models or general sets of theoretical propositions designed to explain or elucidate recurrent relationships and causes existing between classes of events (Allport 1942).

Ultimately, the theories used to evaluate life history data for the purpose of explaining personality are themselves derived from deeplying assumptions that we must understand. These assumptions belong to our *life world* (*Lebenswelt*), an idea suggested by the phenomenologist Husserl (1970). The life world (or the natural attitude from the standpoint of the individual) is the self-evident givenness of mundane experience. As part of living spontaneously in the life world we take for granted that certain things are the way they appear to be without really questioning why this should be so. Husserl has argued that science, like all our knowledge, is grounded in the self-evidence of the life world, and as such its epistemological status is never really put to the question. Theories of personality and the ways they are tested, the phenomenologist would say, are part of the life world too.

In common with other scientific theories, those having to do with personality assume that reality (phenomena) can be treated as separate, definable units that can be broken down, compared, and related to each other. Personality is one such unit in relationship to the organism's larger environment. Indeed, as it is usually defined, personality is a conceptually independent system in its environment. Furthermore, the very operation of personality is generally understandable only in terms of the articulation and relationships of its smaller components or subsystems. Thus, things (or shall we say, phenomenal fields) can be explained and understood by taking them apart and seeing how they fit together. This "fit" implies the assumption that things go together on functional or teleological grounds, that one thing leads to or causes another. These relationships, in turn, are made plausible by the theory or model that defines their saliency or relevancy. In the final analysis, the power of the theory is supported experimentally if the empirical data make sense in terms of the relationships that the theory specifies. When the life history is seen in these terms, it becomes the expression of a category or set of categories in some researcher's mind. Thus, the psychological investigator might conclude that X is a "perfect example of the paranoid adaptation characteristic of his culture." The phenomenon of the life history, in this case that of somebody far removed culturally from the investigator, has been translated into the investigator's familiar conceptual and analytical categories. By establishing relations between these categories according to the specifications of some Freudian psychodynamic model, the researcher then infers the paranoia and justifies the theory to himself. He is making sense of this person—so unlike himself, the product of a different culture—entirely in his own frame of reference. He neither questions the larger context of his scientific operations, nor does he attempt to understand the phenomenon in its own terms.

What is being understood here? Do events really operate in the subjectivity of a person's life the way they are described by the model that the investigator uses? The construct of the personality, when thought of in these terms, may seem arid, artificial, and arbitrary compared with our impression of the living reality of the *person himself* in his true immediacy. By studying the life history to study personality, we often seem to end up understanding a *method* of looking at a life rather than the life itself, or, for that matter, even alternative ways of looking at another life.

The Study of the Individual–Society/Culture Relationship

Another basic etic-nomothetic approach to understanding the life history is to focus on the nexus between the individual and the sociocultural system. The nature of that connection has been variously conceptualized in life history research, but for the most part a functional-dialectic point of view forms the basis of the investigator's theoretical assumptions (although psychological or cognitive variables may be introduced into the analysis). This view regards the individual as a component of a larger system of structured relationships whose ongoing functioning and patterned meanings maintain society in a state of internal equilibrium as well as adaptation to its external environment. In this scheme the individual occupies successively and simultaneously a series of socially defined roles for which he is socialized and whose proper realization has functionally adaptive consequences. This is the functional assumption, we might say. Moreover, the analyst also recognizes that there is likely to be a discrepancy between what individuals *want to do* (their personalities)—at least at some point in their lives and at least in certain respects on many occasions—and what they *should do* (the way society defines their roles).

The dialectic by which the gap is narrowed or bridged as a consequence of social transactions becomes a major point of interest. How does the transformation inherent in this dialectic come about? What are its specific mechanics? Looking at a particular person in the detail of his life and comparing him with others may give us some insight into the process. If the individual is deviant or maladjusted in his group, it can be assumed that deficient socialization, exposure to life experiences unusual for that culture, or personality problems hamper his capacity or desire to interpret and act upon corrective feedback from his environment, making him the kind of deviant he is. By comparing this person, as he emerges in his life history, with other, better-adjusted people in his society, it is theoretically possible to establish the conditions under which the dialectics of socialization and social control in its myriad forms are successful in producing people who can adequately maintain the system in their social functioning. It may be possible even to generate propositions out of this line of research for testing in other societies.

In operating from this angle, the investigator is creating an artificial problem divorced from the life of the subject. While the subject is talking about experience, that is, experience with *subjectively* intended meanings, the investigator is talking about "objective" events, as though he could take these uniquely personal thoughts, feelings, and ideas away from the subject and put them in the realm of pure abstract language, which he alone understands and which he manipulates in his infinite wisdom because he sees something bigger and more important of which the subject is unaware.

What is this bigger problem? It is essentially nothing more than an abstract concept of society and the individual standing in some presumed relationship to each other. The particular quality of any individual relationship to social experience can then be measured by some standard of optimum adjustment and social functioning that exists in the researcher's mind. Recall that as an article of faith he understands society as a functionally articulated whole which, for its own health, must train and motivate individuals to fill certain niches and to conform to preestablished normative codes.

The Phenomenology of Subjective Experience

As we have mentioned, there is an alternative to the etic-nomothetic approach for making sense of the life history. The most obvious things a life history tells us about are the subjective aspects of phenomenal consciousness. If Earle (1972) is right that the autobiography is *only* meaningful as an expression of subjective being in which the individual reflects on what he understands *as himself*, then all other exercises in dealing with the life history are spurious compared with the interpreter's proper efforts to bridge the gap between himself and the life history text, so that he enters into the stream of subjectively recollected experience as unencumbered by prior notions of "personality" or "society" as possible. We are arguing that the fundamental issue of the life history, therefore, is appropriately that of phenomenal consciousness as the individual himself experiences it, mediated through our own interpretive efforts.

The life history makes us aware of a fundamental philosophical issue. What are we interested in, after all, in our attempts to make sense of the world? Is it the phenomenon we are investigating in its own right (in this case, the life history), or how well our models seem to enable us to interpret the world? Both, we would argue, yield vastly different kinds of understanding.

What we understand in any course of study depends to a large extent on what we define as constituting understanding, which is to say, what is important to understand and the methods we use in pursuit of that objective. The etic-nomothetic orientation described by Allport emphasizes generalizing and model building in an abstract frame of reference that is externally imposed on phenomena. On the other hand, the *emic-idiographic* approach, which he contrasts to the etic-nomothetic, concerns itself with the specific and unique richness of a phenomenon, so that we understand the particular (the individual, the subjective) rather than the general. No two cases are alike in their total gestalt. In approaching the life history from this view, we are led inevitably to consider the obvious and compelling subjectivity of its production, for, after all, this is what makes it unique: the personal and irreplaceable creation of one person as he sees his own life, a life unlike that of any other.

In a philosophical sense this is a fundamentally valid alternative to the "scientific" approach to the study of personal documents, which has long dominated research in this area. As we see it, the phenomenological approach, which is concerned with "meaning" and subjective "truth," restores some much-needed balance to the runaway tendency in the social sciences to reduce people to categories and abstractions in the service of model building and model testing. So long as this attitude prevails as the standard for social scientific research, the unique existential texture of phenomena will be reduced to the status of the extraneous, and the individual will eventually be lost in the maze of scientific generalities. While we can see the justification of generalizing approaches in dealing with large-scale social processes and certain kinds of comparative research, there is little reason to accept this tendency in the study of individual lives as subjective products where a reasonable alternative exists.

In subsequent chapters we propose to outline the assumptions and methods of such an approach, which incorporates phenomenological and existential perspectives, and to show how it can be applied interpretively to life history data. We will then critique contrasting approaches, attempting what Ricoeur (1974b) calls a "conflict of interpretations" that seeks to illuminate the nature and limitations of each opponent's position. We shall also consider the specific problem of interpreting the life histories of women, which, because of the various assumptions we hold about women, raises in a challenging way some of the issues and considerations we have just outlined.

Finally we shall reassess the seemingly contradictory positions taken toward the life history. In doing so, we must come to grips with the question of whether or not strategies focusing on the general and theoretical as opposed to those focusing on the unique can be reconciled in life history research so that each approach balances or in some way contributes to the other without necessarily ruling it out. A fruitful way of looking at the problem is to adopt the perspective of some cognitively oriented psychologists who are aware of the *etic/emic* problem in cross-cultural research (cf. Berry 1969; Price-Williams 1974, 1975; Brislin, Bochner, and Lonner 1975). We shall entertain the notion that it is possible and even desirable to see our own scientific models or etic constructs as having a dialectical relationship with the native conceptualization of experience, be it individual or culturally standardized. By being willing to correct our entry categories (or models) in light of units that are meaningful to the native society or individual we are studying, we may be able to cast something that is "real" to the native into something approximating a useful scientific metalanguage we can use for control and comparison.

Thus, the units of phenomenal experience that we advocate as the legitimate focus of study can be reconciled with certain units or categories in an etic model. What remains of the entry category after the emics are considered tells us something about the usefulness and sensitivity of the model in taking account of variations of subjective experience in cultural context. In comparing individual lives from different cultures in their phenomenal richness we may find that the models we customarily use to deal with such experience are too broad and abstract to have anything more than a very limited analytical and descriptive power. We may discover, however, that if we scrupulously compare individual lives in context and check them against our model, instead of confounding model and phenomenon, we open the way for changes in the entry categories that would make them more useful cross-culturally in describing and explaining functional equivalences in individual behavior from the standpoint of its subjective and uniquely textured meaning. We do not advocate that anthropologists abandon the use of individual cases for purposes of generalization and hypothesis testing; we are simply saying that the models we use can and even should be reworked in light of openness to new experience to accommodate the special properties of unique individuals and specific cultural events.

If we do not know the subjective meaning of lives we are comparing and evaluating, then we cannot construct an adequate descriptive framework (based on the emic-etic dialectic) that would have anything more than strongly culture-bound as well as highly abstract and typified significance for us. And by not critically examining what *we* are doing in interpreting the data, we never really grasp what we are actually comparing and understanding. Indeed, it is easy to be content with this state of affairs as long as our conclusions meet the specifications of our models, and since our scientific operations seem natural and inevitable, there is often little impulse to question our equally inescapable "scientific" conclusions.

Thus, our goal will be to show the limitations we impose on our understanding by relying on a scientific, model-oriented method of interpretation, such as psychoanalysis or functionalism. By redirecting attention to the act of interpretation itself in relation to the immediate data, we hope to show that there is, in fact, an alternative method.

Chapter 2
The Life History As a Subjective Document

Anthropological uses of the life history generally ignore the inherent, fundamental issue that such a document poses, namely, the phenomenon of subjective consciousness through which the individual articulates his world. The one thing that the life history tells us about directly is the individual's personal view of his experience as he understands it, bearing in mind that this always occurs within and through a particular cultural context. In this way we encounter the life history without the necessity of understanding it through an elaborately and explicitly formulated network of external constructs.

In his assessment of the personal document as a tool in social scientific research, Allport (1942) comments on the multitude of uses this source of data has served (for Allport's own application see Allport 1965). Significantly, he lists phenomenal investigation first, perhaps because this struck him as the most obvious and compelling:

> If we want to know how other people feel, what they experience and what they remember, what their emotions and motives are like, and the reasons for acting as they do—why not ask them? This is the simple logic of the introspectionist's position that commends itself to many in spite of the scorching displeasure of the behaviorists and objectivists. Personal documents are for the most part introspective protocols, adapted especially to the complexities of phenomenal consciousness. (Allport 1942:37)

Years later, Becker echoed Allport in assigning priority to phenomenal investigation as the task of life history research: "The perspective differs from that of some other social scientists in assigning major importance to the interpretations people place on their experience as an explanation for behavior. To understand why someone behaves as he does you must understand how it looked to him, what he thought he had to contend with, what alternatives he saw open to him" (1966:vi). Becker concluded by emphasizing how important it is to study the "subjective side" of institutional processes and how the life history helps directly in realizing this objective.

The problem with using the life history to talk about "personality," "motivation," "repressed conflict," and the like is that the investigator imposes or infers constructs that are frankly alien to the life history as a subjectively experienced phenomenon. It is of course possible and even desirable in scientific study to make sense of something within the chosen model or frame of reference, using a set of measures external to the phenomenon (as in etic research [see Price-Williams 1974, 1975]). But this must be acknowledged an arbitrary starting point, which once embarked upon generates its appropriate meanings and, in all likelihood, its range of predictable outcomes. With something as alive and vital as the life history document, however, where the individual stands revealed to us through his own choice we have an expressive, self-contained source of information about subjective experience that cries out for understanding. Yet all too often the integrity of the autobiographical account is violated in the very act of interpretation. If explanatory constructs and models are extensively, methodically imposed on the life history, any inferences made from them must depend for their verification on data sources of an entirely different order than the subjective report contained in the life history itself. Projective tests, for example, represent special stimulus materials artificially divorced from the individual's life; structured observations of his life and interviews with him on selected topics are usually organized around preselected categories of analysis, and so on. Thus, when the outlines of the subject's personality ultimately begin to emerge from theoretical interpretation, using these data sources, they may show a disquieting lack of correspondence to the experiential ordering we see in the life history text.

The problem, therefore, is this: the life history is a subjective product, but one that is approached by another subject who himself interprets. To develop fully this basic theme and to determine what it contributes to our understanding of life histories, we must first consider several philosophical schools: phenomenology, existentialism, and hermeneutics.

Phenomenology

Edmund Husserl (1931, 1960, 1970) worked out the essential ground plan of phenomenology in the early decades of this century. His work was continued and applied to the study of social life by Schutz (1967a,

1967b, 1970), Natanson (1966, 1970, 1973), Garfinkel (1967), and Cicourel (1964, 1974), among others.

Husserl's phenomenology was the outcome of his attempt to create a presuppositionless philosophy. Its irreducible starting point is given in the experiences of the conscious human being who lives and acts in a "world" that he perceives and interprets (Wagner 1970: 5). He deals with the world in an active yet natural way through an intentional mode. Consciousness is always *consciousness of something*. The phenomena that constitute experience are therefore in their ultimate nature *intended*, the products of the activity of consciousness itself (Husserl 1931:119–120). This focus on reality as a subjective, conscious act is a view consistent with our belief that the life history must be approached as a subjective product and is no mere assemblage of empirical realities outside the individual.

Schutz (1967b), in attempting to combine Husserl and Weber into a working interpretation of social phenomena, insists that social action is meaningful only when we start with the assumption that the subjective meaning-context through which the individual acts must be understood. He explains that the analysis of common-sense projects necessarily involves our interpretation of the subjective point of view (that is to say, the interpretation of the actor and the setting of social projects—plans and actions in the world—in terms of the actor) (ibid.:34). Understanding the subject's interpretation, therefore, must be a general principle if we wish to reconstruct properly the purposive (in-order-to) nature of common-sense actions.

In the phenomenology of Husserl (1931) human beings live naturally and spontaneously in the routine pursuit of daily affairs. Their acceptance of this world, the product of history and tradition, as given, as taken for granted, is called the *natural attitude*. As an essential mental stance of all human beings it forms the basis of their interpretation of experience. In his later writings Husserl (1970) attempted to identify systematically the properties of the *life world (Lebenswelt)*, which is the world of the natural attitude. The life world can be thought of as the total sphere of experience of the individual, one bound by ideas, objects, persons, and events that continuously orient his pursuit of the basic, everyday objectives of living. According to phenomenology, this is the "ultimate reality" in which people live. People believe that the world of the natural attitude is "out there," and it is unusual for them to question its taken-for-granted status.

The relationship of the individual to the life world is complex. Individuals in the course of daily life choose domains of relevance within the context of the life world. These domains of relevance are selected aspects of specific situations, as well as activities and plans construed through participation in the life world itself, to which the individual ascribes importance (Schutz 1967b:283–286). These domains may change over time and may be given different priorities; moreover, they may be volitional in nature or imposed as a function of participation in the social system.

Schutz's (1967b:120–149) aim in his phenomenological sociology was to map out the nature of the life world and natural attitude and its relevance for studying social interaction and the social construction of reality. This question has been a problem for anthropology as well, although in our discipline we use words like "culture," "tradition," and "culture context" to describe much the same thing, albeit without some of the philosophical implications of phenomenology. In the anthropological life history, to return to our basic problem, what we do indeed bear witness to is the subjectivity of the individual engaged in orientation to the life world. The individual's subjectivity is in fact a subjective "world," since it consists of him talking about himself and his actions within the framework and meaning-context of his culture. As in the "natural attitude," the subject of the life history lives in this world spontaneously, as though it were objectively real.

Schutz (1967b:10–19) attempted to establish the irreducible basis of the life world for sociological inquiry and the task was enormous. We will attempt here not to delineate the range of his thought but rather merely to examine several important concepts related to our own life history enterprise. One of the most important is the notion of *intersubjectivity*. This concept refers, in general, to what is common to individuals.

Sociality as an intersubjective cognitive phenomenon rests on shared assumptions about ideas, plans, and actions through which we can and do understand each other. This shared cognitive orientation itself rests on the preconditions of *typification* and the *reciprocity of perspectives*. A typification refers to a shared meaning of something in its typical, essential, and generally understood form (Natanson 1973:chapter 7). The reciprocity of perspectives means that we can take the role and mental orientation of the other person and that he can assume and understand our own because in their essential form our positions are interchangeable. What is there can be our here, and vice-versa. Intersubjectivity allows us, then, a common ground for understanding and predicting each other's behavior. As we shall see, much of the very fabric of life history conjures up such a world of predictable social experience. As the individual relates his growing up and maturing in various domains of kinship, for example, these networks of social experience seem almost preordained, almost seamless, and their naturalness for us is highlighted when we become aware of an occasional breakdown in the account.

The ultimate objective of Husserl's original phenomenology, however, was to study the essential activity of consciousness itself, and that meant that the empirical nature of phenomena—their status of givenness—had to be transcended in order to be radically inspected. To begin with, the phenomenologist must conduct what Husserl (1931: 110) calls *epoché*, which involves the suspension of belief in the ontological characteristics of experienced objects, the purpose being to inspect their status as objects of conscious activity. Each basic realm of human experience has its particular epoché. *Phenomenological reduction* is a movement toward a more basic phenomenological procedure of bracketing all judgments about the ontological nature of perceived objects; it allows us to disregard their uniqueness and to reduce what is given in cognitive experience to the essentials of its form (eidetic reduction). Ultimately the phenomenologist attempts to bracket the knower himself, the source of consciousness, which brings us to the realm of *transcendental reduction* (Husserl 1960:92–99). With this step we come into contact, in theory at least, with the *transcendental ego*, the pure matrix of consciousness through which the possibilities of thought constitute themselves (ibid.:18–21, 73). Husserl thus believed that the world could be reduced to a correlate of transcendental subjectivity and that in this way the path of the originating constitution of the world could be reconstructed (Husserl 1931:154–55).

There is not a greal deal in phenomenological, and especially transcendental, reduction that is directly relevant to the interpretation of life histories. But some of the ideas are very provocative for our enterprise and bear on the problem of self-reflection, which is central to the subjectivity of the life history.

With epoché the objective status of subjective phenomena is bracketed; phenomena are viewed no longer as *given* but as *intended as given* (Schutz 1967b:106). The average individual who relates his life history does not, as a rule, perform epoché as a matter of course or extend it to many cognitive domains. After all, he is not practicing phenomenology! But to a certain degree all individuals who relate their lives engage in a self-reflective turn. We would say that at various points and in certain ways people adopt a *phenomenological attitude* toward their immersion in the life world as they assess their lives for themselves and/or for another who records it. The phenomenological attitude is the reflexive act that is a part of epoché, where the individual reflects on the value of something given in consciousness and begins to see it as merely intended as given—as, in fact, a product of his complicity in the world, from which he may disengage himself to inspect his active role in it (Natanson 1973:54–62). This action requires his recognition that it is he who sustains the beliefs and idea systems that make up his consciousness of that world. In the phenomenological attitude, as Natanson (1966:10) has remarked, a person renders his perceptual life as though he were aware of the natural attitude itself, giving events a kind of neutrality they do not possess in common-sense terms.

When, in relating his life history, the typical individual engages in limited self-reflection about the meaning of his own thinking, we speak of him assuming the "phenomenological attitude." Thus, phenomenology not only tells us something important about subjectivity *in* the life world; it also comments on the active, dynamic, and hence changing relationship *between* the individual and his pre-given cultural world.

Existentialism

With existentialism rather different (although not entirely distinct) possibilities for life history interpretation present themselves. Here we enter the terrain of the concrete individual, an existent whose life is self-chosen. In interpreting the subjective point of view in life history research, we interpret the experience of a specific subjective being. Moreover, we may try to locate the concrete peculiarities of that subjectivity in the individual's unique biographical situation. However, the individual's unique life plan raises the question of the conditions that made it possible. In that respect existentialism is a relevant commentary on the nature of individual autonomy, an issue that requires us to examine the question of choice and, ultimately, that of human freedom. Unfortunately, some existential writers have seen human choice and human destiny apart from the larger matrix of the life world through which freedom, if it exists, must of necessity express itself.

In our opinion, the single most important work by an existential philosopher is Jean-Paul Sartre's *Being and Nothingness* (1956). In this great work the nature of individual "being" is scrutinized and the possibilities of freedom within the possibilities of that being are examined. Sartre believes that being precedes essence in the sense that individual consciousness creates the meaning of the world and the objects in it rather than itself being the immanent manifestation of transcendental meaning. Outside of individual consciousness we have what Sartre calls *being-in-itself*, which consists of essences that manifest themselves to themselves. Being-in-itself is isolated in its being and does not enter connection with what is not itself. Being-in-itself is forever glued to itself and is filled with itself. It does not refer to itself as self-consciousness does.

Individual consciousness is what Sartre calls *being-for-itself*, which is the absolute basis of human freedom. Being-for-itself is consciousness that is not fixed to itself (that is, to its own being); it transcends its immediate being, which means that it is capable of negating being-in-itself or the fixity of being. This negational aspect of consciousness calls into question itself; it refuses existence. It defines itself to exist in a particular way through the negation of possibilities because it cannot coincide with itself as "being-in-itself" (Sartre 1956:125–126). For-itself, then, exists as a being that perpetually effects in itself a break in being. We might say that being-for-itself is the in-itself losing itself as in-itself in order to find itself in consciousness. Ultimately, this negational aspect of consciousness (being-for-itself) allows us to negate alternatives. It allows us, in other words, to choose our projects.

Our ego (the self, for Sartre) is nothing more than an object of consciousness endowed with qualities according to which consciousness chooses its projects. What all of us experience as beings-for-themselves are the negations of possibilities and opportunities that are not consonant with our chosen self. Sartre says that while it seems to us to be the "I" who is choosing, in actuality the "I" or "self" is only a particular object of our individual consciousness, a kind of illusory subjective "ego," assumed in relation to others. In reality, this "I" with all its projects can always be annihilated by the force of being-for-itself, and new identities and projects can be chosen. Ultimately, asserts Sartre, we are responsible for what we are, and only we can sustain

our situation through our choices because of our capacity for the negation of being, for nothingness. This situation is true for humans
whether they like it or not, or whether they choose to recognize it, because of the very ontological status of being.

The annihilating power of consciousness directed toward ideas,
plans, and projects that are seemingly natural to the individual is reminiscent of the phenomenological attitude we have just discussed, that
bracketing of the world and the self-reflexive turn of consciousness
that inspects the intentional nature of its projects, whose ontological
status seems so "real." So, like existential freedom, the phenomenological attitude of the individual throws into relief his own role in the
thoughts he thinks, the projects he formulates, and the actions in
which he engages. And if individuals do in fact come to this insight
through the phenomenological turn, they may well realize they are
free to think and behave differently.

Sartre (1956:87–92), however, assumes that the awareness of the
awesome freedom we have completely to shape our destiny produces
existential anguish from which we may flee by lying to ourselves (*bad
faith*) that we are what we are not, or that we are not what we are—to
wit, that our choices do not arise from our freedom but are determined
by things, orders, and rules outside ourselves (the life world!). It is always easier to fix the responsibility elsewhere than to confront our authentic selves in our aloneness. Thus, we turn away from the responsibility of freedom rather than acknowledge that it is we, and we alone,
who chose our projects. In the life histories we have seen, we find occasional excursions into freedom from out of the life world and a corresponding movement back into the rationalizations and justifications
of that same world when freedom proves too burdensome or threatening. Perhaps people maintain their culture with such vigor in part because it serves this exact function.

Sartre's metaphor of our waking up to the sound of the alarm tellingly conveys his thinking about the ultimate condition of what it
means to be free:

The alarm which rings in the morning refers to the possibility of
my going to work, which is *my* possibility. But to apprehend the
summons of the alarm as summons is to get up. Therefore the
very act of getting up is reassuring for it eludes the question, "Is
work my possibility?" Consequently, it does not put me in a position to apprehend the possibility of quiescence, or refusing to

work and the possibility of death. In short, to the extent that I
apprehend the meaning of the ringing I am already up at its summons; this apprehension guarantees me against the anguished in-
tuition that it is I who confer on the alarm its requiredness—I
and I alone. (Sartre 1956:75–76)

Sartre's idealism in insisting on seeing the foundations of personal
freedom apart from constraints imposed by the social and cultural context on thinking, deciding, and acting appears to be a limitation on the
possible application of his philosophy to concrete human beings with
empirical egos, rather than mere abstractions removed from personal
histories (see Bowes 1971; Douglas and Johnson 1977).

Merleau-Ponty (1962) has been one of Sartre's sternest critics in
this respect. Man is not always free, he says. Freedom and individual
destiny lie in an intricate transactive exchange between the world pos-
ited in some shape or form and one's own powers of initiative. Man is
not free in all situations, Merleau-Ponty feels, and his decisions cannot create all his situations. In fact, each person's life has a significance that he himself does not create. He is acted upon and yet open
to possibilities, and his situations define his choices so that he is neither totally free nor totally unfree. We can think of this condition as a
set of parameters that varies from one social situation or culture to another. Indeed, this living in the world and being subject to its claims
are reminiscent both of the life world and natural attitude of phenomenology and of the boundedness of the individual to his historically
determined horizon in hermeneutics. Merleau-Ponty goes on to argue
that we determine our freedom for ourselves in interaction with actual situations and meanings that place constraints upon us, and it is
therefore futile to think of freedom in the abstract apart from such concrete situations.

Existentialism asks questions (and in fact answers some of them)
about human "being" and "destiny," without, however, always addressing the problem of how we are to know and recognize these matters through the interpretation of others, and how, if at all, individual
consciousness is related to the larger social world and to history (the
exercise of bad faith suggests one way of joining the individual to his
life world). In any case, we believe that hermeneutics and phenomenology help to provide answers to these unanswered and troublesome
questions posed by existentialism that face us in our attempts to understand life histories.

Hermeneutics

Hermeneutics is a philosophical discipline that, for our purposes, brings into focus (1) the life history as a text or discourse to be interpreted, and (2) the interpreter of the text, whose very subjectivity is historically situated in a meaning-horizon different from that of the text itself. The central ground and essential concern of hermeneutics, however, is with the interpretive process that intervenes between the interpreter and that which is to be interpreted. Hermeneutics claims that understanding of something occurs only as a result of our interpretive activity (Gadamer 1975:274; Boehm 1978:12–13).

Interpretation, indeed, becomes necessary when we encounter something that is alien to us (e.g., a foreign culture, a text) and our usual personal understandings break down and we find ourselves unable to grasp the phenomenon as a coherent and meaningful entity. Palmer has reminded us in defining the scope of hermeneutics that "the various forms of the word hermeneutics suggest the process of bringing a thing or situation from unintelligibility to understanding. . . . Something foreign, strange, separated in space or experience is made familiar, present, comprehensible" (1969:13–14).

Earlier in the history of hermeneutics the emphasis was on the interpretation of texts (in the beginning, biblical ones and later juridical texts) with the objectives of putting oneself in the place of the author of the text and trying to reenact his intentions in writing it (Schleiermacher 1967). Even today there are those who believe we can formulate methods for interpreting texts and establishing canons for determining the validity of these methods. Betti (1962), for example, has exhaustively surveyed the various modes of interpretation in human disciplines and has attempted to formulate a general methodological theory for interpretation. He argues for the objective status of objects of interpretation and the possibility for objectively valid interpretation. It is possible, he says, to reconstruct objectively the meaning that the author was able to embody in the text. Hirsch (1967), going back to Schleiermacher, contends that the author's intentions must be the norm by which the validity of any textual interpretation is measured, and that this intention is a determinate entity about which objective evidence can be gathered. More recently, Ricoeur (1974a) has expanded the discussion by advocating that the meaning of the text can and should be arbitrated by a conflict of opposing interpretations.

All of these writers tend to deemphasize the critical and implicative role of the interpreter himself (Agar 1980). A break with the method-oriented approach to interpretation came with Heidegger's (1962) ontological hermeneutics, which was taken up and elaborated by Gadamer (1971, 1975, 1976a). In Gadamer's work the activity of the interpreter in the process of understanding is given decisive emphasis, an emphasis that we feel is a needed corrective to the traditional positivism and objectivism, for example, of most life history interpretation. In the following discussion, therefore, we shall focus mainly on Gadamer's ontological approach, although we will not neglect the importance and the possibilities of its methodological application.

Gadamer (1975:269–272) recognizes that the problem of interpretation begins when there is a gulf between our horizon and the horizon in which the text (life history, for example) lies embedded; where our ordinary preunderstandings do not allow us to make sufficient sense of what the text "says." The notion of horizon can be likened to the cultural life world in which the individual or text lives, as it is moved by and situated in history. In the movement of history a horizon takes on many different layers of sedimented meaning. If we wish to understand the foreign object, Gadamer argues, we can never completely leave our own familiar context and enter directly into the original intent of the text, for we are bound to our historically determined horizon, which in the beginning mediates the text or object to us. The preunderstandings that constitute our horizon and are mediated by the very language we use are not negative and do not hold us back from interpreting, but rather constitute the initial possibilities for understanding at all (Gadamer 1975:238–239). As Gadamer uses the term "preunderstanding" it appears to refer to the pregiven ideas, judgments, and orientations to the world that are part of our culture-historical horizon.[1]

1. Gadamer uses various terms when he addresses the phenomenon of our preconceived notions that enter the process of interpretation. Most often he uses "prejudice" and "preunderstanding," but "fore-meaning," "fore-understanding," and "bias" (*Voreingenommenheit*, literally, to be within the horizon of preconceived notions) are used as well. Gadamer's concept of prejudice as a positive factor has caused considerable confusion. He discusses at length the historical development and changes in the meanings of the term from pre-Enlightenment times, when it meant simply a judgment before the consideration of all potential information, to post-Englightenment days, when it took on the negative connotations that it has in its modern meaning (1975:240–245). Gadamer (ibid.:240) states explicitly that in its former context "prejudice" did not

When we attempt to interpret an alien text by questioning it, our initial entry point is invariably through our preunderstandings. Gadamer feels that in order to interpret in the first place, we must break through the barriers that separate us from the text. We do this by entering into a "conversation" or dialogue with the text, even though, despite our openness to the dialogue, our initial questions always partake of our preunderstandings. Gadamer (ibid.:263), however, talks of "productive" and "unproductive" preunderstandings: the former allow us to formulate questions that open up a dialogue and allow the text and its world to address us, whereas the latter hinder us from penetrating into that horizon. As the conversation with the text unfolds, we must continuously question our preunderstandings, heeding those that allow us to continue the dialogue, while ignoring or discarding those whose rigidity and closedness prevent the very possibility for that dialogue. To be open to questions from the text as well as from our own preunderstandings becomes one of the central issues: "The hermeneutical task becomes automatically a questioning of things" (ibid.238).

Though he does not spell out exactly how we find the "right" questions appropriate to the context of an alien object, questions with true potential for dialogue, Gadamer (1967:108; 1975:238) does talk about the essential qualities of imagination and openness in the formulation of questions and the necessity for critically questioning ourselves and our own horizon.[2]

The hermeneutical endeavor requires a basic distinction between

----

convey a positive or negative meaning but represented an open position from which the one who attempted to understand could proceed in different directions. Coreth (1969:100), however, has argued that the term "prejudice" in contemporary thinking does not express the basic potential associated with "preunderstandings" as used in Gadamer's work, that is, their open and continuously changing character, which makes space for new and different meanings in the process of interpretation. He suggests that instead "preunderstanding" should be used as the more appropriate expression. We agree with this position since we assume that most contemporary readers will not reenact the historical journey of the term "prejudice."

2. Kaiser in an attempt to demonstrate the systematic nature of the hermeneutical effort, explains how this questioning of horizons comes about and makes understanding possible: "The hermeneutical effort questions its epistemological perspective, i.e., its expectation-horizons, and by doing so makes it actually possible to consider these horizons" (1978:430). Thus, according to Kaiser, "scientific interpretation," as compared with "reading as an aesthetic experience"—which means "just being in the horizon"—becomes possible.

"methodical" and "dialectical" questioning in the process of understanding.[3] Methodical questioning or analysis tends not to call into question its own guiding presuppositions but rather operates within a system, so that the answer is always potentially present and expected within that system (Palmer 1969:233). This activity, then, is a form not so much of true questioning as of testing. Dialectical questioning, however, breaks the barriers of its own context. We often learn from it that the phenomenon is different than what we expected it to be. In dialectical questioning, questions open up the potential of the conversation so that the text in its turn speaks to its dialogue partner of its world.

In the movement of conversation the interpreter puts to risk his preunderstandings in the form of questions (after self-critical scrutiny), seeking ever to modify and refine them in the course of the exchange in order to continue the dialogue. In the process, as the text addresses the interpreter and begins to reveal its world to him through his questions, it poses its own questions in turn, thus requiring the interpreter to reexamine his understandings and, if necessary, to change the context of his own questions to assimilate better what the text has to say (Gadamer 1975:239). Gadamer likens the conversation to the game. Players are focused on the back-and-forth movement of the game itself, just as the interpreter and the text as dialogue partners are focused in their conversation on the exchange centered in their common concern (ibid.:446).

The productive nature of the dialogue is made possible by language itself, which is the medium of exchange and the embodiment of the dialogue partners' respective horizons. Each horizon is given prereflectively in language and we possess the world linguistically. Speech allows us to make ourselves understandable to others regarding a given subject matter. Language as conversation presses against the limits of established conventions and moves between the sedimented meanings and usages that are its basis and the new that it strives to express (Gadamer 1976b). Its flexibility as a semantic system opens up the inherent possibilities of dialogue. Indeed, the concrete use of language in conversation is the foundation of the very fluidity of our horizons of understanding. Ultimately, understanding is essentially linguistic, but in such fashion that it transcends the limits of any particular language,

3. Here we follow Palmer's (1969:233) terminology, which we feel expresses best the problems faced by the anthropologist collecting a life history.

thus mediating between the familiar and the alien. Our language, in fact, is not closed off against what is foreign to it: rather it is porous and open to expansion and absorption of ever-new mediated content in the dialogue situation (Gadamer 1975:363–364).

These important hermeneutical issues are related to our own work of life history interpretation. If the interpretive purpose for engaging the life history is, as we have advocated, to capture something of the subjectivity and individuality of its author within the horizon of the text, any kind of methodical questioning bound to rigid theoretical preunderstandings (such as psychoanalytic theory) imposes an alien set of meanings on the enterprise and in so doing fails to bring out the subject's own truth of himself. Existential and phenomenological interpretations better open up dialectical questioning to this end, thus initiating a dialogue that allows the life history to converse about the particular subjective character of the author's world. In this case, and for this type of understanding, therefore, some kinds of interpretive preunderstandings are more likely to engender a fruitful exchange of views and result in a more meaningful mediation of horizons than do other interpretive systems.

The result of dialectical questioning is that, while we never totally abandon our preunderstandings, we come to enlarge the meaning of the text, integrating it into the framework of our present but changed understanding so that "we understand in a different way, if we understand at all" (Gadamer 1975:264). This situation refers to the hermeneutical circle because it is a bridging back and forth between horizons, in the process of which we move in concentric circles away from an original horizon, bridging our world and that of the text until they are integrated (ibid.:259).[4] Using the example of understanding different historical periods, Gadamer explains that this becomes possible when we "perform the transposition that the concepts of the past undergo when we try to think in them" (ibid.:358). This process, for Gadamer, defines the ontological character of all understanding. It

---

4. Bauman also stresses the implicative activity of the interpreter in the process of understanding. He feels that understanding of alien forms of life comes not from immersion in their specific uniqueness but by spotting the general in the particular, by "enlarging both the alien and one's own experience so as to construct a larger system in which each makes sense to the other" (1978:218). We believe, however, that in the dialogical process some of that special uniqueness is brought out even if it must be cast in forms of understanding generated from our own experience.

happens as we interpret and understand beyond our willing and sometimes beyond our knowing. We remain creatures of our historically
determined situation, but we are also creatures who can also understand the difference of others (ibid.:269–274).

One of the cardinal tenets of hermeneutics is that when we interpret
and understand a text, like a life history, we see it in both unitary
fashion—as a whole—and in terms of the parts that make it up.
Thus, we cannot understand the whole without the parts, nor the parts
except in reference to the whole (Gusdorf 1980:43). The construction
of the thematic relationship of parts to whole is one of the most important meanings of the hermeneutical circle (Gadamer 1975:258–261).

As we interpret we build upon our knowledge of the parts of the
text to grasp the whole. As the meaning of the whole emerges, we are
better able to correct our interpretation of the significance of the parts.
For example, the individual parts of a typical Guajiro Indian life history, such as the obsessive fear of poverty, begin to take on thematic
unity and make sense only as they are related to the larger cultural
world of class injustice and personal debasement of the poor before the rich as this world reveals itself in the text through our interpretive activity.

Grasping the dialectic interplay of parts and wholes emerges out of
true dialectical questioning. By asking questions appropriate to the
text, and by listening to its answers and the questions that it addresses
to us, we create a dialogue in which it is possible to correct continuously the direction of interpretation, until through our changed understanding (that is, through the broadened contexts we have fashioned),
the parts begin to relate meaningfully to each other and to the whole
and reveal their underlying subjective integrity.

In the final analysis, Gadamer seems to give no clear answer as to
what ideally constitutes understanding. It is the work of hermeneutics,
not to develop a procedure of understanding, "but to clarify the conditions in which understanding takes place" (ibid.:263).[5] For him interpretation is open-ended and never complete in the absolute sense, as
he states in the finishing words of the third (expanded) edition of *Truth
and Method*: "But I am breaking off. The dialogue which is in prog-

5. Nonetheless, Gadamer does imply that while mediation of horizons always
occurs as part of interpretation, some mediations are better than others and
more fully capture what the text wants to say about *its* world.

ress evades definition. A bad hermeneuticist who believes he could or should have the last word" (1972:541).

An interesting comment on the unfinished business of living and understanding a life comes from Gusdorf in his discussion of autobiography:

> Autobiography is . . . never the finished image or the fixing forever of an individual life: the human being is always a making, a doing; memoirs look to an essence beyond existence, and in manifesting it they serve to create it. In the dialogue with himself, the writer does not seek to say a final word that would complete his life; he strives only to embrace more closely the always secret but never refused sense of his own identity. (1980:47)

Like the incompleteness of the autobiographer's own self-rendering, textual interpretation itself has no true end, either, for it never really reaches a final stasis that can be definitively arbitrated. Indeed, future interpretations attempt to probe ever deeper in order to yield ever more coherent meaning unities, even if exact standards for evaluating them, of the kind argued by hermeneuticists other than Gadamer, are lacking. Kaiser has expressed this belief in continuous refinement of interpretation in his discussion of the scientific understanding of texts. He perceives "the process of interpretation as advancing forever more complete, more differentiated and deeper probing interpretations," which becomes possible through the ability of the hermeneutical approach to incorporate as many different "problem-positions of interpretation" (possible interpretive constructions) as possible (1978:432).

We agree with Gadamer's ontological approach. In fact, we see this process happening experientially in our own efforts to interpret and understand life history texts. The problem remains, though, that in doing specific interpretations one must be guided by an interpretive system that allows questions to be posed in the first place. Our interpretive activity, while always in motion, should in fact be sufficiently defined at any stage of the process so that it aids us in our efforts to synthesize and evaluate the text's own questions and answers. By being flexible within possibilities mapped out by our interpretive systems, we can begin the long and challenging process of integrating parts and wholes to make understandable the world of which the text speaks.

The Problem of the Text

With the anthropological life history text we have a vast cultural distance, not merely different phases in our own Western historical tradition, to bridge. The exoticism of the venture is intensified because as anthropologists we often experience life histories first as free-wheeling oral discourse when we either have an imperfect knowledge of the native language or must use an interpreter. How then do we bring this encounter with discourse into a frame that makes sense in our cultural tradition of chronological histories and written documents?

Two phases of interpretation, under these circumstances, are normally involved. First, the oral discourse is interpreted as it is transcribed and integrated into textual form. At some point this process involves translation from the native language. Then the written document itself is interpreted. Geertz (1973a, 1976) points out that our attempts to reconstruct meaning in other cultures are interpretations of other peoples' interpretations; but we would argue, with the life history in mind, that our search for understanding consists of an interpretation of an interpretation of an interpretation. Initially the native informant interprets his situation and his culture for us; we then translate his discourse into our language and interpret it in a certain way by textualizing it; and, finally, we must interpret the text itself as a fixed form whose meanings cannot be extricated from the interpretive scheme through which it is mediated to us (textualized) and by which it actually addresses itself to us.

Gadamer sees the understanding of the text as the greatest challenge to interpretation: "There is nothing so strange and at the same time so demanding as the written word. Not even the encounter with speakers of a foreign language can be compared with this strangeness, since the language of gesture and sound always contains an element of immediate understanding" (1975:145). While he obviously minimizes the difficulties associated with the understanding of non-verbal communications and their culture-bound characteristics, he is focusing on one of the central issues: the immediacy of the message that has been alienated, separated from the writer: "Written texts present the real hermeneutical task. Writing involves self-alienation. Its overcoming, the reading of the text, is thus the highest task of understanding" (ibid.:352). This task is accomplished by bridging the text back "into the living presence of conversation, whose fundamental procedure is always question and answer" (ibid.:331); that is, writing must be changed back into speech and meaning (ibid.:354).

Ricoeur's discussion of the oral discourse and the text sheds light on the difficulties and questions involved in this bridging between text and oral discourse. As Ricoeur (1979) points out, texts are of a different order from oral discourse and pose their own particular kinds of interpretive challenges. (Indeed, all the life histories that we will be interpreting or reinterpreting in the remainder of the essay exist as texts, even though in several instances we collected the life history data ourselves and so command some perspective on the subject's original activity and our own recording and editing of it.) Ricoeur mentions four attributes that emerge when discourse becomes text:

1. The fixation of meaning. When writing fixes discourse in the form of the text, it fixes what is "said" in speech and arrests the inevitable disappearance of discourse, which is a fleeting event. Aspects of the speech act are codified, gathered into paradigms, where, consequently, they can be identified and reidentified as having the same meaning. Once we have fixed the life history into the form of a text, for example, it ceases to have the openness of the original dialogue and becomes inspectable as a limited and unchanging set of ordered significances; it is there for others in the same form as it is for those who affixed it.

2. The dissociation of the text from the mental intentions of the author. Discourse is self-referential; the subjective intention of the speaking subject and the meaning of the discourse overlap each other in such a way that to understand what the speaker meant and to understand what his discourse means are practically the same thing. But fixed as text, that discourse escapes the finite horizon of the author, and what the text says now matters more than what the author meant to say. Ricoeur feels that every interpretation of a text operates within a circumference of meaning that has broken its moorings to the psychology of the author and that now comes to exist as a world for others.

Although the author of the life history is very much present in his account, thus rendering his intentions a potential object for interpretation, we see in the hermeneutical situation defined by Ricoeur that the text is speaking about a *world* in which the author may or may not reveal himself; and it is the primacy of that world *as text*, through which the author speaks, that should be the main concern of textual exegesis.

3. The display of non-ostensive references. In spoken discourse the dialogue ultimately refers to the situation common to the interlocutors. Reference is ostensive. The text, however, opens up an ensemble of nonsituational references that outlive the immediate reference. This larger world that the text points to beyond its immediate situation, therefore, is there for us as "symbolic dimensions" of our "being-in-the-world" (Ricoeur 1979:79); entering it can illuminate our world as well.

One might think of the life history text as a world, albeit one articulated by a particular individual, that reveals to us the possibilities of our own situation and leads us to self-understanding. The original discourse of the dialogue situation and its meaning may be lost to us, but the world contained in and revealed through the text itself, whose inner meanings are potentially decipherable, is still there for us.

4. The universal range of address of the text. The discourse is addressed to someone who is present, immediate to the sayer. The text as something written is addressed to an audience, an unknown audience that it creates itself: "In escaping the momentary character of the event, the bounds lived by the author, and the narrowness of ostensive reference, discourse (as text) escapes the limits of being face to face" (Ricoeur 1979:80). A life history text, then, would no longer be just the subject addressing a particular anthropologist interpreter. It would exist for others who knew nothing of the original discourse to interpret, each potential interpreter finding that the text addressed him in a unique way according to his own initial preunderstandings and his own special capacities for initiating and maintaining the dialogue.

While Ricoeur's observations are valid to a degree, they underplay the real possibility that the anthropological interpreter may establish some of the background of the original discourse (the situation) and find it possible to reconstruct at least some of the outlines of subjective intent where information on the data-collecting setting, the motivations involved, and the personality of the author is known. Moreover, the "world" of the life history text itself, unlike that of most other texts, is primarily self-referential and should be understood, therefore, in those terms. The author speaks about *his subjective world*, which includes his interpretations of himself and his experience, and this occurs even when we know little or nothing about the encounter, the dialogue, or the exact properties of original subjective intentions. Indeed, we can legitimately work toward reconstructing subjective intent by regarding the life history text as a statement about the dialectical interplay of the individual with the meaningful world of personal experience he seeks to recreate.[6] As Gadamer reminds us, the interpretive endeavor itself is mediated through our own conversation *with* the text, so that through the dialogue it is possible to join the text in recreating something of its subjective dimensions.

We can, in fact, bring out some of the unique and special subjectivity of a life history by working mainly within the text, but we should supplement our knowledge with whatever we know about how it has been translated into written form from the original discourse. As anthropologists we are not committed to accepting Ricoeur's contentions that the text is necessarily dissociated from subjective intent and that its reference is non-ostensive and directed away from the original dialogue encounter.

Ricoeur argues that texts yield their significance, within limits, according to the methods and interpretive perspectives that we employ, despite the dialectical and unanticipated quality of understanding. Each interpretive endeavor, moreover, follows from a body of stated or implicit principles and theory (Ricoeur 1974b). The meaning of the text is arbitrated when conflicting interpretations proceeding from different principles confront each other, within the limited field of possible constructions of the text. Criteria of relative superiority for arbitrating interpretations can be derived from the logic of subjective probability (Ricoeur 1979:91). Exactly what that logic is remains unclear in Ricoeur's discussion because in his examples different interpretations appear equally plausible but in different ways. Ricoeur then offers the following tentative way out of the dilemma: "It is always possible to argue for or against an interpretation, to confront interpretations, to arbitrate between them, and *to seek for an agreement, even if this agreement remains beyond our reach*" (ibid.:91; italics ours).

In discussing the conflict of psychoanalytic and phenomenological interpretations of texts (life histories would be good examples), Ricoeur says that the former yield the possibility of underlying disguised structures, while the latter lay open the revelatory possibility of being by bringing out the meaning through which the text speaks and orients

6. Gusdorf's comments on the interplay between autobiography and the individual who reveals his life also hold true for the life history. "It is a moment of the life that it recounts; it struggles to draw all meaning from that life, but it is itself a meaning in the life" (1980:43). Thus the text is testimony to the dialectics of the person's battle to recount this life and give meaning to it. In this sense the life history as text "turns back on the life and affects it by a kind of boomerang" (ibid.:47).

itself to the world. Each, it seems, reveals the limitations of the other;
yet the two interpretive schemes seem to be reconcilable as a commentary of origin, on one hand, working toward an immanent existential
truth disclosed in being, on the other, each of which is revealed within
its own methods (Ricoeur 1974c, 1974d).

In summary, then, we accept four points in regard to life history interpretation: (1) while the life history as text poses special problems,
sufficient additional information on the personality and immediate
culture context of the author may enable us to approach the text not
merely as a "world" but as a subjective individual experience speaking
"through a world," one mediated and comprehensible in terms of the
particular dialogue situation of the author and his interlocutor; (2)
through a phenomenological and existential approach to the text we
can achieve a greater (albeit imperfect) understanding of the unique
subjectivity of the individual and the possibilities for his freedom than
would be possible with other approaches; (3) in the process of interpretation our understanding is always a mediation or integration of the
horizon of the author and his world with our own, so that in a sense
the text speaks through our changed self-understanding to an unknown
audience; and (4) by confronting other interpretations of anthropological life histories with our own, we hermeneutically broaden the very
understanding we seek.

Hermeneutical Issues in Interpretation:
The Case of Tuhami

Tuhami: Portrait of a Moroccan (1980) by Vincent Crapanzano is an
ambitious and largely successful attempt to examine the hermeneutical
issues at stake in our efforts to understand the life of another. In more
immediate terms, the book represents the author's self-appointed task
to work these issues out for himself in the special circumstances of his
encounter with Tuhami and his world.

Tuhami is a Moroccan tile-maker whose life is ruled by saints and a
host of she-demons, particularly one camel-footed 'A'isha Qandisha,
who keeps him from marrying and having a normal social life appropriate to a man of his age and position. His is the life story of an
alienated, marginal individual whose existence has a seemingly unreal
and fragmented quality, but which at the same time is highly complex

and convoluted. It is that nature that challenges our interpretive attempts to make sense of him. Crapanzano's undertaking must be seen in the light of the manifold complexities of Tuhami's experiential situation and the shifting dynamics of the interpersonal circumstances through which this situation was expressed.

Crapanzano wishes to make sense of what Tuhami related to him and to understand how he articulated his world and situated himself within it (ibid:xi). Crapanzano's interpretation raises the question of Tuhami's freedom and the constraints on his freedom. But perhaps above all *Tuhami* as a text and as the experiences of a human being raises the problematics of life history construction and the ethnographic encounter.

We shall confine ourselves to some general observations on the book as it relates to the main issues we have taken up in earlier discussion, and we will not try to render in any way a detailed account of the contents of the study. Our critique, therefore, will make most sense to those who have already read *Tuhami* and pondered it for themselves, and we urge those who have not read it to do so, for it is a sensitive and richly articulated portrayal of two men coming to know and understand each other.

Crapanzano utilizes some of the interpretive perspectives we have advocated, particularly the existentialism of Sartre and the phenomenology of Schutz. In an effort to find a broad enough interpretive base to engage the demands of this life history, Crapanzano integrates phenomenology and existentialism with several other approaches: the anthropology of symbolism, and the theories of Simmel and G. H. Mead. All these theoretical approaches, it must be added, are framed within the larger hermeneutical ground of how we are to know the "other" and how our own activities produce the "known." To some extent Crapanzano's hermeneutics is reminiscent of Geertz's (1973b) "thick description" of culture but applied here to the individual *in situ*. Rather than using his theories to test anything, Crapanzano explains,

I use specific theoretical approaches here rhetorically—to illuminate the space of encounter and what, I believe, from my essentially skewed perspective, transpired within it. My reference, then, to theorists and theories resembles more the references that literary critics, in their interpretation of a specific text, make to other authors than it resembles the references that anthropolo-

52 Interpreting Life Histories

gists and other social scientists make in their development of theory. For the critic the text has a primacy that data—the social scientist's text—do not have. (Ibid.:xiii)

The interpretive thrust here is sophisticatedly eclectic, and different approaches are utilized at different times in various ways to shed light on the meanings of Tuhami's utterances as they changed over time in the dynamic give and take of the dialogue situation. Because various theoretical perspectives were used and because Crapanzano's perspective changed with his altered self-understanding, the interpretive results sometimes seem rather fragmented and unintegrated—indeed, far removed from his claims for the elegance and coherence of his approach. For Crapanzano the whole scaffolding of his interpretation probably sprang from a unified vision of his activity and, perhaps, from a sense that the different interpretive forays reinforced each other. The reader is apt to find it difficult to integrate the author's interpretations as he tentatively approaches the book with his own hermeneutics. The real point that should be underscored, though, is that Crapanzano's interpretation is never static, and as it moves forward through the book it cancels out or modifies previous stances and prior understandings (though the dynamics of this very process, the ways in which understandings are corrected and changed, are not spelled out).

Tuhami's life as it is presented to us is a retreat from the world, a kind of living death. It takes the form of a static dialectic with the female jinns, male spirits, and the ghosts of saints that dominate his life and prevent him from making practical adjustments to accomplish things that he advocated in his conscious life and were in accord with Moroccan values, such as marriage and family. As Crapanzano explains, Tuhami chose to lead his life in terms of a frozen symbol of a now irrelevant cultural code rather than to be cast adrift in the flux of meaningless social activity, where he would take his chances and perhaps risk everything (ibid.:83–84). This life choice, it would seem, gives Tuhami his reason for being, his individuality, even if it is that of a suffering victim.

Does this mean that Tuhami authentically chooses the projects through which he defines his life, or is this life a flight into "bad faith," an escape into the irreality of supernatural enslavement that would absolve him of the necessity to make choices in the everyday pragmatic world? It is, indeed, a difficult question to resolve, and Crapanzano provides us with no easy answers. Yet, if Tuhami's recitation of the "real" and fantasy all mixed into one is regarded as a metaphor for the "truth" of his life, as Crapanzano says, then we may have to consider the possibility that he freely chooses to embrace these images and to imbue them with the power they have over his life. He is paradoxically exercising freedom to be not free. Ultimately, however, we feel this truth of his life is an expression of his freedom because it is reaffirmed continuously in the choices of his life and in his rendering of himself to others. Tuhami finds meaning in life in the very way he constructs it as an ongoing process.

This summary is but a minute specimen of some of the interpretive insights in the book and the larger hermeneutical issues they raise when the reader questions them and attempts his own critical reinterpretation.

Crapanzano's interpretations of the meaning of Tuhami's subjective world seem to be played out on a hermeneutical level of textual exegesis rather different from the level of the interpretive commentary he provides on the negotiated nature of text construction that occurs within the encounter with the other in the field situation. That the two are not always satisfactorily integrated, in our opinion, can in no way detract from Crapanzano's skill or sensitivity; it is rather a statement on the virtual impossibility of interpretation to account fully for the construction *and* reinterpretation of texts, beginning with tentative and unstructured human relations in the field and ending with intellectualization on an already highly edited and interpreted text that has been forged in the dynamics of human encounter.

In our own view the most striking insights to emerge in the book, encompassing various levels of interpretive activity, are the following:

1. Crapanzano places a clear emphasis on the hermeneutics of the encounter so that the meanings that emerge to define this event are seen as an agreement negotiated by the partners in the dialogue situation. That agreement is the common meeting ground for text construction and is somewhat, although not fully, analogous to the process by which different horizons are integrated in the course of the dialogue, as in Gadamer's hermeneutics.

2. Crapanzano discovered that the reality of Tuhami's life could not be grasped within the framework of our concept of the "real"; rather, the events and experiences described, whether "real" or "fantasy," were metaphors for the essential truth of his existence.

3. Finally, Crapanzano came to realize that the very truth of Tuhami's life was itself changing, being negotiated; in fact, insofar as it

was mediated through their particular relationship, "truth" was relative
to the encounter itself.

We now wish to shift gears and proceed with our own brief commentary of the author's hermeneutics. We do this in the spirit of a
quest to understand the book, not to undermine or detract from this
very significant endeavor. Our critique essentially falls under three
headings: (1) the incompleteness of the life history text; (2) the
problem of wholes and parts in interpretive reconstruction; and
(3) the dialogue-like character of interpretation, bringing into play the
preunderstandings of opposing or different horizons and their eventual
mediation through the process of conversation and dialectical correction.

1. The incompleteness of the life history text. The life history text of
Tuhami unfolds in a series of interviews; thus, the personal data in
textual form is an elicited and subsequently edited recitation. In Crapanzano's interpretation Tuhami is made to speak through the world of
the text, but because the final text itself is reduced to certain subjects,
avoids others, and has no true narrative continuity, the subject's inner
horizon in its unfolding complexity is not fully captured. In fact,
Tuhami's inner life, when it does emerge, derives mainly from Crapanzano's interpretive horizon rather than from his own recitation of
his own personal meaning horizon. Thus Crapanzano often overinter-
prets subjective meaning. Tuhami's life seems rather flat and incomplete at times; closure occurs, where needed in such circumstances, by
interpretive "filling in."

If we are to situate Tuhami in his world, to understand that world
through the particular subjectivity of his life, a good deal more personal data has to be presented. The frame of the text as an interview
certainly gives insight into the field situation and may be an accurate
portrayal of what happened there, but the little actual textual information about the multiple and interlocking dimensions of Tuhami's
subjective humanness is insufficient to allow us that deep and reassuring glimpse.

2. Wholes and parts. In an earlier discussion we talked about correcting our understanding of wholes and parts in terms of the dialectics
of their interaction as we come to reconstruct the process interpretively. There are several problems in this respect in Crapanzano's account of Tuhami. Because the life history text itself is incomplete (the
part, here), Crapanzano tends to reconstruct Tuhami's inner life by
overinterpreting it as a reflection of Moroccan culture (the whole),

which he has culled in large measure from sources other than Tuhami's own account. This overinterpretation results in a diminishment of the dialectic we advocate, where, by understanding the rich inner life of the subject through an examination of a detailed and sustained narrative, we are more fully able to reconstruct the particularistic features of the personal culture from which he draws his sense of being in the world.

An opposite problem sometimes occurs when Crapanzano attempts to interpret the meaning of an event (the part) in relationship to the larger themes that make up Tuhami's life (the whole). Here the problem characteristically involves a failure to trace out the connection between part and whole, to make plausible the process of interpretation that made such an integrated vision possible in the end. For example, in a sudden insight Crapanzano claims that the death of Tuhami's friend by drowning (the part) "was *the* event [and a "real" one] that was central to him, the subject of his persistent metamorphoses [the whole, or other larger parts of the whole], the root of his emptiness, his impotence, his being as dead" (ibid.:129). Evidently, Crapanzano had seen a similarity between this "infinitesimal and sacred void that concluded a death and began a horrible metamorphosis" in the life of Genet as interpreted by Sartre and in that of Tuhami (ibid.). For some reason, unexplained in the book, Crapanzano felt justified in applying Sartre's interpretive schema for Genet to Tuhami. Why? Because they were both misfits, men without women, men who recreated the world metaphorically through fantasy? Who knows? Crapanzano never really does show just how this "central" event was related to Tuhami's metamorphoses, nor does he tell us, furthermore, the nature of those very metamorphoses that derive from this experience (though one could make some good guesses from context). We are left then with interpretive statements about parts and wholes but without any explanation of why and in what ways they are connected.

3. The dialogical character of interpretation. The ground of hermeneutics can be divided for the present purpose into four areas: (1) the horizon of the individual and his production (the text); (2) the horizon of the interpreter and his role in text construction; (3) the process of interpretation; and (4) the products of interpretation, that is, the interpretive results that presumably reflect the final position of processes in which the horizons of the dialogue partners (text and interpreter) have been dialectically integrated.

Crapanzano is very strong and convincing in his treatment of the cultural horizons of the text, even if the inner life of the subject is not fully revealed, and he provides us with many examples of the products of interpretive activity, that is, actual interpretations of Tuhami and his world. However, we learn very little about Crapanzano's personal or even cultural horizon, except for his observations on his role in the field relationship, and we learn less than we should about implicit pre-understandings and the more specific biases that he brings into play in his encounter with Tuhami.

Furthermore, although the interpretations themselves are there for us to see, we have little knowledge of how they came into being through the dialectic process of Crapanzano's interpretive activity, involving, as it must have, a kind o' "conversation" (trying out understandings) with Tuhami, and later with his life history text. As in all dialogues, the process moves forward through "prejudices" posed as questions that were tried, corrected, rephrased, and corrected again, until an interpretation that was meaningful to Crapanzano's changed self-understanding in his particular human relationship to Tuhami could emerge. We are not referring here so much to the original dialogue, which is preserved in the book in textual form (although that too had already been interpreted and edited in all probability); we are saying that Crapanzano himself did things, tried things out from his initial position, abandoned certain preconceptions, entertained other possibilities, while developing explanations for his memories of Tuhami and the notes he recorded, until he forged these efforts into the fixed texts and interpretive statements we read.

He tells us practically nothing about his own background, or even about his intellectual roots. The choice of literary models is apparently a product of experience and self-chosen interests. And if indeed that assumption is correct, why then did he choose Sartre and why Sartre's study of Genet? In what ways and at what point in his understanding of Tuhami were these particular figures chosen and engaged in the dialectic and made to speak of Tuhami through him? Were these theoretical prejudices imposed on the material early in the going and reconfirmed as Tuhami was made to conform to them, or were they taken up, worked out in conversation with the text only after other, less satisfactory interpretive possibilities were exhausted?

Perhaps Crapanzano did not really know for sure. We should commend him for his honesty in making the following statement about his work: "I do not know when my theoretical confabulations, my observations, and explications result immediately from the encounter and when they result from the literary reencounter" (ibid.:139–140).

Nonetheless, it is not unreasonable to suppose that with his hermeneutical interest Crapanzano could well have given us a self-reflective interpretation of at least some of his own interpretive activity. If, as we believe, Gadamer's ontological hermeneutics defines the way interpretation operates over and above our willing or desiring, then a self-reflective turn on the author's part toward the very being of his developing understanding could have illuminated much of the process for us.

Tuhami, though certainly a problematic book and not without flaws, represents a significant contribution because it addresses in a singular and forceful way the naive epistemological assumptions that have traditionally characterized our anthropological understanding of what life histories mean as texts and as human documents born of deeply motivated interpersonal encounters. We can only applaud that effort and hope that when others read *Tuhami* they come away from the experience with a greater self-critical understanding of themselves and their interpretations of the world.

Chapter 3
The Subjective World of a Life History

In this chapter we shall attempt to make use of phenomenological and existential perspectives, situating them in the larger ground of hermeneutical activity, in order to understand the particular subjective world of a Guajiro Indian woman as she presents herself in the life history text she and we have constructed together.

Though hermeneutics could just as well take a Freudian or behavioristic slant, phenomenological and existential approaches are the ones most likely to yield interpretive insights into the unique subjective world of the author of the text and are the least likely to distort or skew our understanding. Our phenomenological and existential starting points are a meaningful hermeneutics for the very reason that they give explicit recognition to the status of the text (e.g., the life history) as a subjective product equal in its importance to the interpreter's whole subjective bag of preunderstandings. Our interpretive approach, therefore, becomes an encounter of two distinct but equal horizons. The life history that we wish to interpret is something whose meaning is revealed, not by imposing massive external constructs, but by "making room" (listening) to accommodate the foreign frame of reference that brought it into being (Winch 1964).

That our eventual understanding will remain incomplete is to be expected; that it will be integrated into and mediated through our world and speak through us is part of the hermeneutical process.

Interpretive Categories for a Framework of Understanding

Our aim is to define and elaborate a set of categories for hermeneutically engaging the life history through phenomenology and existentialism. The first five categories relate to the fundamental hermeneutical problem, the next six to phenomenological and existential hermeneutics, specifically. Nevertheless, all eleven represent in a sense a single arc leading from the interpreter's own horizon (that is to say, the preunderstandings of his world) to some approximation of an eventual understanding of the subjectivity of the life history production.

1. The sociocultural context. The hermeneutical position asserts that an understanding of an event or phenomenon cannot be divorced from the whole of which it forms a part (the hermeneutical circle; see Watson-Franke and Watson 1975). If we are to remain faithful to the holistic interpretation implied by the hermeneutical circle, it is important for us to know as much as possible about the large sociocultural context (horizon, life world) of the individual in approaching the life history. The details of economics, family structure, politics, educational transmission, and general ideological orientation, for example, must all be known, at least in theory, to comprehend fully the contextual meaning of events and experiences that the life history describes. No event, however seemingly remote, may be dismissed a priori as irrelevant in our search to discover the significance of any other event, for together they form a single intricate chain that has no true, self-evident beginning or end. Knowledge of the larger context and the interrelationship of its parts enables us better to correct our interpretations as we project them onto the text and attempt to work them out within that complex matrix in our quest for understanding.

2. The individual life in context. At still another level of interpretive activity we can identify the particular context that defines the interplay between the individual and his culture. In hermeneutics it is not enough merely to know the general context of an event, work, or text (like the totality of Greek culture, say, for a particular statue); in addition we must know the more particular context that gives rise to it and encloses it (e.g., the artist who made the statue and his special milieu in Greek culture). Specifically, we want to know what it is like to be a certain kind of person in the culture and the quality and texture of that person's participation in his cultural world. Also, what kinds of developments and changes could a certain kind of individual expect in the course of his life? Here, any life cycle data and personal documents other than the ones to be examined in depth should be studied (if available) to get some overall feeling for the dimensions of the individual-culture relationship. A sufficient understanding of the cultural context of different individuals, as revealed in life cycle accounts and life histories, helps to establish the variability of experience in the culture along age, sexual, class, and occupational lines; and it may also reveal the range of deviation from typical events that various individuals exhibit. We may, for instance, find that the life of women is fundamentally different from that of men in many essential respects, that women's range of deviation from typical life events is wider or narrower, and that women come to terms with their life experiences (some of which they share with men) in very different ways.

3. *The immediate context of life history construction.* The context of encounter in which the life history has been elicited and negotiated must be identified. The information should include such matters as the conditions under which the informant enters the relationship; the physical and social setting in which the life history is related; the role of the translator, if one is used; the informant's perception of the encounter; the ethnographer's definition of the situation; and, finally, the working out of a life history text through the complex interactive process of negotiated meanings between the various parties.

Admittedly, our knowledge of that total context will forever remain incomplete; nevertheless, we should strive to describe as many relevant events and their subjective definitions as possible. Only if we have some understanding of this context will we gain insight into (1) how the individual's immediate phenomenal field influences the nature and meaning of his selection of his recollected experience into culturally typified categories (the natural attitude), and his self-reflective interpretive departures from the life world (that is, the phenomenological attitude); (2) how the native translator, if one is used, renders these events in turn through his own experience in the act of translating the informant's discourse; and (3) the activities of the ethnographer in attempting to penetrate into the subject's world, not least of which is his encounter with the other that defines the initial meanings of the events he is recording and fixing in textual form.

4. *The preunderstandings of the researcher.* We take preunderstandings to mean in the hermeneutical sense preconceptions about the life experience to be interpreted and held by the ethnographer or other outside investigator. They may also include deep-seated assumptions about space, time, causality, and the person that are removed from or inaccessible to conscious reflection but that nevertheless enter into the interpretive process and in their unexamined ways contribute to the results. Hermeneutically, however, it is important to question and examine as wide a range of such ideas as we can, and, if necessary, to change them in light of how we come to grasp the immediate person and his life in the encounter. Fixed preunderstandings prevent us from productively questioning our dialogue partner (the text, for instance; see Gadamer 1975). Hermeneutics makes us aware that true under-

standing can never come if our preunderstandings close us off from what the life history text has to say, for under those circumstances we understand only or mainly in terms of what we already know. This limitation, in fact, prevents us from understanding the life history in its own immediate context and larger culture-historical horizon.

In approaching the life history a total commitment to a Freudian view of character structure would enable us to understand the phenomenon very well in Freudian terms, and we might end up understanding some aspect of Freudian theory the better for the "testing" we had done. But, after all, does psychoanalytic theory describe "reality" or help us understand the reality of a foreign meaning-context? Would we, in truth, through this body of theory necessarily understand the events that the subject was interpreting in his own frame of reference?

5. *The dialectical relationship.* Once the life history is seen in its total context, and as the investigator formulates and questions his preunderstandings, he must bridge the distance that separates him from it by assuming a dialectical relationship with the life history, establishing a dialogue of questions and answers in which he moves back and forth between his own position and that of the life history text. In this unfolding dialectic he adds accumulative meanings to the text as it speaks to him and becomes transformed into his own world. This process is part of working out an interpretation against the backdrop of a foreign context. The ultimate product in the hermeneutical sense is a synthesis in which the interpreter, while never totally abandoning his own preunderstandings, now understands the life history and himself in a qualitatively different way, incorporating something of the subjective reference and context world of the text and merging it with his own.

6. *The life world and the phenomenological attitude.* In the act of interpreting, the nature of the phenomena in consciousness (what *is* in the life history) must themselves be grasped. The *life world* (revealed in the "natural attitude") and the *phenomenological attitude,* as we call it, are not particularly easy to disentangle, although distinctions have been made in phenomenology (Husserl 1931:106; Natanson 1973:61). It may prove problematic to determine what aspects of phenomenal consciousness in the life history are taken for granted, that is, are not reflected upon and are assumed a priori to be valid, and what aspects genuinely reflect the operation of self-reflective intentionality that brackets the pre-given meanings of experience. In a sense, all there is in a life history (noema) represents the results of selectively intentional

processes (noesis); yet, within the apparent ordering of life events, the flow of the subject's consciousness may suggest more or less natural, self-evident chains of thinking, the selective character of which (judged by an outsider's standards) the narrator of events is largely unaware of. To ascertain this sort of "natural attitude" in the life history we should consider specific aspects of phenomenal consciousness in relationship to whole contexts. Thus, we may assume something to reflect the life world if its significance is not intentionally changed to suit different contexts and if it does not undergo reflective elaboration or experience critical reappraisal.

By approaching the life history from a phenomenological standpoint, we become aware of events, people, feelings, self-images, and objects as they stand out in the individual's recollected experience and how these are meaningfully intended and interrelated. This approach is rather analogous to an attempt to reconstruct the properties of the "mazeway,"

> a unique mental image of a complex system of objects, dynamically interrelated, which includes the body in which the brain is housed, various other surrounding things. . . . Its content consists of an extremely large number of assemblages or cognitive residues of perception. It is used, by its holder, as a true and more or less complete representation of the operating characteristics of the real world. (Wallace 1970:15)

The life world, in part, might also be likened to Wallace's notion of mental schemata, some of which constitute programmed but highly axiomatic assumptions of which the individual is not aware and which must be inferred.

The next five points, essentially, relate to aspects of phenomenal consciousness (with existential implications) that may be regarded as pertaining either to the natural attitude and the life world or to the self-reflective and bracketing activities we define as the phenomenological attitude. Deciding which is which depends on the application of our interpretive framework working through hermeneutical principles.

7. Cognition. In studying cognition we are concerned with the apparent organization of perceptual experience that characterizes the autobiographical account. Some of the important elements of perceptual organization include the following: (1) the selective effects of memory —in part culturally determined; (2) the particular manner in which events and objects are categorized according to culturally determined schemes; (3) the idiosyncratic conceptualization of experience, involving a reworking of cultural categories; and (4) the significant imputation of meaning, including affect, to categories and relations of experience as they are remembered and organized conceptually. Understanding the degree to which cultural as opposed to individual factors have an influence on the selective process by which such experience is organized will depend on our ability to reconstruct the larger cultural context and the individual's relationship to it. In any event, it is clear that the recollected life history has come into existence as a result of subjective intentionality, which, we may assume, reflects some sort of selective process at work. The problem is then to discover, if possible, the level of consciousness and self-awareness at which this intentionality operates.

8. *Self-identity*. In any life history document the subject will tell us to some extent, unwittingly or knowingly, what he thinks he is like. This self-rendering is a differentiated portion of the larger cognitive and phenomenal field (Rogers 1951). There are probably aspects of himself that he is either unaware of or consciously conceals from the anthropologist in the ethnographic encounter. At an immediate level we may be able to extract statements from the subject's account that suggest he recovers himself as an object to himself through the act of self-reflection and consciously makes decisions on the basis of who he thinks he is. His actions are thus partly, and perhaps largely, determined by the limits set by his own self-awareness. This "unique" self-identity, moreover, may be as much a product of internalized cultural definitions of the "person" as it is a matter of pure individual expression, and what we see in the life history is probably some sort of dialectical resolution of cultural and idiosyncratic processes operating in the individual (Rosaldo 1976).

To assess hidden or repressed identities, on the other hand, it is generally necessary to go to sources of information beyond the life history itself and to make inferences of various kinds. In the hermeneutical view, one gains a greater understanding of the part (here, the identity) by considering it in relationship to the whole (the total life and experience of the person). The individual's overall psychic life, including possible unconscious factors, may not emerge unless we look at measures of that individual's activity outside his recollected life history. Dreams, projective test performance, and observation of the person's behavior under stress may reveal repressed self-images that help us account for difficult or obscure passages in the subject's life history recitation. Therefore, while phenomenological investigations of identity can in theory be carried out with the life history alone, the investigator may wish to supplement his understanding by expanding his framework of interpretation and the sources of information from which he attempts his reconstructions.

9. *Conflicts and doubts.* Conflict seems to be an inherent part of the human condition, no matter how it may be experienced symbolically in other cultures. There is never a perfect fit between human desire and social demand, and human desires are themselves in conflict. The individual is aware of the disparity between his self-image, his needs, his hopes, and the reality of the world that thwarts and contradicts his intentions; this awareness sets into motion the recognition of conflict. The mere fact that the individual for purposes of social adaptation appraises his actual performance against normatively defined standards that he accepts (Hallowell 1955) suggests to us that conflict may indeed be an intrinsically human condition. When conflict is intense and prolonged, disrupting the individual's ability to function, it may create malaise, uncertainty, and, ultimately perhaps, fundamental doubt, which may result in a radical self-reflective turn (the phenomenological attitude), causing the person to question the givenness of his life world and his stance within it. He may say: "I am in conflict because I have allowed this to happen to me. What I want is something else." Basically, in the phenomenological attitude the person, by doubting, brackets part of his experience: "I intended this; it can be changed" (as we shall see this is rather explicit in Blanca's case). This process of moving into the realm of conflict and doubt, in our view, can become the basis for the individual's awareness of his freedom.

10. *Choices.* All human beings make choices of various kinds during their lives and some of them have profound implications. Does choice proceed from their awareness of freedom to determine their projects, or is it part of their natural attitude, their taken-for-granted life plan with its accepted options and ranges of reasonable alternatives? (In this sense, perhaps, hiding behind culture can sometimes be an act of "bad faith.") It is important to determine whether some self-reflective attitude lies at the basis of choices, to uncover the level of self-reflective intentionality. Evidence for making an interpretation one way or the other way may be gathered by asking certain questions of the text and scanning it for particular patterns. We are more likely to have existential freedom (in Sartre's meaning) if we find in the text an arrested flow of narrative; explicit self-awareness of conflict and al-

ternative possibilities for action, including unconventional ones; and an explicit awareness on the part of the individual of how his decisions have created and can create his personal destiny.

11. The unity of phenomenal consciousness with interpretation. The interpretive categories of the life world, and self-reflective excursions from it, are not discrete units; they should be seen as they articulate together to form a whole, a unity that flows along in the individual's consciousness as ongoing process. We must not lose sight of this larger unity in favor of emphasizing the smaller view, however tempting it may be to do so. Ultimately, by means of interpretation, this unity is bound together through and in the self-understanding of the one who interprets.

Interpreting a Particular Life History: Blanca Gonzalez

Thus far we have argued that the life history may be regarded as a source for understanding the subjective aspects of individual experience articulated through the presentation of a subjective world. In attempting to apply our perspective to a specific life history, it has been necessary, for reasons of time or space, not to present either the entire sociocultural horizon of the individual or the total life history itself, although we will try to give all aspects a balanced treatment. Although we find it necessary to edit and condense the presentation in this way, we feel we have retained enough information to justify our attempt to interpret it. Ideally, our endeavor should serve as a brief demonstration of what kind of understanding can be obtained through the application of the basic principles of phenomenology, existentialism, and hermeneutics we have just outlined.

The narrative material is presented as a case history, consisting of illustrative extracts and schematic summaries marshaled together by an outsider from the original life history text in the service of his analysis, evaluation, or interpretation. We have chosen our highlights and representation to conform as closely as possible to continuities and sequences in the autobiographical narrative.

The life history in question is that of Blanca Gonzalez, a thirty-six-year-old Guajiro woman living in the Baja Guajira of Venezuela; she related her life history to the senior author, through a translator, over a four-month period in 1965. Translation was from Guajiro to Spanish.

Blanca was a rather solemn woman with a sad, careworn face. Her smiles and laughter always seemed to have a dry, bitter quality. When she did smile or laugh, the senior author was always aware of the incongruity that one of her front teeth was capped in gold, while the other one was missing.

Blanca was a poor woman who owned neither land nor cattle, and her husband was currently unemployed and away looking for a job as a laborer in Perija, to the south of the Baja Guajira where she lived. She had four children who lived with her: two older girls, who were fourteen and twelve years old, a boy, eight, and a little daughter, about three. She articulated no particular hopes for herself or her children, but she was anxious that her husband should soon secure employment. Blanca, like many Guajiro mothers, was harsh and distant with her children and frequently beat them. For the senior author, defined as a social superior, however, she was all smiles and the model of the ideal informant. These traits suggested that there might have been an authoritarian streak in her personality. She lived from hand to mouth in the most uncertain circumstances imaginable, but, strangely, rarely complained about her current situation except when she commented on her children's insubordinate behavior. The family lived in a small one-room house constructed of branches and matting, about forty miles northeast of Paraguaipoa in the Venezuelan Baja Guajira.

In order to put the events of her life, as she related them, in proper perspective, it is essential first to consider the general cultural background that constituted Blanca's horizon, one in which all traditional Guajiro live, as well as the more specific ethnographic encounter and the interpersonal situation in which the life story was elicited.

Perhaps the most immediate and striking feature of Guajiro culture is the nomadic pastoral adaptation to the arid, desertlike environment of La Guajira Peninsula in northwestern Venezuela and northern Colombia. Soon after the Spaniards arrived with cattle and other domesticated animals, the Guajiro abandoned their hunting and gathering subsistence patterns and took to raising cattle, sheep, and goats acquired from the Spaniards through trade and theft. The Guajiro also adopted agriculture where it was practicable.

Also striking is the matrilineal principle of social organization that permeates the fabric of Guajiro cultural life, resounding like a leitmotiv in virtually all areas in which the Guajiro conduct their affairs. Each Guajiro matrilineage is exogamous and has its own internal structure consisting of smaller, interrelated minilineages, and each matrilineage possesses a corporate character. The lineage is headed politically by a cacique, or chief, who inherits his position from the maternal uncle. The cacique is the political mediator of the group's internal affairs and acts as the legal representative of the lineage in its dealings with other lineages.

Marriage arrangements between lineages represent the basis of political security; it is customary for chiefs to marry off their daughters and sororal nieces to other caciques in an attempt to build up political and military alliances for the protection of their group. In Guajiro society, a small lineage without friends and allies is considered fair game for the predatory instincts of larger, more powerful lineages, who exploit their superior strength at the expense of defenseless groups in the absence of centralized political authority. Even when no political considerations are involved, marriage in Guajiro society is always an economic and social arrangement between the families of bride and groom. Formal marriage occurs only under conditions in which the groom's lineage makes a bride payment in cattle, horses, mules, and jewelry to the bride's family, the exact amount of which has been agreed upon beforehand.

Guajiro society is rigidly stratified in terms of wealth in livestock, retainers, and access to political power. The chiefly or noble class controls the outcome of political conflict and the redistribution of wealth in society (especially in their own lineages), and they manipulate for their own advantage those whose interests they protect. The commoners, while they have their own resources, are under the nobles' protection and are dominated by them. There is also a retainer class that serves the nobles, and a class of slaves who have been acquired through war, sold to remove a debt, or born to their position.

The supernatural system is characterized by the importance attached to dreams and the acquisition of power through dreaming. Magical fetishes that the individual obtains through dreams enable him, for example, to protect himself from real and supernatural danger, to enhance his sexual attractiveness, and to amass wealth in cattle and other valuables, thus raising his social status.

The individual in Guajiro society plays out his life in the shadow of his matrilineal kin group. He is born as the child of his mother into the *eiruku* (lineage; literally, "flesh of the mother"), and he is socialized to feel primary responsibility to the lineage; he learns that if he conforms to the expectations of his kinsmen he will eventually inherit from them. Even his marriage is not a personal matter involving his private feelings but rather the affair of the lineage and its chiefly authority. Conflict in the lineage is ruled out by normative definition, but if it occurs it is sanctioned by disinheritance and ostracism. Antisocial behavior, especially aggression, tends to be projected onto or displaced against outsiders (Watson 1974).

Any criminal act committed by a member of the lineage (rape, murder, theft, insult) is the responsibility of the group as a whole, and collective action becomes the obligation of each and every individual. When a Guajiro dies his property is redistributed among members of the lineage and his body is buried in the lineage cemetery. The soul goes on a long journey to a cave in an island off Cabo de la Vela to join the spirits of other departed members of his lineage, with whom he lives forever in peace and harmony, always remaining in the social position he had in his mortal life.

While kinship sets the dominant tone of the individual-culture relationship in this society, the individual's role in the division of labor also has pronounced consequences for the quality of his life. The most obvious determinant of the general course of the individual life other than kinship is sexual identity. Male and female roles are very dissimilar in this culture, as they are in most cultures, and presuppose very different kinds of socialization.

Men attend to the herding of the animals, build the houses and corrals, and determine movements to new pastures. Men administer family property, are more or less actively involved in political decisions depending on their social status, and defend the integrity and interests of their lineage against hostile groups. Going to war to avenge an unresolved criminal act committed by a member of another group against one of their own and fighting to destroy a weak competitor group at the behest of the chief represent activities that virtually all Guajiro men become involved in at some point in their lives.

In some respects men lead a dualistic existence. On the one hand, a man lives matrilocally with his wife or wives at certain times of the year, administering the property in livestock he has left in his wife's care for her support and that of her children; on the other hand, he must also visit his mother, sisters, and maternal aunts and uncles and dispense his obligations to his matrilineal kin. Men are thus simultaneously involved in two very different forms of social participation, and they must try to balance their involvement to take account of their primary allegiance to the matrilineal kin group without, however, forgetting the wife and her family, who are important political allies who must be treated with circumspection, respect, and consideration to avoid losing their goodwill.

While she owns her property in domesticated animals and may supervise their care when the husband is away, the Guajiro woman is not herself ordinarily responsible for pasturing and watering the livestock. She is primarily responsible for domestic upkeep, care of the children, cooking, processing dairy products, acting as official hostess for the family, and weaving articles of clothing and daily use for her family and for sale for her own profit. The respectable, responsible, and admired wife in Guajiro culture is economically proficient, impeccable in moral behavior, and adept in the social graces (see Gutierrez de Pineda 1950).

In preparation for adult married life, the Guajiro woman must at the time of her first menses undergo a period of confinement that lasts one to several years. During this time her social activities are restricted; she is subjected to various food and behavior taboos; and she receives explicit instruction in moral, economic, and social responsibilities (Watson-Franke 1976a). Advanced training in weaving is also given at this time (see Watson-Franke 1974).

When she is finally brought out of confinement, the girl is ready for marriage. To a large extent, the Guajiro woman is a pawn in her family's attempts to arrange a suitable marriage for her; marriage brings with it a sizable bride payment and connections with another family who, it is hoped, will render political favors. She has little or no choice of a husband, for he has been selected for her by familial authorities on the basis of economic and political considerations. This choice may inspire disagreement if not outright rebellion in the bride-to-be if she dislikes the man in question, but there is usually not much she can do except to resign herself to the decision of the family, unless she is prepared to flee the security of the lineage and seek her fortune in the city or with some other group. In some families, however, it may be possible for the woman to argue effectively against an arranged marriage; but this generally occurs only when the parents recognize that the girl's right to determine her own destiny is more important than the collective interests of the family, a decidedly unusual phenomenon in this culture with its collectivistic, lineage-oriented thinking.

Occupational specialization and social class also influence the nature of individual experience in Guajiro culture. In discussing occupational specialization, we might briefly consider the role of political leader, whose attributes have well-defined cultural properties. The chief (*alaulaa*), or cacique, represents his lineage in legal and political matters, resolving internal disputes and settling conflict between his group and other groups through diplomacy or warfare, depending on which option he feels he has. The office usually passes from maternal uncle to eldest sororal nephew within the highest ranking line of the lineage, although a certain leeway of choice is given the chief to insure selection of the best-qualified candidate (Watson 1976b).

Once the candidate is chosen for instruction in *cacicazgo*, his life changes dramatically and takes on a very special quality. At this point he usually moves in with his maternal uncle — a departure from the usual pattern of matrilocal residence — and intensive training begins. At first the candidate learns the theory of being a chief, that is, how to conduct himself in public, how to interpret the law, how to talk properly, and the like. When he has mastered this theory, he watches his uncle at work and accompanies him to political events, learning the practical applications of what he has been taught.

The cacique, unlike the average Guajiro, has a more complex cognition of the way the sociocultural system operates, in that he sees more significant relationships and complex implications arising out of behavior. He must know how to apply the ideal culture to any contingency, but he must be aware of the way people behave under stressful situations and he may have to bend the rules to fit individual needs and motivations. In other words, he must make difficult decisions affecting life and property with which the average man need not concern himself, and he must struggle with the temptation to use his power and authority to consolidate his own private advantage. This conflict of interests between private and collective needs also does not touch the ordinary man in this culture except in a marginal way.

Social class position likewise significantly affects the subjective nature of experience. The upper-class person, who is more likely to be involved in political decisions, assumes more responsibility for protecting and sustaining the well-being of his lineage group than the average person, but he is also given more opportunity to be irresponsible and selfish if he chooses to abuse his power in political and economic matters. An attitude of disciplined responsibility, however, seems the predominant solution to this inherent conflict. Upper-class people generally act in a very controlled manner, channeling their behavior into the forms prescribed by social norms. The upper-class woman, for example, usually behaves with the utmost propriety; she is careful not to let a breath of scandal touch her and she is ever mindful of the need to adopt a reserved, distant circumspection in her dealing with men. In her role as hostess, however, she treats men and women alike with consideration and grace, observing all the rules of hospitality to the letter.

The noble of either sex is more aware than the average person of the consequences of behavior in social and political contexts. He realizes the profound implications of his acts as an individual and their possible moral and legal consequences, and he monitors his behavior accordingly.

The commoner adopts a more compliant, less responsible mode of dealing with his environment. Knowing full well he is under the protection of the chief and nobles of his lineage, he looks to them for support and protection and he learns to assume a subservient, obedient demeanor to elicit their consideration and to avoid falling into their bad graces. His attention is focused on the more concrete problems of his immediate life situation. With outsiders he is cautious and respectful, a strategy designed to protect him from aggressive acts.

Technically, there is no longer slavery in Guajiro society, although de facto slavery still exists. The Guajiro nowadays refer only to their "retainers." The slave has no power of self-determination at all, and the commoner who has indentured himself as a retainer to a noble has very little liberty. A slave or retainer is cared for and protected by the noble only because he is a valuable piece of property; in the strict sense he has little or no worth as a person in his own right, for his role is not sanctioned by kinship obligations. He must submit to the demands of his master no matter what these involve and however much they may demean his integrity as a person. A model of degradation for all Guajiro is implicit in the servant-master relationship.

It is probably safe to assume that in certain important respects, at least, the slave or retainer must see life as outside his own control—a view that invites a sense of powerlessness and alienation—for there is little hope that he will ever leave his special circumstances except, possibly, through a desperate act fraught with potentially disastrous consequences. Yet there may be positive feelings associated with this kind of experience. The slave or retainer may feel protected and secure in the knowledge that there is no escape.

While the foregoing description of the culture context and the individual-culture nexus is admittedly sketchy, it serves to give some of the background necessary for the kind of holistic interpretation of experience advocated by hermeneutics. We now turn to the immediate context in which the particular life history of Blanca Gonzalez was originally collected. Since one of us, Watson, collected the original data, made the initial observations, and edited the text, these circumstances will be described by him. The following is Watson's account of what happened as he saw it.

I will attempt here to delineate briefly the circumstances under which the field situation in question was brought about, my impressions of what went on in the encounter leading up to the elicitation of the life history material, and my initial attempts to make sense of the recorded text.

A month or so after I had been in the field I became acquainted with a very powerful chief who suggested that his son, Nemecio, might work as my assistant and translator. Since I had initially been having difficulties establishing contact with the Guajiro and had gathered little data, I eagerly seized the opportunity to advance my work, thinking that a person with connections would be very helpful. The son and I made contact and he agreed to work for me at a weekly salary for as long as I needed him. Nemecio proved to be very adept, indeed, in his job as translator, informant, and contact man. He was aggressive, intelligent, resourceful, and unafraid; and he was absolutely masterful in playing on the reputation of his father to motivate potential informants to cooperate with us.

One day as we were walking among the cacti and divi-divi trees in the Guajiro desert, we chanced upon a small rancho located somewhat off the beaten path. Determined not to lose the chance to do some anthropology, I suggested to Nemecio that we stop and see whether we could persuade the people to help us in our research. I needed to find more Guajiro mothers and children to continue my study of socialization and personality development.

We went over to the rancho. Nemecio called out the greeting in Guajiro. After several moments a Guajiro woman in her thirties, rather shabbily dressed, appeared in the doorway. She answered in Guajiro. Nemecio proceeded to explain, as best I could tell with my limited Guajiro, that I was a white "doctor" who wanted to learn about the Guajiro, and he wondered whether she would be willing to help. I was prepared, he added, to pay her for her time and effort.

The woman invited us inside and slung some hammocks for us. I learned that her name was Blanca Gonzalez, that she was married, and that she had four children. Her husband was presently unemployed, and since the family had no livestock, the man was out looking for work. The family was obviously in bad financial straits; in fact, there was very little food in the house and I suspected they were going hungry. Blanca was eager to cooperate. She explained that she and her family were more than willing to help an important *arejuna* (white) doctor who was the friend of old chief Raul.

This much at the very outset suggested some of the motivations behind Blanca's decision to enter into the informant relationship. It was clear that the prospect of receiving payment to meet the family's serious economic needs must have been an influencing factor. It represented a potential way out of difficulties and may have activated fantasies about receiving unlimited, gratuitous nurturance. It was also clear that this consideration alone might not have been enough to overcome Blanca's suspiciousness, an important factor that emerged in subsequent conversation with her. Since I entered the relationship under the auspices, so to speak, of a greatly respected and feared cacique, however, his sponsorship undoubtedly helped to elicit compliant behavior and countered the subject's anxieties about my intentions. Her emphasis in the life story on the abuses she had suffered in the past may have been in part related to her perception of me as somebody who would shower her with favor out of pity and sympathy.

My feelings for Blanca in turn were positive and anticipatory. When I saw that she tried to be friendly to me and willingly supplied me with detailed information, I looked forward to my visits with her. In the beginning I experienced a twinge of nervousness as we felt each other out, and I was always afraid I would say the wrong thing and disrupt the relationship. But the situation seemed to improve with every visit and I began to think my fears were groundless. At some point—I cannot remember exactly when—I came to regard her as my best informant, as somebody from whom I could get almost unlimited data. This may not have been true, but it seemed that way when I compared Blanca with other informants who supplied me with far less data and who did so with much greater reluctance. I am sure, I was affected, too, by my sympathy for her plight, and I undoubtedly overreacted at times in my anxious concern to believe any and all her tales of woe. I was hesitant to question her critically about these events or to ask her to resolve some of the discrepancies I discovered in the account of her life she gave me. I was simply afraid of seeming unsympathetic in the context of the helpfulness and trust we had created together with Nemecio's assistance.

The presence of my translator, Nemecio, and the role he played in the encounter were extremely critical. Since Blanca spoke virtually no Spanish and since my Guajiro was very limited at the time, Nemecio became the medium through which we did most of our communicating with each other. Nemecio, being the kind of person he was, elicited support and trust in others. His pleasant, joking behavior warmed Blanca to the task of talking with us. But being the son of a chief, Nemecio undoubtedly hindered the subject from expressing certain kinds of attitudes and emotions (e.g., hostility toward formal authorities and whites) of which he would have disapproved. Blanca must have realized that Nemecio could persuade me not to continue a relationship with an informant if he judged that the informant was not honest or was not cooperating. Nemecio had the habit of conveying that kind of authority to people, and Blanca was anxious for her own reasons to keep the interviews going.

Nemecio, in turn, was accountable to me, and I knew he felt he should provide me with "good" data for the wages he received. He did this by selecting good informants and motivating them to cooperate, and occasionally by overdramatizing and distorting in his translation what the informant related, as I subsequently learned and which I had to correct. Thus, the life history of Blanca as it finally reached me had undergone a series of changes in the process, with Blanca talking with me through Nemecio and predicating her behavior on her perception of our expectations, and with Nemecio editing the material to conform to my needs and his at the same time. This complex situation persisted over several months, but the mutual understanding, rapport, and camaraderie that we had built up over this time seemed to resolve potentially serious misunderstandings and to reduce the distorting effects of the "translation" process.

To give the reader some idea of the tone of our later encounters, along with the particular pleasures they afforded, I am including the following exchange taken from my field notes. The humor, trust, and good fun are readily apparent, I think, within the serious business of doing ethnography:

LW: *You were saying last time that you used to be afraid of going to the lagoon to draw water when you were about twelve and living near ———.*
B: *Yes, mama used to send me there late in the day as night was falling. There were bad things, dangerous things near the well.*

LW: *What were they?*
B: *Different things. People said that the* wanülu *[evil spirits]
went to the well at night to kill innocent people, and once when I
was out late and about ready to go back—it was already dark
—I saw Keralia [a large luminous lizard who rapes women with
his tail and kills them]. I was really scared because I knew he
would impregnate me with his tail and I would give birth to
maggots and die. I saw him from afar and I didn't think he saw
me. I managed to get home all right.*
LW: *What else was bad about the well?*
B: *There was a young man who hung around there who would
have intercourse with animals. He had a big penis. The girls
were scared when he was there because if he didn't have it with
a burro he would force a girl to submit to him and he would in-
jure her.*
N: *That guy sounds like a cousin of mine. But he actually married a girl and then wouldn't sleep with his wife because he only
liked it with his burro. [We all laugh.]*
LW: *Well, we have people like that all over the streets at night
in our cities and they're not wanülu either.*

This mixture of straight reportage, fantasy, and humor was very
characteristic of our encounters and we all seemed to enjoy
them immensely.

I am in a much better position to discuss my own preunderstandings
than those of Blanca or Nemecio. The most serious of these, I suspect,
was my insistence, at least in the beginning, on directing the flow of
personal narrative into certain preestablished categories, such as the
socialization of dependency, or aggression training, which I wished to
investigate as part of my research design. I believed that data bearing
on these themes were "good," "important," "worthwhile," and that
other kinds of data, while interesting, were essentially irrelevant for
my purposes. The life history, which I elicited apart from data on the
culture and child rearing, was the only source of data where I tapped
to any degree a free recall, and even here I would sometimes concen-
trate on certain aspects of Blanca's situation that I considered to be of
special interest to my research. I realize now that I saw the life history
primarily as a supplementary source of data on socialization experiences. That this was, in fact, a kind of "prejudice" (an unproductive
preunderstanding) was quite possible, for although I was willing to

admit my preunderstanding was an arbitrary one and grew out of certain theoretical commitments, I was insistent on settling for the sort of understanding generated within the reassuring confines of my system. I use the word "prejudice" with caution, because it is a retrospective judgment and because I now feel that it forced me into methodical questioning and did not allow me to hear the questions posed by Blanca in *her world*.

Another preunderstanding had to do with my view of the Guajiro, formed through my reading of published accounts of their culture. This preunderstanding was both productive and unproductive. Because I knew them as aloof, touchy people who were easily offended and who would not forgive a slight or oversight, my preunderstanding helped me to appear socially sensitive, allowed me to maintain rapport, and enabled me to elicit data. But it also inhibited me to a great degree, perhaps because I overread these characteristics and imagined them to be more threatening than they were. Since I feared offending them, I felt with most Guajiro that I could not get them to talk about certain supposedly "sensitive" areas such as sex or family conflict. (Probably my assumptions were not strictly warranted in all cases.) Nor did I feel I could challenge their statements with impunity, as I might have with somebody from my own culture. I knew the Guajiro were accustomed to ask compensation for damages for insults to their persons, and I had already had one unpleasant encounter with an informant who threatened to sue me because I had shown her disrespect. In essence, my preunderstanding made me believe that only certain kinds of information could be safely obtained.

A third preunderstanding, if not to say prejudice, was my largely unquestioned assumption that data elicited in fieldwork were "real" and had some kind of ultimate or fixed validity that was basically independent of the circumstances in which they were evoked and the vagaries of the translation process that all data necessarily undergo. I assumed that these bits and pieces of information, even those in the life history, could be treated as discrete facts that related to empirical events, rather than statements whose true significance lay in the way they had been negotiated in the encounter. I was not at that time prepared to question my basic epistemological presuppositions. The texts simply spoke for themselves; my operations did not have to be examined in assessing their meaning.

The upshot of all this is that my preunderstandings in the field dictated (1) that only certain kinds of information would be elicited; (2)

that these had to make sense in terms of my analytical categories; and (3) that data reflected real events in the experiences of the subject and were divorced from what happened in the encounter.

I actually carried one other preunderstanding, I now realize, that accounts for the way I am presently approaching Blanca's life history: I felt, in truth, alienated from my own research design. At some vaguely conscious level I felt forced to follow it, and I felt victimized as the existential man who could not exercise his freedom. Why had I not embraced my freedom to choose something closer to my authentic interests in existentialism, in concrete people, in the aesthetic rendition of experience? I must have thought in my truly rigid, compulsive way that the academic community would have disapproved had I given in to these threatening interests, which in a very real way defined my true but not always self-acknowledged identity. Now, however, that same hidden preunderstanding has come into the forefront of my consciousness and provides the ground through which I can allow myself to be hermeneutically self-reflective. It has become the interpretive medium through which I retrospectively capture the aloneness and alienation of Blanca and mediate it as part of my own changed horizon of self-understanding.

Framing these immediate personal preunderstandings are, of course, my own deeply held notions of such matters as time, causality, and history, which were pre-given in my own culture and which I no doubt internalized and have subsequently used in orienting my sense of what a life history means and what interpretive operations can be performed on it. I must add that the nature and influence of these preunderstandings are difficult to reconstruct exactly since they lie beyond the usual and immediate level of self-reflection. In any case, my preunderstandings of time and individual history as some kind of orderly chronological sequence leading the individual from birth to old age and death certainly account for the organization of the original text and I believe, bear to some degree on the interpretive presentation that takes Blanca's life to the break with her father. Indeed, I have retained some of the original linear rendering in relating sequences of actions and reaction whose underlying coherence appears to reside in the individual as an autonomous psychological entity acting on experience, which is itself a Western notion.

In the interpretation that follows, it has been difficult for us to suspend this orientation entirely. However, because the priorities compellingly articulated by Blanca in her subjective world forced us to recognize a rather different pattern, we have had to organize causal explanations around key events of importance to Blanca and her culture and then work backward and forward in time from them to explore their significant interconnections and ramifications for her. Meaningful "inner time" for Blanca seems integrated into a temporally indeterminate matrix of significant happenings from which she draws meaning through basic Guajiro preunderstandings of the nature of honor, the problem of evil, and survival. To engage Blanca interpretively in her own notions of time, personal history, and autonomy, we have had to alter hermeneutically the original linear narrative characteristic of the life history text itself and to portray events and human actions as meaningfully integrated largely in the frame of Blanca's subjective rendering of her own dialectical encounter with experience, which is less bound to strict linear chronology and deterministic sequences than we are accustomed to.

To engage in a dialogue with the life history text, in this case, is certainly no easy task, taking into consideration the many complex interacting factors that eventually determined its character, including the respective preunderstandings of the subject, the translator, and the anthropologist, and of course their dialectical interplay. These issues constitute the essential background or context in which the life history should be approached. Yet, as we look at Blanca's life history, it is precisely that—the text of that frail life—that claims our attention, our interest. What is it? What does it mean? We realize now that prior preunderstandings were misleading. The text as we have it, the very events that make it up, what it seems to say and mean, all were negotiated, consciously and unconsciously in the original encounter. Questions were asked and answered in the process, but always within certain frames of tacit agreement we had assumed. It is now impossible after so many years to reconstruct them fully and understand them, but some features are clear. The domains of tacit understanding began with methodical questions based on my research interests and Blanca's cooperation as an informant. After all, I was a "doctor" and my requests were "reasonable." A neutral ground was created on which information was exchanged. The information conformed to Blanca's sense of personal adequacy as an informant and my critical expectations as an ethnographer. The life history data of the first few months seem, indeed, to be neutrally informative. But as I developed a true feeling for Blanca, born of trust and respect, I tried increasingly to grasp her situation and her dilemmas. This effort was a purely human movement toward mutual engagement.

The meaning-context of our initial encounters, because of our common interests, seemed to assume the elements of a commentary on "growing up," on reaching "competency" in certain areas of life, on learning to cope with the threats and dangers involved, such as the necessity and difficulty of controlling disruptive impulses like sex and aggression, and on learning to assert personal autonomy without being insubordinate.

Later, after we had come to engage each other as two human beings, through Nemecio (another person important to us both), our true possibilities and interests came more into play and our negotiated understandings became increasingly oriented toward defining the meaning of the individual as he seeks to find his place in the world, to cope with disappointment and degradation, and to overcome alienation through personal responsibility. Ultimately, I realize, Blanca articulated values and attitudes that were meaningful to me as a person and not just as an anthropologist.

Let us now consider Blanca's life history as a fixed text whose form and meaning were in part negotiated in the encounter we have described. Hermeneutically speaking, it is unknowable as a subjective document in any kind of definitive sense. If we are to capture Blanca's particular subjective world by overarching the difference between it and ourselves, we must be willing to question our categories of scientific analysis and look at the text as conscious phenomena produced through her intentionality. Our phenomenological and existential hermeneutics pose the possibility of a dialogue through which some of that subjectively intended world can be interpreted, even though ultimately we are the ones who speak about it in our own partially bracketed life world.

At this point we should add a few words about the general course of our engagement with the accomplished text of Blanca's life history, and our interpretive stance toward it, before we get into the actual interpretation of specific events and experiences in the text. As we considered the life history the first time, several years after it was recorded, the subjective context eluded us. Even then, however, we noticed the subject's obsession with certain themes, and her stance within the text began to form a shadowy but integrated pattern that defined aspects of her subjective world. But for us, this growing awareness happened in an offhand sort of way, and our own research interests and theoretical biases kept reducing all of our knowledge of her subjectivity to a marginal status.

Looking at the same life history again years later, we began to establish a different kind of dialectical relationship to the text. We bracketed some of our own prejudices (which were no longer so strong), were open to existential and phenomenological points of view, and engaged in a self-reflective hermeneutics, where we began to pose different questions that seemed to open up the personal and cultural horizons of the text. Doing this, we sensed, created a new world that had heretofore remained largely hidden. It now seemed as if Blanca were really communicating her possibilities, and they were centrally important and comprehensible within her world. The information conveyed by the text was no longer merely a reflection of more important underlying patterns of socialization and character development, nor could we view the material any longer as merely compliant responses to the "methodical" questions of the original research design. Blanca as a subjective being in the world was beginning to emerge. Looking back, we suspect that our growing awareness of the subjective dimensions of the text had something to do with the more personalized, existential quality that began to dominate at the end of the narrative. We were finally convinced, as we hope our subsequent interpretation shows, that there was a coherent reality that our scientific constructs did not enable us to understand.

In Blanca's life history the life world is the Guajiro frame of reference, whose basic operating principles are never seriously questioned; indeed, this life world possesses, as any life world should, a taken-for-granted rightness and inevitability. It is a world of kinspeople, with the individual assuming especially heavy responsibilities toward his matrilineal kin group, to which he is bound and to which he is accountable for his actions. It is also a world of social and economic inequality, with those in power (relatives and nonrelatives alike) wielding control over the dependent, the helpless, the less fortunate. These premises form an integral part of what is essentially Blanca's prereflective awareness of her own condition.

It is the alternation of this world of restrictive kin control and constant demand with the less structured world of the bush and peer-group play activities, where experimentation with forbidden desires and the release of tension occur, that lends a special quality to Guajiro childhood and growing up in general, and to Blanca's memories of her own childhood in particular. These opposing elements do not so much perfectly balance each other as they represent the possibility for Guajiros to work out dialectically the conflicting requirements of duty and desire, which finds its culmination in the adult world in the search for sexual domination, security, wealth, and political power.

In Blanca's account this quality of the Guajiro life world already makes its imprint on her recollected experiences of childhood. The following passages are illustrative:

> *I remember when I was little my parents expected me to work from early morning until dark. If I was not helping with the cooking, tending the fire, or helping bring water, I was scolded or sometimes beaten: "You must learn your lesson," my mother would say, "because we Guajiros must be able to work hard with discipline and concentration to master our lives. This way we keep our families strong and keep our enemies from dominating us." These words made a great impression on me and I tried very hard to always be working.*
>
> *My favorite job was taking the goats to pasture. This was very important for the maintenance of our family and I was always proud to be entrusted with this responsibility. But it was always fun, too, for we children would meet at the well and fool around—both boys and girls. Since our parents weren't around we'd joke with each other and throw cactus fruit and play games. We also had romantic meetings. Boys and girls would kiss and touch each other. Boys would ask for our vaginas. We would get very excited but it was very important not to yield to temptation, for our bodies belonged to our family and not to us. I would say, "If you want my vagina you must ask my parents" [they arrange a marriage, involving a payment of cattle and jewelry]. Often I became sexually aroused but I was too afraid to ever do anything except exchange a few innocent kisses. Girls who "played too hard" always got into trouble. . . . Sometimes we got so carried away by our excitement we became negligent and lost animals; then our parents beat us and curtailed our liberties. Even though these games were full of danger we looked forward to them.*

Certain basic values seem to constitute part of the life world that Blanca accepts. As the above passage already intimates, security is surely one of the most important of these values. Security means to be protected and provided for by one's parents and by the larger matrilineal kin group. These people are the ones who provide not only livestock and other essential materials by which adults support themselves but also protection from outside aggression. That outsiders are threatening and dangerous Blanca accepts as a natural concomitant of existence (outsiders include even the boys who asked for her vagina!). Thus the individual is vulnerable to their potentially evil, self-seeking designs unless he can count on the backing of an interested and concerned kin group.

As Blanca tells it, the respect of others is another critical value. This value pervades a Guajiro's sense of self-worth in all encounters with the world. The respect of others is not merely enacted in the rendering of protection and security: respect is the very basis for significant social support and imparts a finality to it. While protection and security, according to Blanca, eliminate or at least diminish fears of being abandoned and exploited by other people, the respect that ideally accompanies the fulfillment of social obligations serves the more positive need of enhancing self-esteem. Blanca stated at one point:

> One is nobody unless that person can count on the respect of others. It is not enough to find shelter in the family if a person is considered an unreliable fool and is only tolerated. When we Guajiros are young we learn that we must win respect through our actions. If we do not learn the rules, and apply them, we will never get it. And if that happens, our whole life becomes poor and miserable.

Except in certain extreme instances, as we shall see later, Blanca does not question the essential rightness of the ties that bind her to her family and kin group, and indeed to her cultural world. She is obviously conscious of these bonds at a certain level of awareness, but she does not see them in everyday experience as existential possibilities she can choose or reject. It might be accurate to say that she reinterprets the conditions of social life within the limits set by her normal subjective stance toward the world. We might say that these bonds, contracts, and conditions are the taken-for-granted sedimentation of her life world.

Other aspects of that same life world, even more remote from conscious reflection—notions of causality, styles of thinking, and the categorization of experience in semantic space—would have to be inferred from an in-depth analysis of the subject's linguistic behavior.

These aspects are not something we could reasonably expect Blanca to comment upon. They are beyond the task of our interpretation, but nevertheless highly interesting.

We feel that Blanca was unable seriously to censor or distort her life world, even if she did alter the significance and sequence of specific events that took place within it. An important part of understanding the life history text is to identify the uncritical, prereflective attitude that comes through the description of many events and experiences that Blanca did not seem to think she needed to manage or rearrange to create a favorable impression, since they were already "real" and required no commentary on her part. This is a different matter, as we shall see, from her attitude toward other specific events whose meanings she critically reflected upon and manipulated in behavioral terms.

A knowledge of Blanca's own cultural background and familiarity with other Guajiro life histories helps us to assess the difference between the unique aspects of her specific experience—her particular way of making sense of events—and cultural patterns of behavior she shares with other Guajiro, patterns of thought and action that make up intersubjective reality and that are usually presented with a spontaneous conviction. Generally speaking, this common life world is neither elaborated along uniquely idiosyncratic lines nor changed significantly through self-reflection in Blanca's account.

Guajiro culture assuredly selects, censors, and distorts the nature of experience as it is retrospectively retrieved through memory. Like other Guajiro, Blanca tends to remember and emphasize the threatening and negative, stressing the times she was wronged, abused, and misunderstood by others through no fault of her own (Watson 1974). The tensions and frustrations of always living up to the demands of others, of trying to elicit their respect and ward off their contempt, no doubt have a very strong bearing on why the negative, even the occasional failure, stands so prominently in the foreground. Moreover, the meaning of the data-collecting setting for Blanca is a kind of constraint that selectively limits her rendition. The focus on the negative may have been stimulated by her desire to inspire sympathy and good will in a powerful, respected outsider, but it may also have arisen from Blanca's modeling her behavior on other poor individuals who debased themselves before power because they had no alternative.

Blanca, like other Guajiro, also favors certain types of experience, whether positive or negative, stressing the practical, everyday world of economic striving and collective social activity at the expense of the

intensely personal and mystical. In her life story Blanca squarely
places herself in the world of the everyday with only occasional forays
into what we would regard as the "supernatural" realm.

Blanca's particular social position also influences her selectively to
edit her recollected experience. Like most Guajiro wives of our ac-
quaintance whose life histories were also taken, Blanca dwells on her
marriage and the problems of adjustment it posed for her. And like
other poor Guajiro, she emphasizes the difficulties and deprivations of
poverty and her generally frustrating and unsuccessful attempts to deal
with them, which brings us back to the predominantly negative tenor
of the life history. Because that negativity was shared with other Guajiro who were better off and more self-secure, we must see this quality
as part of a common ethos and not merely as a by-product of one particular individual's sense of being frustrated and exploited.

Although Blanca's life reveals much of the "natural attitude," the
narrative also evidences the effects of self-reflective activity upon the
natural attitude. We have the firm impression that Blanca has worked
over in her own unique terms certain experiences she is presenting after she has critically appraised their significance for herself and others.
And in some instances Blanca's reflection upon her experiences (conflicting and frustrating as they are) has thrown into phenomenological
doubt the very givenness of various typified events in her life. Indeed,
as she reconstitutes these events by bracketing their giveness for herself, they come to stand out as merely intended possibilities for her in
a field of action rather than things she is condemned to repeat because
they are compellingly and inevitably real. These events have become
part of Blanca's self-reflective intentionality and as such have become
subject to her freely exercised choice.

While the kinship order can be regarded as forming part of the life
world, the provisional and contractual quality that implicitly adheres
to kinship obligations emerges as an essential ingredient in Blanca's
critical self-reflective experience. The volitional quality undergirding
the real world of kinship is revealed as Blanca adopts the phenomenological attitude. In the earlier part of her narrative, before she seriously questioned her life world, she accepted that kinsmen had legitimate claims on the individual, who was obliged as a member of the
kin group to comply with others' rightful expectations and to submit to
the decisions of constituted authority. In return, she as an individual
would be nurtured, provided for, protected, and, yes, respected. Security and respect, the cardinal values of Guajiro social life, were sim-

ply *there* for those who had adopted the compliant and dutiful posture for which they had been socialized. However, in Blanca's movement toward self-reflexivity, these obligations came to assume the quality of a rule rather than a stable, unchanging truth, for, as she makes clear, specific kinship obligations, like rules, can actually be broken.

In describing her earlier years and her marriage in particular, under very interested and probing questioning, she indicated that in her case the contracts binding human relationships in Guajiro culture were violated without legitimate reason, and usually because of the cruelty and selfishness of human character. At one point Blanca described how her father "sold" her when she was a young woman, marrying her off to a rich Guajiro for a handsome bride payment in livestock, jewelry, and whiskey. Blanca complied with the arrangement, even though she did not know the man, for, as she explained:

> *My kinsmen owned me and had the right to choose a husband for me. I was the eldest daughter so my father got most of the bride payment for himself. We Guajiro women know this is our fate and we submit to it. We only hope that the man our relatives select for us is reasonably kind and has enough resources to maintain us. We fear neglect and drunken beatings.*

Given the cultural definitions of the situation that Blanca herself accepted, we can see that it was only proper for her to submit to this decision in good faith.

Unfortunately the man to whom she was sold, true to her worst fears, was cruel and sadistic and would beat her for no reason when he was drunk:

> *He would come home after drinking with his friends, staggering, his breath stinking of rum. He would usually say something like, "I know you've been fucking so-and-so and you like it because you're hot and have to have it. I can smell it when another man has been with you, you filthy whore. I'll teach you who owns your vagina." Then he'd start beating me with a strap or the flat part of his machete, or with his fists till I screamed for mercy or he became afraid he'd done me serious injury. This happened more often than I'd care to remember.*

Finally, in despair, she left her husband and came back to her father seeking his protection, which she had every right to do within the framework of Guajiro conceptions of redress for marital abuse. The father listened sympathetically and promised support:

> *"Look," he said, "I'm going to protect you from this guy, but let's wait and see if we can't work this thing out. Basically I think your husband is all right."*

Blanca had some serious misgivings about her father at that point. Why all the concern about getting her back to a brutal man in what seemed to be an impossible situation? As Blanca recalled:

> *When he talked that way to me, a chill went down my back and my whole body began to tremble. It seemed to me that my father had made up his mind about this thing. God, was he really going to make me stick this out, knowing it was impossible for me? I felt sick in heart and spirit.*

The husband soon came looking for her, contrite and sorrowful, bringing a present of several cows and some rum for the father. He apologized to the father and promised to stop drinking and not mistreat Blanca in the future. The father talked to her and finally persuaded her to return, but only after he promised that if she were ever mistreated again, he would never let the man have her back. Blanca remembered:

> *My father took my position and I felt somewhat reassured. He said that he loved his beautiful daughter more than life itself and that my suffering was an injury to his own soul. He was warning my husband that the next time something bad happened he would reclaim his daughter for good. He was so positive and forceful I thought he really meant what he said.*

Soon therefter, contrary to his promise, the husband got drunk again and beat Blanca severely, knocking out her front tooth, and accusing her, as usual, of having illicit sexual relations with another man. This time, before she lost consciousness from the beating, he threatened to kill her. When she recovered and was physically able, she resolved to flee and return to her father's house. Gathering her few possessions together, she left under the cover of darkness with the help of an older woman who sympathized with her plight. Her sole comfort in this difficult time was the memory of her father's reassuring promise. When she finally returned and her father saw her battered face and tearful eyes, he was profoundly disturbed:

*He even broke down and wept before me because he was so
grieved by my terrible story. He told me I did not have to return
a second time. I could put all my trust in him, my own father
who loved me with all his heart.*

A day or so later Blanca's husband sent a messenger with another
gift requesting the father to return Blanca to him. He explained that
the father could keep the gift if he cooperated; if he did not, however,
the husband would take back the bride payment he had made for the
girl. At first the father refused, but then his resolution began to waver.
As Blanca remembered, with much bitterness in her voice:

He began to think of all his fat cattle and all that good cher-
rinche *[rum], and my needs did not seem so very important
anymore. The first seeds of doubt were planted in my mind: was
he, in fact, to be trusted with my life?*

Finally, Blanca's father asked her to return to her husband once
again, confirming her worst fears. He assured her that "things would
work out all right." Blanca was horrified by her father's callous disregard for her feelings and well-being. How could he put his cattle before her? Oh, if only she still had a mother to protect her.

*I just couldn't believe what was happening to me. Nothing really
had ever prepared me for this. Sure, I was beaten when I didn't
do my work or didn't mind, but when I was good and did what I
was told, I was always treated well by my parents and relatives.
Father was always particularly supportive; if anything, it was
mother who could sometimes be cold and critical. This reaction
from my father shocked me so much, I remember I almost
fainted from the force of it.*

In a reaction of deepest despair, Blanca threatened her father that if
he tried to make her go back she would kill herself. But the father was
adamant and ignored her appeals. She was being unreasonable and he
was taking her back. She was to get her things ready for the trip.

At this point, Blanca stated, her father had *broken the contract*. The
provisional quality of their relationship and the contingent nature of
her compliance to him had become the focus of a radically self-reflective turn and had surged, with all its hideously negative implications,
into a terrible awareness of what the situation really meant *for her*. Indeed at this point, as the taken-for-grantedness of the relationship was

placed in fundamental doubt, Blanca began in an existentially meaningful way to question some of the basic givens in her life and her personal involvement with them, whereas before she had dutifully accepted this world as naturally and ultimately her own.

Up until now Blanca had complied faithfully and honorably, for she
had taken the father's goodwill more or less for granted, but in the
moment of truth her father totally failed to reciprocate by giving her
the security and protection she rightfully expected, indeed, had a legitimate claim to. It was clear in Blanca's account that she felt her father
failed to live up to his obligations because he put his selfish material
interests before her emotional and physical welfare.

Since violation of the "agreement" had occurred *in extremis*,
Blanca's initial impulse, stemming from a sense of despair and hope-
lessness, was to overreact by ending the very being of this conflict:
she would kill herself.

> *I wanted to commit suicide. This was my first reaction, as I re-
> member. That was the only way out and I was so terribly des-
> perate, without hope, really. But then in a moment of clarity I
> thought to myself, "Why should I let this happen to me? Why
> should I allow them to destroy me?" I realized it was a terrible
> thing to die. And for what and for whom would I die? I knew,
> then, that if I committed suicide I would die for* nothing, *for lit-
> tle more than these people's selfish ambitions, like the poor little
> goat who is sacrificed by the shaman to feed the evil spirits who
> have attacked the sick person in order to eat his soul. This death
> does not benefit the goat, only the others.*

However, once her fundamental aloneness and personal responsibility
to herself had become an issue in her desperate self-scrutiny, there
was no turning back. Suicide was no solution at all. Rejecting the easy
way out, Blanca now came to recognize the existential responsibility
she had to assume for her own possibilities. No longer could she take
flight into bad faith by insisting on her helplessness or by imbuing the
family with the power to rule her life when these same people had already violated her very existence. Now, perhaps, for the first time,
and only under the greatest duress, she was aware that she could forge
a destiny for herself apart from the cultural definitions and constraints
she had naturally accepted in the past.

If we cast this interpretation into the language of self-identity, we
could say that in the aftermath of these terrible events, the easy secur-

ity of her traditional self-image was shattered in the recognition of her aloneness. Yet paradoxically, the very awareness of personal freedom that came from radical self-reflection in the face of doubt and despair, as she questioned her stance to the life world, offered the possibility of a new integration of her identity, molded in conformity with her own emerging, honestly acknowledged self-interests. Cast adrift on the sea of her personal freedom by virtue of the extremity of this violation of herself, Blanca resolved to act on the basis of her own selfish needs, regardless of whether such action jeopardized the relationship with her father. After all, had not events revealed this relationship to be rotten to the core?

The basic but unstated conflict inherent in all Guajiro relationships had now assumed an irreversible character in Blanca's self-reflection and had to be acted upon. Any decision to minimize the bad treatment she had received and return to her husband, thereby securing her father's approval, was now rendered impossible given her definition of the situation and her newfound sense of autonomy. Really, the only course of action was to flee and start life anew. She could justify her decision to herself easily enough on the basis of her father's failure to respect her essential human dignity. However, in exercising personal freedom in such awesome form, she would lose her father's regard and perhaps the support of her whole family. But she would certainly escape her husband's capricious abuse by leaving, and she might create for herself a more meaningful, personally fulfilling future.

Freedom was not easy. Blanca saw herself as helpless to a large extent and knew that any decision she made would be fraught with risks, but she knew the customary sources no longer offered her security:

After I had rejected suicide and knew that I wanted to live, nothing mattered more than taking my life into my own hands, just leaving, going anywhere, but being able to say to myself, "I can do something. I don't need to depend on bad people."

Having little to lose, Blanca voided the contract binding her to her husband and father—for, after all, had they themselves not made this possible by violating the basic conditions of it? She had finally reached the point where the only decision was to seek her future, whatever it offered, poor and without support, on her own terms. Human beings in their misery, she seemed to be saying, can be driven to desperate courses of action.

The ethnographer, through his probing and insistent questioning at this point in the relationship, probably stimulated Blanca into this self-reflective turn. Moving from a neutral to a highly charged personal encounter, both informant and ethnographer were now working through the material at hand in a context of greater self-awareness and honesty. Perhaps Blanca would have described the same situation in the same terms had there been no human encounter, no relentless pressure at the end toward self-examination. We are inclined to think, however, that without that particular experience, through which interaction came to be understood, this material would not have been evoked at all, or, at best, only a very little. It would, we feel, have remained an unsaid part of the life recitation.

As we remove ourselves from the original discourse, we apply our phenomenology toward understanding the underlying, hidden significance of text events that hermeneutical activity seeks to uncover (Ricoeur 1970). Our own interpretive stance, stressing the revealed possibilities of self-examination and freedom to choose, now becomes the means by which the "unsaid" of the text articulates its meanings through the "said" of the fixed discourse that we are mediating in the hermeneutical encounter. The nature of our endeavor is revealed: first the discourse was forged into a particular meaning-form through the mediated preunderstandings of ethnographer and subject, becoming the text with which we work; now we seem to repeat these same operations, as the text is engaged, on a higher and more explicit interpretive level in our search for subjective meaning. We strive, nonetheless, to remain faithful to the requirements of the hermeneutical dialogue as we pursue that elusive objective.

When Blanca left her father's house she gave up the support world of her family and lineage group. As an uprooted person she sought employment as a domestic in the homes of wealthy Guajiros and Venezuelans. According to her account she quit jobs time and time again if it suited her economic needs, or if the conditions of employment violated her sense of personal dignity. After a number of years on her own she met and married her present husband, a man of completely different character from the first, with whom she has had a family and has been able to stabilize the conditions of her life:

> *I am satisfied now. We are poor. We have enough to get by. My husband treats me well and keeps his drinking down. My children fear the rod and obey me. I feel that while things are lacking, I have some control over my life.*

At other, subsequent points in her life history, but in less extreme instances, Blanca felt that she could afford to continue discharging her responsibilities in a relationship, even though the other party might warrant the voiding of the contract by his own selfish behavior. Thus Blanca could validate her own worth as a good and moral person in an evil world and shame others for their lapses. While she was, therefore, free to reject those who violated social contracts, she was also free to rise above the very conditions she had set for maintaining her personal dignity if it suited her need for moral superiority and could be reasonably worked to her advantage. This manipulative quality stood out in stark contrast to the compliance and rigidity she had previously exhibited in her attitude toward others.

In her life history Blanca recalled a critical incident where her brother refused to give her food when she was hungry, and even denied that she was his sister. Several months after this incident, however, the brother experienced difficulties and came to Blanca seeking economic assistance:

> *My heart leapt for joy when my evil brother one day came to me in need. He used to live not too far from here, you know. At the time his children were sick and he was out of work. He never had anything for me when things were going well, no matter how much I suffered. Remember, he had denied me. I was in a position to deny him now, but that is not what I wanted. I took it upon myself to make him examine the evil of his own nature. I told him, "You denied that I was your sister when I came to you, but I don't forget quite so easily. You are my brother and I will give you food because I still love you."*

Even if this episode were pure fantasy, we feel it comments on a subjective truth of Blanca's life. She had, out of past experience, come to define herself as capable of feeling morally superior in a world of criminals, fools, and madmen. This sense had seemingly become a very real part of her self-identity, and she made her actions in the world conform to these images.

Blanca accepted as a reality the negative, rejecting character of much of her world, but she did not uncritically take it for granted. Blanca speculated that the baser nature of human beings might prevail in the absence (and even in the presence) of kinship contracts, and yet she was also aware that people could act compassionately and considerately if they had received a proper upbringing. At such moments in

her rendition she was selecting a category of behavior and reflecting
upon it, drawing certain conclusions and adjusting her perception and
adaptive responses accordingly. At a deeper level Blanca was really
accepting a basic conflict between good and evil in human nature,
with evil (in the form of selfishness and malice) expected to win out
most but not all of the time. Proper socialization, as Blanca saw it,
provided the antidote to this eternal problem. Her own life had served
her as a model for the "good."

However personally reflective this perspective seems to be, it was
nonetheless a typified Guajiro solution to the problem of evil. Blanca's
life merely illustrated a personal reworking of this common theme. Indeed, Blanca's account of her life, like those of other Guajiros, contained many statements regarding the importance of severe discipline
to insure that a child learn correct behavior to counteract his bestial,
antisocial proclivities. Blanca, like other Guajiros, seemed unaware
that the parent's own harsh, aggressive treatment provided an unfortu-
nate model for the child to follow in his dealings with the helpless and
less fortunate. In any case, being "good" in the prevailing Guajiro
scheme of things meant overcoming the recognized temptation to be
nasty, aggressive, and exploitive, as Blanca demonstrated to telling effect in her forgiving treatment of her brother after she had every right
to bear him malice:

> *Guajiro sometimes grow up to be thoughtless, selfish people,*
> *even vicious criminals, because they were never disciplined and*
> *punished when they acted bad as children. If the parents and*
> *relatives assert their authority, the child is afraid to show his*
> *evil; he must control it. Eventually, perhaps this evil in his na-*
> *ture will disappear if the family is constant in their expectations.*
> *It is important for us never to relax our vigilance, for as soon as*
> *we do, our children will become insubordinate and then they*
> *will do whatever their bad nature tells them to do.*

Blanca herself had been rigorously trained by her parents to behave
respectfully and responsibly; unlike other Guajiros, however, she
seemed fortunate insofar as she learned to appreciate the values of her
socialization and subsequently internalized them. She has attempted to
do the same with her own children, but with imperfect results.

Blanca had evidently forgotten that her own compliant, submissive
behavior, her own "goodness," which we presume stemmed from the

propriety of her upbringing, had not necessarily netted her much consideration when it came to the true test. Why, then, should children be good to begin with? These are precisely the kinds of contradictions on which human activity seems so often to turn. The limits of human lucidity and consistency are profound. For Blanca the way out of any such potential contradiction was by validating to herself her moral superiority, even if her goodness was not always rewarded in practical terms.

Two preoccupations dominate Blanca's recollected life experience, and they apply to her life before and after the critical events that led her to leave her family and seek her own way in the world. These preoccupations are poverty and sexuality. They are, we feel, rather intimately associated first with her particular social position within Guajiro society, and later with her somewhat marginal status as a Guajiro, although her manner of expressing these concerns is certainly unique. These preoccupations do not necessarily characterize Guajiros in other social categories.

Blanca selected poverty for special emphasis in recollecting her life story, and she did so virtually from the beginning of the ethnographic encounter. One of her most telling statements had to do with her early hardships and hunger:

> *I remember many times when there was no food and I went hungry. Sometimes I would wake up in the morning with my stomach hurting because I had not eaten for days. It was awful to know that I would have to go out and do my chores when I was already weak from hunger.*[1]

She also recalled the abuse of the poor by the rich; the necessity of working long and hard to earn money, and the difficulty of making ends meet; and her present husband's unemployment and the problems it caused.

Blanca believed that her poverty had been the major cause of the

---

1. The emphasis on her early poverty contradicts Blanca's statements about her father's relative prosperity later on, when she feels he sold her out because of greed. He may actually still have been a poor man who was ready to sacrifice his daughter for his paltry herds, which may have come largely from the bride payment he received for her. Perhaps it was more acceptable for Blanca to think that her father betrayed her through greed for more, rather than through fear of the rich man or pure economic necessity.

mistreatment she had received in life, the specific abuses of which she
catalogued in considerable and minute detail. If she had been rich, she
felt, nobody would have dared to treat her improperly:

> *I see now that if I had been wealthy—had lots of animals and
> jewelry—everybody would have been nice to me because they
> would have been afraid of me or greedy for my property. They
> would have come waiting on me: "Señora Blanca, how are you?
> We hear you have not been feeling too well. It is so good to
> see you. We hope you are well now!" Because, on the con-
> trary, I was poor, nobody ever did that; they treated us only
> with contempt.*

In describing her woes Blanca threw into relief the life style and behavior of the wealthy and powerful by contrasting their self-assured
and self-righteous arrogance and inhumanity with her own empathy
for the poor and downtrodden, which came out of her immediate subjective knowledge of their desperate condition.

That the subject perceived the ethnographer as a sympathetic and
generous listener, as we remarked elsewhere, undoubtedly motivated
her to stress her difficult situation, although this theme might have
come out even in other circumstances. In any event, unburdening herself in this way served (1) to justify her position to a neutral but sympathetic bystander; (2) to elicit sympathy and compassion; and (3) to
secure financial assistance that alleviated her economic problems to
some extent. We feel that it is impossible to understand fully this emphasis on poverty in Blanca's story without considering the way she
defined the immediate data-collecting situation and evaluated the positive feedback she received. This definition of the situation must have
called forth certain types of need and response priorities.

Blanca's view of her sexual feelings was one she shared with most
other Guajiro women and was a striking theme that ran through her
life history account (she repeated the attitudes she learned and applied
as a child with her own daughters). Sexuality, Blanca insisted, was
not the Guajiro woman's right to control and dispense as a free agent.
The reality of people's attitudes had to be taken into account. Rights
of sexual access to a woman, she explained, were held by her family
and were conferred to a man only through formal marriage. Thereafter
only the husband had the right to sleep with her, for he had bought her
sexuality. Blanca feared the sexual temptation that she experienced as
a young, unmarried woman and was indignant (but secretly excited)

when boys made obscene advances. Blanca always reminded herself and her tempter that her body was not her own: if a man wanted to have sexual relations with her, he had to talk with the people who owned her.

Blanca recognized, of course, that as an unmarried woman she had sexual needs, but she always had them firmly under control. While she might bestow a few innocent kisses on a boy she favored—she was only human—she made it clear that she could and would not go further. Unlike other girls, it seems, she had learned the desperate consequences of improper sexual behavior. When she was on the verge of losing her head, she always recalled these terrible punishments of her childhood, and these memories sufficiently inhibited dangerous temptations.[2] She also selectively recalled and obsessively rendered a number of negative role models, women who had not learned to behave according to the rules of sexual propriety and who suffered for it. Particularly striking examples were the blatantly homosexual wife of one of her uncles and a deaf and mute girl who promiscuously sought out sex. Later, in her disastrous first marriage and her successful second marriage, she accepted the exclusive sexual rights that her husbands held in her, despite the abuse of the first and the unemployment of the second. Moreover, despite changes in the Guajiro way of life, she felt she owned her daughters until some man married them by making her a bride payment. Thus, although Blanca had discovered freedom in some areas of her life, the choice of her own sexual projects was evidently not among them.

Blanca's awareness of her conflicts and her carefully considered choice of methods to adapt to stress and overcome it, with that final shattering recognition of her own freedom to change the world, seem to form an unbroken chain in her recollected experience, beginning with her earliest memories and continuing into her adolescence and adult life. At the center is Blanca herself, as we have rendered her, a self-reflective being who is maintaining an identity and whose actions we and she have made to appear internally consistent and meaningful. By the end of the life story recitation Blanca seems to be saying to us: "This is the kind of person I am, and I am the product of my subjec-

2. Once Blanca was hung upside down from the rafters of the house in a carrying bag for several hours because she talked to a boy and had come home late with the firewood. During her ordeal she had to urinate but her mother was unrelenting. Blanca remembers urinating all over herself, the urine trickling down her face and burning her eyes.

tive interaction with experience, which is, however, sometimes beyond my control. My life is its own justification. Try to accept this
and respond to it as if it were true, even if you cannot privately suspend disbelief."

Conclusions

Our goal in understanding Blanca has been to grasp the complexity of
her life in its subjective immediacy. To this end we have tried to see
the unique character of the subject's phenomenal consciousness as a
product of past events, but one nevertheless transmitted in the context
of the particular conditions she defined as her ongoing reality. Our understanding of her life, however, is surely not something we have entered into directly from a blank, ahistorical starting point. The process
of interpretation by which understanding is achieved presupposes
events, conditions, and negotiated meanings: the unfolding dialogue
between the ethnographer and the subject; the dialogue between the
subject and the translator; the translation process itself; and the dialogue between all of these parties and the expectant environment that
surrounds them and that changes as it moves with them through time.
Each of us, in a sense, has been integrated into a common endeavor
despite our illusion of control, and each of us in a sense is a prisoner
of the meanings he has created with the other. Nonetheless, each seeks
to make sense of what is going on in his own way and so each ar-
rives at his own eventual understanding after a process of fumbling
and groping.

As interpreters of the life history, therefore, we "understand" when,
in recreating Blanca dialectically through an act of our own self-understanding, we grasp her foreignness within our changed horizon. We
join Blanca in our own efforts to overcome alienation and to choose a
destiny for ourselves according to our authentic interests. This is the
self-reflective turn that has brought us to understand how Blanca situated herself in her world, first in the discourse, and later in the final
text itself. We have partially succeeded in our interpretive efforts to
eliminate Blanca's strangeness by including her in our world, now
changed irreversibly through that very encounter.

Much ethnographic research lacks a true feeling for human life as it
is subjectively experienced by individuals. We know the richness and
complexity of our own inner life, and when we compare this to the

many tedious, dehumanizing accounts of life in other cultures (and that includes our work, too), we may feel an acute sense of disinterest and even outright alienation (which is an alienation from ourselves, as well). All too often the real thing seems to get lost in the obfuscation of the investigator playing God with his constructs. Blanca's case is instructive. Her particular Guajiro despair is also our human despair, and her anguish at people's inhumanity and her attempts to think well of herself in a corrupt, vicious world are the very things that impress us about her life, because that is what her life seems really to be saying as a subjective truth in addressing us.

We are tempted to turn to the great works of fiction, which are imbued with the author's thoughts and feelings distilled through the immediacy of the creative process into living characters, for insights into the human condition. In *The Age of Reason* by Jean Paul Sartre (1947), for example, the richness of a man's existential situation is revealed as he contemplates his freedom in a world where bad faith and ready-made solutions threaten to snap asunder his will to act and create his own destiny. Surely this situation is applicable not only to the limited sphere of French existential man: the flow of subjective experience magically recreated by Sartre in this novel cries out for a much fuller measure. To render Blanca and other individuals in the full force of their existential dilemma, as Sartre does in his novel, would be to enlarge in a significant way the explicitly human and concrete dimensions of the subject's world and engage the human possibilities of the interpretive endeavor as well. Perhaps it would not be amiss, in conclusion, to suggest that the study of the individual in anthropology could benefit by imitating art, by following the artistic and imaginative re-creation that occurs in fiction.

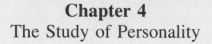

Chapter 4
The Study of Personality

One of the main uses of the life history is the investigation of individual personalities and the mechanics of personality function in general. The investigator works deductively from a set of abstract propositions that define the dynamic and predictive properties of his theoretical model. In the process, the data of the life history must be translated into the appropriate analytical categories. Through this activity the data are converted into the abstract, highly symbolic forms or typifications that represent the true or hidden significance of the data (Natanson 1970: chapter 3). Once this is accomplished, the investigator looks for a coherence or pattern in his analytical categories (that is, the translated data) that conforms to the specifications of some part of the model. If he can reassemble or reconstruct the model in whole or in part after he has translated the life history into the proper symbols and put them in the appropriate analytical frames, he takes this reconstruction as proof that the model makes sense, describes the reality, or isolates causal processes and significant relationships.

The personality model assumes that experience determines intrapsychic events, but *certain kinds* of experience (reinforcements or Oedipal traumas, for example) are seen as decisive in their invariant effects on character. The model thus establishes particular kinds of preexisting scales or dimensions by which testing and measurement must proceed, and the data are scanned and placed on these dimensions. Personality and experience are therefore two different things interacting in predictable ways along measureable categories, with personality simply being a set of variables whose saliency derives directly from the priorities set by the theory. In other words, we understand personality to be a certain kind of thing related causally or functionally to other things. Its attributes can be described in terms of certain dynamically interrelated dimensions that together constitute it.

However, interpreting the life history from the standpoint of some personality theory that relies heavily on constructs external to the phenomenal consciousness of the individual studied can become a form of testing rather than an attempt to engage and understand his world through the dialogue, because the answers are already embedded within the structure of a predefined context. The answers, we might say, are potentially present within the system that generates the questions (Palmer 1969:233), and the subjective integrity of the life history is thus violated. That approach treats events that are subjectively meaningful to a person in the context of his own life as though they were objective stimuli of the kind manipulated in a laboratory experiment. If they were such, of course, we could properly assign them the absolute meanings insisted upon by the theory acting through the requirements of the experiment. But all of this neglects the very real possibility that such events are meaningful only as they are organized in the individual's consciousness of his own life. The very act of intending these events is the way that person subjectively recovers himself in his experienced social world. In taking behavior from the life history and manipulating it in the forms required by theoretical constructs, the phenomena in the true immediacy of their subjective meanings are lost to a large extent.

Let us take an example to illustrate what we mean. Kardiner (1939, 1945) formulated the concept of the basic personality structure, which he defined as the "effective adaptive tools" of the individual that he shares with other members of his culture. This concept arises from the assumption that during infancy and childhood the members of a common culture have all been exposed to similar nuclear experiences that were generally frustrating or conflict producing. By "adaptive" Kardiner means the ability of the individual to deal defensively with his interdicted needs and anxieties in a way that makes sense in the culture to which he belongs. He further states that early maternal care is critical in determining later ego strength and adequacy of adaptation. If it is bad, (that is, conflict producing), as defined by such and such standards, one "reactive" system, as defined by such and such behavior, follows; if it is good, a more healthy adaptation ensues.

In evaluating life histories of individual subjects from the small East Indian Island of Alor (in the Indonesian Archipelago) collected by Cora DuBois (1944) in 1938–1939, Kardiner finds evidence that his theory accounts for the relationship of experience (poor maternal care) and aspects of personality development (weak ego organization). But to do this, certain kinds of early experience have been coded as representing "poor" maternal care (e.g., neglect of the child because of economic duties). These events may indeed make the kind of sense

Kardiner intends them to have, judged by our own standards, but would they necessarily be interpreted by Alorese subjects in the same terms? By forcing these events to mean what the investigator thinks they mean, Kardiner loses the meaning they had for the person to whom they happened. For the Alorese, their maternal care is natural and has predictable, manageable implications.

With weak ego organization, for which Kardiner believes he has found ample and predictable evidence, we are on even shakier ground. Certain Alorese behaviors suggest to Kardiner a weak ego structure and ineffective defensive techniques stemming from early deficiencies in maternal care and other learning experiences. Kardiner talks of lack of perseverence, feelings of helplessness, disorganization, shallow affectivity, and meaningless or trivial attempts to overcompensate, on the basis of the apparent brittleness and lack of affect in Alorese social relations and lack or underdevelopment of social cooperation by Western standards. But Kardiner is measuring ego adaptation and mental health against standards that have currency in his own culture. There is, in fact, ample evidence in the subjective narrative of events by the Alorese themselves of seeming self-initiative and resourcefulness in the larger cultural context that makes sense to *them*. This is true in such diverse areas as financial activity, gardening, and mystical experience.

Kardiner, like many others who use the life history to study personality, seems to have managed to make sense of personality events in the framework of his theory. If there is a mistake in his method, it is the fundamental one of assuming that the theory describes another's reality; it would be more accurate, however, simply to say the theory describes the world through itself. Wittgenstein (1968) would say that we understand things through the words or metalanguage we use to describe them.

The Hermeneutics of Psychoanalytic Theory

The life history accounts that we shall attempt to interpretively re-engage in this chapter through phenomenological and existential hermeneutics have already been interpreted from psychoanalytic perspectives. In retrospect we see that our own first understanding of the subject's personality as presented in the account, and therefore our sense of the "true" meaning of the subject's actions, came from our initial inclination to read the life history with the analyst's interpretive intent in mind. The presentation of the subject's personality as we originally came to understand it, then, was clearly intelligible only within that interpretive framework.

Ricoeur (1970), in his monumental interpretive critique of Freud, maintains that psychoanalytic theory is merely one type of hermeneutics. If the aim of a more general hermeneutics, as he says, is to decipher the double or hidden meaning of symbols fixed in text, then psychoanalytic theory stakes out its own claim by approaching the essential phenomena of human consciousness and activity as illusion or mystification; the text of human life is written in symbols that disguise and conceal the true underlying meaning of man's existence (e.g., Oedipal conflicts and death instincts). Freud posits an "archaeological" approach in his hermeneutics, seeking to uncover the meaning of the present as disguises for the threatening archaic images of childhood traumas and conflicts.

Recently Crapanzano (1981) has expanded the hermeneutical engagement with psychoanalytic theory and has proposed a somewhat different reading of Freud. He approaches psychoanalytic hermeneutics as an interpretation of the dynamics of the patient-analyst encounter, which reveals a process of self-construction through the "other" that is masked referentially by the fixation of the biography into the written word of text so that past is assimilated into present. This effort represents an interesting extension of the hermeneutics of the ethnographic encounter (e.g., with Tuhami) into the domain of psychoanalysis, which as interpretive reconstruction has the character of dialogue.

Ricoeur feels it essential to the hermeneutical endeavor to confront conflicting approaches with each other, to arbitrate between them, and, if possible, to find a dialectic reconciliation between them: "By showing in what way each method expresses the form of a theory, philosophical hermeneutics justifies each method within the limits of its own theoretical circumscription" (1974b:15).

He confronts psychoanalysis with a phenomenological hermeneutics, as we will also attempt to do, that aims to determine the progression of human consciousness toward the truth of its own being (the "teleological" approach). Meaning is therefore discovered as something disclosed and revealed in the very nature of the thing itself. The text, for example, can be opened up for us to see what it says about its own being. In the life history that being is a profoundly subjective one. Ricoeur's (1970:515–518) splendid confrontation of his own and Freud's hermeneutics in order to make sense of Sophocles' *Oedipus Rex* is a classic example of how the two approaches can be reconciled by showing how a man's life can be understood by meanings extending from his present position into the past and into the future.

Our own enterprise, like all others, derives from a particular starting point that limits the nature of understanding itself. Nevertheless, we feel that a phenomenological and existential hermeneutics better satisfies the essential direction in the being of understanding. Freudian theory does not engage the text in the form of dialectic questioning; rather, the preunderstandings are imposed on the text and the text or discourse is rigidly assimilated into them to reveal its hidden meaning. Since we follow Gadamer's emphasis on the dialogue in his ontological hermeneutics, we believe that some dialectical mediations capture more of what the world of the text is saying than do others.[1] Phenomenology and existentialism are hermeneutics that offer a greater possibility for dialectical questioning to occur; it is this questioning, we hope, that will allow us to encounter the text in its own world, on its own terms, and, in the case of the life history, in its own intrinsic subjectiveness. We believe that by confronting psychoanalytic perspectives with our own (to bring Ricoeur back into the discussion), we reveal the possibilities of our own hermeneutics and the limitations imposed on understanding in all efforts to interpret life histories through psychological, and especially psychoanalytic, approaches. Perhaps we are merely appealing to other hermeneuticists who feel that

---

1. Lang, in an article on language and psychoanalytic theory states that a contemporary theory of psychoanalytic treatment must bring into visibility its hermeneutic basis, which is hidden behind all the "bio-physicalism" of psychoanalytic therapeutic methods (1978:262). He points out how interested Freud was in "the talking cure" of Breuer's patient, Anna O. Breuer would listen to her, helping her thus to use a personal language, since he did not insist on applying beforehand his own scientific prejudices (ibid.:255). Later, Freud would stress the importance of language in psychoanalysis, which relied on the power of words rather than on drugs and tools. Freud moved away from even hypnosis and toward his free-association approach using words: "In psychoanalytic treatment nothing else happens than that an exchange of words takes place between the analysed and the doctor. . . . Nothing else happens among them than that they talk with each other" (ibid.:256–258). But, as Lang points out, Freud did not perceive this process as a hermeneutical act since his understanding of language was based in the empirical tradition (ibid.:258).

the reconstruction of the subjective intent of the text is the most legitimate standard we can apply for judging the validity of interpretations.

Some readers may not be convinced by our reinterpretive effort, and they should consult the original works we critique and weigh the respective merits of the two contrasting interpretations for themselves. Our readers may discover, as Ricoeur does, that through the self-reflective process we may find a higher complementarity in two seemingly irreconcilable approaches that ultimately enhances understanding.

Ricoeur is willing at least to arbitrate psychoanalytics and phenomenology, even though it often seems as if the two hermeneutics are talking at cross-purposes. Sartre (1956:92–94), on the other hand, brings existentialism to bear as a radical critique of Freudian theory, ruling it out on the basis of a faulty epistemology. (We should add that this Freudian epistemology is weak only from the standpoint of Sartre's own epistemology, and so we come back to Ricoeur). Sartre questions the basic premise of "repression" and hence the very status of the "conscious" and the "unconscious" as real entities. He asks how the ego (censor) can block impulses if it is an ego of consciousness. He argues that the ego, as censor, in order to apply its activity with discernment, must know what it is repressing. Moreover, how can the censor discern the impulses needing to be repressed without being conscious of discerning them. Thus Sartre poses the question: "How can we conceive of a knowledge that is ignorant of itself?" (ibid.:93). All knowing is ultimately consciousness of knowing. Sartre then answers that the very self-consciousness of the censor is in bad faith because it is trying not to be conscious of the consciousness of needing to repress the impulses: "Psychoanalysis has not gained anything for us since in order to overcome bad faith, it has established between the unconscious and consciousness an autonomous consciousness in bad faith" (ibid.:94).

We will not try to explore the implications of this radical critique or deny the possibility of unconscious processes. Instead, we will adopt the assumption in our own hermeneutics that the individual is conscious of his choices at some level, but that bad faith, when it occurs, may or may not be initiated in actual empirical consciousness and may or may not be transparent to self-reflection. Accepting this premise, however, does not in any way compromise our belief that there is an inherent subjective truth in the life history account itself.

Sartre has suggested a resolution to the dilemma of psychoanalysis by proposing "existential psychoanalysis" (ibid.:722), which is an examination of the irreducible projects of being in human totality that *are* the life history we wish to understand, unencumbered by an a priori psychology. With this approach we are in fundamental agreement, and it will be reflected in some of our subsequent critiques.

Basic Approaches

While all efforts of using the life history to study personality share certain fundamental presuppositions about the nature of experience, several distinct kinds of problems or issues concerned with personality have been investigated in and through the personal document. These concerns can be organized essentially into two basic groups. We shall try to identify briefly the characteristic research interests involving personality that pertain to these two categories. In order to elucidate the interpretive problems posed by these approaches, we shall reexamine several specific personality studies of life histories. In the process we shall focus on general theoretical constructs that these studies embody, as well as epistemological and methodological issues they raise. We shall be adopting the attitude throughout that there may be other ways of making sense of autobiographical data if we proceed according to the hermeneutical and phenomenological assumptions outlined in the previous chapter.

The first group consists of studies that attempt to use the life history to understand the distinctive personality of a particular person because he is intrinsically interesting as an individual in his own right, because of his social or political importance, or because of the investigator's clinical or therapeutic interest in the person. The investigator customarily works with a set of explicit or unstated theoretical propositions (e.g., mainly psychoanalytic ones) that guide the way he deduces the personality of the subject, using the life history as his data laboratory, but sometimes supplementing this with other data as well.

In the second category are life histories that have been analyzed to test assumptions, whether developmental or psychodynamic, of some personality theory. The theory is not really used to understand the life history; rather, the life history functions as an independent measure of the predictive power of the theory in question. Here, of course, the life history may be only one of several measures used as independent assessment of the theory. As we shall see, one important type of theory has to do with formulations of national or social character, and thus for testing or experimentation purposes a range of life histories is utilized for comparison.

Studying the Individual Personality

One group of studies in this area, consists of attempts to use life history data to understand the distinctive personality of a particular person for some of the reasons we have just suggested. The investigator customarily uses a set of theoretical premises for figuring out the personality of the subject, using the life history alone or in conjunction with other personal documents and measures. The model, however, may exist in the investigator's mind in varying degrees of explicitness. Where its use is highly explicit and follows formulated procedures, the model may become the conscious, closely reasoned basis for systematically inferring personality from the life history. In such cases the evidence of the life history as gleaned through its analysis is taken as "objective" proof that the theory works the way it is supposed to work. Validation of the theory may be claimed even though data and interpretation have become hopelessly confounded.

Some attempts have been made in anthropology to understand the character dynamics of a person from another culture through his life history. Studies done by Sachs (1947), Leighton and Leighton (1949), and Devereux (1969) are representative. Of course, the number of such detailed studies is small compared with the large number of life histories that are simply collected and published for their own sake or with a meager attempt at character analysis.

In order to talk about sufficiently important personality studies in life history research, it will be necessary to abandon a narrow definition of the life history as a coherent, strictly chronological account by a person in his own words about his own life in favor of one that includes any kind of record of an individual life over time that involves some subjective self-reporting. This expanded meaning of the life history applies to two studies of individual personality we will be looking at in some detail. Sachs's work is cast in the form of a biography interspersed with interpretive remarks, although in many passages the subject speaks for himself; it is a fascinating document. The Devereux work is a psychiatric life history; the material represents responses to a series of therapeutic, psychiatrically oriented interviews, and there is no consistent narrative thread, but the subject is doing a lot of interesting talking about himself.

While not all studies of the life history clearly state their theoretical biases, both Sachs and Devereux approach the autobiographical data in terms of explicitly stated psychoanalytic assumptions that constitute the basis of their interpretive framework. Indeed, both authors are firmly committed to Freudian views of personality and reaffirm this commitment as a matter of faith. Our interest in reevaluating the Devereux and Sachs studies is more than merely to illustrate a particular kind of personality study in life history research. We wish to investigate interpretive presuppositions in these approaches and their adequacy in dealing with the individual in the life history from the different vantage points we have been suggesting.

The Life History, Character Neurosis, and Psychotherapy

Reality and Dream: Psychotherapy of a Plains Indian by George Devereux, a psychoanalytically trained anthropologist, is an account of his attempts to help Jimmy P., a Wolf Indian, overcome an incapacitating neurosis. *Reality and Dream* is not a true life history in the narrow sense but is rather a full record of Devereux's interviews with the patient, accompanied by a description of the theoretical setting, a review of the patient's cultural background, and a very complicated analysis of the psychodynamics of the neurosis and a rationalization for the therapeutic strategy. Enough autobiographical data were elicited during the interviews, however, to justify the inclusion of this study, for our purposes, under the rubric of the life history.

There is an immediate advantage working with life history data elicited in this kind of format. While the account of the life is piecemeal, the date themselves are unmistakably related to the behavorial context that evoked them. We see the patient recounting aspects of his past life in response to the analyst's questions and expectations, which he perceives as having certain meanings that call for particular reactions on his part.

In *Reality and Dream* we are able to see the life history data unfold before us as a product of a definable and extended dialogue in which what each party says to the other seems really to matter in significant interpersonal terms. How often is the social or interpersonal context of data gathering defined with the clarity and exquisite detail that it is here? How often are we able to understand the relationship of what is said in the life history to the conditions of the dialogue request as exactly as we do in this case? Of course, to a large extent the nature of the study itself determined the central importance attached to spelling out these interpersonal factors in the therapeutic relationship. Nevertheless, the whole thing has been brought off in a very illuminating way. Whether or not we agree with Devereux's point of view or his methods is one thing; we do, however, have the opportunity to examine his biases as a therapist and analyst, and we can reappraise the significance of the form and content of the extant life history in that light.

The form of the dialogue and the meanings it generated must be seen in terms of Devereux's self-defined role as therapist. Being an anthropologist and respecting Jimmy's Indian identity, Devereux familiarized himself thoroughly with the patient's tribal background to find a therapeutic strategy that would be understandable to the patient in his own cultural frame of reference. This effort is probably the most compelling facet of the dialogue situation and perhaps the one most responsible for getting the patient to look freely and critically at his past in light of the therapist's suggestive interpretation of the events leading up to his present problems.

Nonetheless, there was no real dialogue in the hermeneutical sense of an exchange centered on an issue in which the patient's viewpoint was respected. What the patient said was important primarily in relationship to the conditions and limitations imposed on the dialogue by the investigator, who knew that the patient was disturbed and that the analyst, in his professional wisdom, had the framework and the techniques to realize a necessary, predefined goal of cure. In defining his position as one of helping the subject, Devereux manipulates the meanings of autobiographical events to establish the problem and the dimensions of treatment within which the patient could understand and work through the symptoms of his neurosis (conversion reaction, impotence) back to the original neurosis itself (Oedipal conflict, repressed rage toward women).

Although it is simple enough to see the structuring of the data as the therapist's attempt to put the patient's life in a Freudian frame of interpretation, we are hard pressed to see much of the patient's life spontaneously recollected from *his* point of reference. Any meaningful chains of reminiscence or association outside those that Devereux wishes to explore are soon broken in the service of the therapeutic objective.

By artfully manipulating Freudian psychodynamics, Devereux integrates the events of Jimmy P.'s life with his neurotic symptoms to
make certain causal sequences appear plausible. Thus, for example, a
pattern such as his early unresolved Oedipal conflict (castration anxiety), which was exacerbated by the traumatic event of his wife's infi-
delity, is linked to his injury in the army, his fear of high places, his
impotence, the latent content of his dreams, and so forth. Because
these events appear dynamically integrated, they are imbued with a
singular emphasis that other life events, because they are of peripheral
importance to the neurosis, are not accorded. The life of Jimmy P.
thus has meaning only from the anthropologist's perspective; the life
account lacks inherent vitality, in our opinion, because the subject's
interpretations of events, which are *his* reality, are regarded only as rationalizations and defenses that disguise their true meaning (Cioffi
1971, for example, has pointed to this loophole in Freudian analysis
for making any event, no matter how seemingly contradictory, consistent with its assumptions).

It is true that Devereux, unlike most psychotherapists, is fully aware
of the subject's culture, and in part the therapy is predicated on suggesting insights that make sense in the patient's frame of reference.
But while Devereux helps Jimmy P. to understand through his own
value system, these values are still being reduced to and manipulated
into a Freudian matrix, which is totally alien to the reality and conscious interest of Wolf culture and Jimmy's situation in particular. The
fact that Jimmy frequently could not understand or sympathize with
the author's interpretations suggests this very strongly, particularly
since these feelings and discontents are most strongly verbalized after
the patient felt himself strong enough to stand up to Devereux.

One reason the interpretation seems so reasonable, we suspect, is
because for a good part of the therapy the patient meekly allowed
Devereux to define his reality for him (with his dream interpretations,
for example). Is it not possible, despite the emphasis of the study on
"truth" and "objectivity," that the therapeutic setting obscured the *patient's truth* by eliciting compliant modes of behavior that made it impossible, or at least very difficult, for the subject to disagree with this
very-clever white doctor, who knew all the answers and who seemed
so sympathetic and anxious to help him?

A careful perusal of the interview protocols raises several important
questions. First, did Jimmy's "problems" really have the meaning
Devereux said they did? In other words, did the nightmares and impo-

tence take their genesis from the alleged traumatic events in the patient's life? Much of the interpretation hangs on the crucial traumatic significance of the five-year-old Jimmy seeing his mother having sex with a man. But was Jimmy really old enough and sufficiently aware to attribute to this event, unconsciously or consciously, the very complex meanings he was supposed to have given it?

That the patient is obviously angry and resentful of the mother does not necessarily imply the deep-seated dynamic and sexual importance that Devereux assumes (i.e., Oedipal and castration fears that structure all subsequent life experiences). Indeed, before being pressured, the subject could hardly remember the incident in which he surprised his mother in bed with a man. But through the meanings Devereux provided, Jimmy retrospectively came to recognize the enormous implications of this experience. One might compare the passage in which the patient dumbly and rather sadly assents to the author's interpretation (page 418) with his earlier recollection: "My mother never took care of me. I say this from my own experience. It is lucky that my sister and brother-in-law took care of me" (page 357). Here the conscious, spontaneously recollected significance has to do with the mother's caretaking rather than sexual functions.

An alternative explanation might relate these symptoms to the subject's consciously experienced anxiety about his interpersonal adequacy. It is only natural that his self-esteem would have suffered as a result of his inability to find work, a problem that preoccupies him. Jimmy's self-definition of his own existential problems provides the self-reflexive meanings that determined the behavior we are trying to understand. Devereux might well have spent more time looking for the subject's ongoing interpretation of his reality, instead of reconstructing a pseudoreality for him out of events filtered through the meaning of Freudian theory.

Second, what indication is there that the patient would have been any different or worse off without the therapy? Before, the patient had always been able to work through his problems on his own without the benefit of psychoanalytic insights. His neurotic problems may have been a passing disturbance brought about by the self-defined difficulties of his life. If, at that time, Jimmy himself had been able to change his life for the better (which was well within his power), the psychological difficulties might well have disappeared in whole or in part. But as it is, the patient's life is arrested by the therapist in midstream, a problem is created, and a solution is suggested without which, so it seems, the patient could not have gone on without experiencing serious disabilities.

Whenever Jimmy does talk about experience in terms of his own understandings (his interpretation of white people's behavior, for example), he is immediately told that such thinking represents problems, defenses, and unreal ways of looking at the world, an insight which, if he could only understand and accept it, would enable him to resolve his difficulties and find a happier and more efficient life. This insight is particularly manifest at the end, when, after feeling somehow attacked by the therapist but by now more confident of his ability to speak up, he criticizes the staff at the hospital for their lack of consideration in dealing with him. Even Devereux himself is not excluded in this criticism, the particular charge against him being that he had undermined the patient's faith in religion when the patient wanted to believe that there was a higher power that was more than just merely the "power he had in himself." Yet for Devereux, this reaction was all part of the therapeutic process, an inevitable aspect of the transference relationship. By defining himself successfully as a superior authority, and by using clever word magic, he makes Jimmy see that he was wrong and immature in holding these ideas. And this is the whole tenor of Jimmy's life history as he comes to "understand" it retrospectively through Devereux's guidance.

Perhaps the most blatant example of Devereux's unwillingness to accept events in the life history at their obvious face value for the subject is his insistence on interpreting Jimmy's recollections of Schultz, a famous white writer about the Plains Indians whom Jimmy very much admired, as a sublimated representation of the patient's Oedipal transference to the therapist. The patient's liking for Schultz's son in this context was a symbolic way of replacing this transference with a friendly relationship between equals. What appears to be Jimmy's innocent and long-standing interest in this writer is made to appear as meaningful only in the matrix Devereux has identified as characterizing the patient-therapist dynamics. If the event has any "ultimate" meaning, however, perhaps it was simply Jimmy's way of symbolically showing Devereux that he had learned from their relationship that the anthropologist, like Schultz, was a decent man who was genuinely interested in *him*, just as Schultz had earlier been interested in the Blackfeet, and that it was only now that he realized he felt that way. Devereux may have made a fundamental mistake in assuming that the patient's prejudice against whites (but not the neurosis!) was not that important and could easily be overcome, whereas in reality this receptivity to whites came about after considerable difficulty only at the end of the relationship. Our knowledge of ethnic minorities shows that this kind of typification of experience is at once a powerful protective device and a method of cognitive control that cannot be easily eliminated.

While we are critical of Devereux's approach, our criticism is mainly directed to what we see as his uncritical acceptance of the epistemological status of his interpretation of the patient's life. He says, in essence: "I am taking Freud and with him I am going to understand a life." But it is not just any life; it is a life far removed in experience from Devereux and from Freud. The understandings that the author then devises, while ingenious and sophisticated in their own terms, are misleading when we go back to the actual data of this man's life and begin to see events falling into a meaningfully integrated pattern from his standpoint. The fact that the context defining the form and content of the life history was a therapeutic one must certainly be recognized, and it was not Devereux's intention to collect a coherent life history for its own sake. Yet Devereux's interpretive excesses in the application of theory are by no means unique in life history analysis and may therefore be instructive for our purposes.

Some aspects of the patient's behavior, for example, defensiveness in dealing with Devereux, may indeed have a psychodynamic aspect. But this explanation simply cannot be the whole of the reality of this man's life. The author's interpretation is rather like a segmented construct of bits and parts artificially detached for consideration. How ramifying the unconscious is—and Devereux is saying it is very ramifying—we have no real way of knowing for certain, because propositions about this question are not falsifiable in any way that matters. As Cioffi (1971) has charged, Freudian theory always has a ready explanation of why things are not the way the theory says they should be. Indeed, procedures of Freudian psychoanalytic theory are designed functionally to obstruct the discovery of disconfirmatory states of affairs.

Finally, apart from any doubtful Freudian explanation, we have incontrovertibly another kind of *subjective* integrity in the life account, which is there if we only attend to it. Jimmy is the sole author of his own destiny and the many shifting events that constitute it, whether or not these things have any deeper or hidden significance outside the organizing powers of his conscious mind. The little of the life history that has not been engineered by Devereux in the interests of Jimmy's cure bespeaks other interests and concerns that have defined the course of this man's life up to his hospitalization.

The Life History, Personality, and Adaptation to Change

Wulf Sachs's *Black Hamlet* (later retitled *Black Anger*), the life story of a tribal medicine man living in racist South Africa, is a remarkable book. Like *Reality and Dream*, it aims to understand a man from an alien culture in a "civilized" world through his life history, dreams, and observations of his ongoing behavior. Like the Devereux book, it has a therapeutic intent although that intent is not so marked. While it is true that Sachs, a psychiatrist, is concerned with helping John Chavafambira, a Manyika medicine man, overcome the problems of his life, this aspect is of strictly secondary importance. Essentially, Sachs finds John an intrinsically interesting psychological subject.

As an essay in life history interpretation, *Black Hamlet* is well worth examining, even though it does not fulfill the narrow criterion for a life history, lacking as it does the subject's view of his life in his own words. John is allowed to speak about himself directly only from time to time; basically, this book is John's life as Sachs sees it. Most of the information on which the biography is based, it is true, comes from the subject's own report of his experiences over the years. What were originally purely autobiographical materials have been confounded to such an extent by Sachs's interpretation that it is hard to know what the subject said, did, and thought, and what Sachs thinks happened. Some of the conclusions and opinions attributed to John were obviously Sachs's inferences and readings between the lines. In addition, some parts of the biography are based on Sachs's observations of the man and on what other people told him about John; these parts are not always carefully differentiated in the book from the subject's report.

Yet, in spite of these problems, the author is remarkably careful in spelling out for the reader his relationship with the subject and the circumstances in which the life history data, as well as his own observations and conclusions, were elicited. We have, in effect, the social context of this life history laid out in detailed exactitude. The vicissitudes of John's life in the book come to take on their meanings in the context of the author's involved but ever changing relationship to his subject. This relationship developed over a ten-year period in the subject's life and encompassed much of his entire life situation, unlike the limited time span and peripheral involvement that characterized the relationship of Devereux to his Wolf Indian subject. Sachs does not have to depend entirely on what John tells him, as did Devereux with Jimmy. His direct involvement in all phases of John's life enable him to make sense of John's verbal reports in the larger experiential context to which these reports referred. This approach is one of the most significant features of the book and one of its greatest hermeneutical advantages, in our opinion.

We are not saying this study is better or worse than Devereux's. That is not the point, for the two investigators attempt to accomplish very different objectives with their subjects. We have defined our task as one of simply looking at the ways in which they attempt to use the data to interpret, understand, or explain their subjects' lives. At a general but in some respects superficial level, each study is concerned with reconstructing character dynamics to understand the direction each subject's life has taken; and since both authors are psychoanalytically trained, their interpretations show a strong Freudian bias. Sachs, however, is less consistent in applying Freudian theory than Devereux, and his analysis suggests other perspectives. In fact, Sachs's approach is a curious amalgamation of orthodox Freudian psychoanalytic interpretation with phenomenological and existential approaches, a mixture that, as we shall see, gets Sachs into some interpretive difficulties.

Sachs attempts to explain John's inability to master his environment, his penchant for running away from trouble, and his tendency to blame others for his misfortune as being related to a powerful but unresolved Oedipal conflict. According to Sachs's reading of the data, this complex had been precipitated by the nurturant and excessively loving behavior of John's mother, Nesta, coupled with his father's untimely death and replacement by John's hated uncle Charlie, who married the mother according to Manyika custom. There may be something to Sachs's assertion that John sublimates his sexual interest in his mother by idealizing her qualities in his search for other women, and that he hates the "bad father" Charlie and probably tends to generalize some of these attitudes to other authority figures. Sachs, however, says that John's inability to work through his nuclear conflicts and to sublimate properly these repressed interests with ego-directed, reality-oriented strivings has made him immature and irresponsible, a mere child unable to assert himself in an adult world. His willpower is blunted because energy is diverted for his neurotic fantasies and other symptoms. Sachs repeatedly maintains that John's Oedipal fixation has kept him from reaching the genital stage of healthy personality development of the typical European, characterized by the capacity to test reality, to gratify needs within the framework of socially adaptive sublimations, and to form altruistic, socially relevant (as opposed to narcissistic) relationships. John, he says, goes through life depending on internalized parents to make decisions for him, parents he can blame for his failures.

And yet, in the context of his close, involved, and prolonged association with John, Sachs is impressed by his ability to rise to challenges, to make the hard but right decision; he is impressed by John's nobility and poise. Since John is no mere subject on the psychoanalyst's couch, but a real man seen *in situ*, in the fullness and complexity of his life, he takes on perforce the qualities of a whole, integrated person who has both strengths and weaknesses, but who in any case is always himself and no simple puppet.

Toward the end of his book Sachs mentions how John, at great effort and personal risk, attempted to resolve a dispute between the Shanghaan and the Basuto in one of the native locations in Johannesburg. Sachs interprets this effort as a significant index of psychological growth, a manifestation of John's emergent maturity and responsibility; but he treats it as though it were a new and startling development in his subject's character. In actuality, if we go back to the data and disregard the interpretation, John had always demonstrated, even in the "dark days" of his immaturity and selfishness, a capacity to take risks and sacrifice himself for the good of others, although this capacity was cast in the idiom of his tribal values. In the very beginning of his travels to Johannesburg, for example, John was persuaded to use his medicines to help a disease-striken community poisoned by a witch. John undertook this heavy responsibility although he knew his dead father did not yet feel he was old enough and wise enough to practice as an *nganga* (medicine man), and the witch posed dangers to his life. That the thing ended badly and that John had to run away for his own self-preservation do not detract from the positive and altruistic way he defined the situation and acted upon it.

Why should we make such a fuss over a point as "minor" as this? For one thing, the issue is not insignificant, for we are dealing with Sachs's interpretation of a man's life, and whether a man is or is not able to assume authentic responsibility for his actions is a crucial point in our assessment of him. If Sachs had been able to suspend his Freudian prejudices and had been more sensitive to the cultural context and to the seriousness with which his subject defined his role as an *nganga*, he would have seen that the basis had always existed for this man's appraisal of his own actions in the context of a deep belief in service to the community. In his role of *nganga* John directly assumed responsibility for the community's well-being. John took this role seriously and lived his life by it, albeit imperfectly at times.

Sachs sometimes adopts what appears to be an existential-phenomenological perspective in making sense of John's life, although he uses this perspective as little more than an occasional excuse for John's deficiencies and limitations when he tires of his Freudian burden. For example, he will say something like the following: "It looked that way to John, and since the ancestors and witches were an ever-present reality to John, he really had no alternative but to behave the way he did." But this faith is not intrinsically negative from the standpoint of this man's life, in our estimation. His belief in his power to control witches and to contact the ancestors was positive and soul satisfying in its ultimacy to explain and renew the world. Certainly this belief was as meaningful to him as was Sachs's conviction in the power of psychoanalysis. Indeed, Sachs explains that his respect for the subject's existential reality was the actual reason why he never encouraged John to give up his practice as a medicine man. After all, as Sachs so cogently argues, if John gave up his practice he would be giving up the fundamental meaning through which he reconstitutes his life, the source of his hope and self-esteem, and the basis for his strong sense of duty in helping others.

It is our impression that as John moved through life, as he suffered and overcame suffering, he drew upon his sense of himself as an *nganga* to establish an ever wider experiential and operational base from which to dispense service to others in the new conditions that defined his ongoing reality. At the end of the book John has left behind the *nganga* whose self-defined mission was exclusively to throw bones and give medicines to people; he has learned to use the influence and powers of his chosen role to advise, to counsel, to act as peacemaker and guide in the context of the larger processes and events that he has come to see are changing an oppressed people.

For us the book is invaluable because it allows the reader to see the dialectics of the investigator-subject relationship in the kind of detail that gives insight into the workings of a man's life. We will never know just how profound was Sachs's influence, as compared with other influences, in shaping the course of John's life in its adaptive vicissitudes. But there can be no doubt it made a significant qualitative difference in the texture of John's thought and experience, and in Sachs's too! We suspect that John learned from Sachs the lesson that doctors could change people's lives and their worlds through talking and helping them to analyze their situation. This knowledge may in fact have provided John with the impetus, as well as the model, for resynthesizing his old identity as an *nganga* and building it into something responsive to changing conditions of life and the black man's need for unity and purpose to go on.

Unlike *Reality and Dream, Black Hamlet* contains no unswervingly rigid commitment to one interpretive perspective. Through some strange chemistry of the author's involved relationship to John, any such rigid interpretive intent gives way to the need for a larger sense of understanding. This relationship, perhaps, more than anything else, explains the author's changed perception of John at the end and his willingness, to some extent at least, to suspend his psychoanalytic prejudices and to see things from John's point of view. It is not just that John had changed; Sachs's perspective as an interpreter of events changed too, as he himself admits. As his concern and friendship for John deepened, John became a real man—a friend—and not just a subject for psychoanalytic investigation. Sachs's awareness opened up a whole new interpretive horizon whose insights could not sit comfortably with any smug, doctrinaire Freudian perspective. However, even at the end the analyst is trying to salvage his theory despite his sense of the disquieting limits of his interpretive framework. Almost desperately he insists that John's character changes can be understood in Freudian terms as a progression from a pregenital to a mature, genital character structure.

But what is far more important than this bow to his Freudian past is that Sachs in the end is describing John from the vantage point of their own changed relationship as men, one in which John has forever and irreversibly become different for Sachs. This relationship is no longer a matter of manipulation and interpretation; it has become a vital matter of understanding. Sachs slowly realizes that John's life possesses its coherent integrity and dignity, which is revealed in the choices John freely and authentically makes. No amount of psychoanalytic pyrotechnics can explain this away.

In *Reality and Dream* the characteristics of Devereux's relationship with Jimmy P. never altered the framework through which the author undertook to interpret his patient, except to provide increasing information for the building of ever more plausible interpretations of his neurosis. We have, it is true, the subject's actual account to work with, but its usefulness has been vitiated by the degree to which Jimmy was dominated by the author's understandable commitment to directing the exchange along channels he felt would benefit the patient. However, we can at least see that this is so from the meticulous record kept of the dialogue. In *Black Hamlet* the opposite seems to have occured. The interpretive framework, while apparently rigid, does change as a result of the dialectics of the human relationship to the subject, which is beautifully described; but the data themselves are hopelessly confounded with the interpretations so that the reader has no way of separating *explanandum* from *explanans*. We have no way of going back and judging for ourselves independently, except insofar as the author occasionally seems to be describing things that are minimally distorted by his preunderstandings, at least compared with his more obvious attempts to provide psychoanalytic explanations for underlying dynamics, motivations, and so on.

In summary, both of these studies of life histories have reduced their subjects' lives in varying degrees to the analytic categories of Freudian theory. Both men, as it turns out, suffer from unresolved Oedipal problems; their problems and character deficiencies can be taken back to these earlier events. But making a case for one's theories by integrating the life history data into a plausible pattern is a different issue and a different epistemological problem from showing that these constructs correspond to the experiential reality of these two subjects.

Studying Theories of Social Character

As we indicated earlier in the chapter, the life histories of several individuals from a given culture have sometimes been used to test or demonstrate assumptions about basic personality or social character (social character has been arrived at by applying some general psychodynamic theory to various sorts of data, such as child training and cultural products, collected from that cultural setting). While the specific aim may be to establish or test the utility of the general theory by showing its predictive capacity in yet another culture, more often than not, in fact, the underlying theory is simply used as a tool to derive the presumed existence of some "real" social character or basic personality in that particular society as it is reflected in the life histories and other behavioral projections of individual people.

The Life History and Basic Personality

The People of Alor: A Social-Psychological Study of an East Indian Island by Cora DuBois, with analyses by Abram Kardiner, is a remarkable study in its complexity and exploratory use of a multidisciplinary approach involving the collection of different kinds of data, including life histories, and their interpretation by experts in various fields. The basic aim of the study was to test Kardiner's theory of basic personality as exhaustively and as systematically as possible with data from a single society. DuBois's fieldwork provided the necessary data for a systematic "test" of the theory. This data included various psychological tests, the results of which were subsequently turned over to experts for independent evaluation. Their evaluations provided a check on Kardiner's psychodynamic reconstruction of the basic personality of the Alorese from cultural data supplied by the ethnographer.

In this study eight "complete" life histories (of four men and four women) were taken, and Kardiner analyzes each in some depth to reconstruct the individual's character structure, using an essentially neo-Freudian approach. The purposes of this exercise are to determine the range of individual variation in the society and to assess the extent to which aspects of the basic personality derived from cultural data are still shared despite these variations. However, far from being a true test of the theory, the analysis of the life histories in Kardiner's own words is more of a check on the extent to which the basic institutions responsible for personality formation in Alorese culture intervene in the experiences of individual subjects.

The conditions under which these life histories were recorded are briefly but not sufficiently spelled out by DuBois. One of the most interesting things she tells us in her brief introduction to the autobiographies is that only deviant, less successful members of the community were willing to spare the time to help her. The more successful people of the community were too busy. We should keep in mind, however, that the unusual, the deviant in the community, may have been the more successful Alorese, not DuBois's informants, who in fact cover a wide range of character types but whose frustrations and anxieties are described as typical for the culture.

Those whose life histories she did record came to her at her house early in the morning before they began the day's activity, and these sessions generally lasted for about an hour. DuBois used a Malay-speaking translator throughout, although her fluency in the native language (Abui) reached a point where she was able to check the accuracy of the interpretation and to ask for clarification from the translator. The strict time format and the presence of the translator no doubt critically influenced what was said. DuBois's passing remarks in the autobiographical texts themselves reveal how she thought the translator's presence was affecting what the informant said and how he said it. Unfortunately, she does not discuss the possible influences of the temporal and physical settings, except for noting that some of the informants considered it an honor to come to the "fancy" house of the *nonya* (white lady) and evidently wished to impress her since she was a person of power and stature.

DuBois states that she has reproduced the autobiographies as they were originally related to her without any serious editing or rearranging so that the chains of association and characteristic thinking patterns of her subjects would be preserved for whatever light they might shed on cognitive processes, attitudes, and personality dynamics. By contrast, most life histories of "primitive" peoples are heavily edited, the events of the life rearranged into an orderly temporal sequence to meet Western readers' standards of proper chronology. This feature, to us, is one of the most valuable aspects of these Alorese life histories. They give us some idea of how the people actually and spontaneously talk about themselves and their experiences.

DuBois also inserts in the text in brackets the questions she asked and probings she initiated in order, for example, to clarify obscure references, to help the informant over mental blocks, and to redirect the subject's reminiscences away from descriptions of impersonal events to more personal experiences. Thus we can clearly see in what ways the content of the life history material was determined by the ethnographer's operations. We can determine for ourselves what material was volunteered freely and what was triggered by the ethnographer's interests (for example, sibling attitudes and memories of the parent, these being important categories in Kardiner's model) and biases.

Unfortunately, DuBois gives us none of her observations about her feelings for the informants, the ways she interacted with them, and how they may have taken their cues from her behavior in formulating their responses. Surely DuBois's reactions to her informants must have been differential, which would have reinforced differences in behavior. We believe that specifying some of these interpersonal currents would have made the life histories a good deal more intelligible as products of behavioral settings than they are. DuBois does at least interject occasional observations about the gestures of the informant, as well as his tone of voice, mood, state of mind that day, and any significant interaction with the translator. Still, DuBois exempts herself from scrutiny, as though she occupied some privileged position in these proceedings.

Kardiner himself is very interested in the relationship of the informant to the ethnographer and makes a great deal of it in his analysis (almost as though it were some kind of transference reaction). However, in the absence of explicit statements about the relationship, Kardiner has to rely on indirect measures such as dreams and fantasies that "reveal" the subject's underlying attitude to DuBois and the key to his personality dynamics. It is hard to believe that DuBois did not have more to say on this subject, particularly in view of its seeming importance to the research design. In any case, these insights are absent from the published record and the reader is the loser.

Kardiner's analyses of the life histories are of great interest because they represent, for all their incisiveness, an exaggerated example of overcommitment to a theoretical model to understand the subjective life of another. As we said, his self-defined task in evaluating these life histories is to see how Alorese basic personality structure, as reconstructed from abstract institutional patterns, coheres in individual character adaptation. The analysis, then, becomes a kind of test of his formulations, most specifically, his assumption that primary institutions are pervasive in a culture and are shared by its members. That certain institutions, however, have predictable effects on the outcome of character formation is taken for granted and is never independently tested. The psychodynamic model is treated as though its predictive powers were already a foregone conclusion and could be used to make sense out of any specific body of data.

What does this mean in terms of Kardiner's operations upon the Alorese autobiographies? As we see it, Kardiner has succeeded in translating each life history in the book into the components and categories (e.g., reactive systems, superego, defenses) of his psychodynamic model, and it is through this translation process that the life events take on their ultimate value. When these operations are finally completed, virtually nothing remains of the subjective quality that distinguishes the individual's account of his life.

The fundamental limitation of this theory (or model) is that its normative statements (e.g., given condition A, then A^1) are based completely on Western clinical observations and ultimately rest on our own culture-bound notions that there is a standard of healthy personality functioning, with various neurotic departures from this ideal stemming from disturbances in early socialization. In other words, certain kinds of maternal and paternal care, which are measured in this theory in highly abstract terms, indicate "good" care and are clinically assumed to elicit successful ego adaptations and superego control, which can be assessed from an individual's subsequent dispositions, attitudes, and behaviors in a whole host of critical areas.

For example, Kardiner would say that a strict, just, but contingently loving parent administering clear-cut rewards to his child in a clearly defined moral, social, and family order enables that child to internalize a sense of responsibility and right and wrong (paternal imago) and to develop ego skills to pursue his needs through proper, socially sublimated channels. The conceptualization and description of these processes, clearly, have a distinctively Western coloring. In effect, we have the model of the typical male middle-class Central European of Kardiner's and Freud's own background.

The Alorese, of course, do not fully measure up to these standards; this model condemns them to look very much like half-baked versions of Western neurotics in their character adaptations. Apparently, the Alorese suffer from the same kinds of childhood frustrations and disturbances in parental care (although these are standardized!) that are typical for Western neurotics. It is interesting that the Alorese informant judged to have the greatest ego strength is the most Westernized. This man (Fantan, the translator), because of his greater Western contract, simply adjusted more "properly" (in a Western sense) to the ethnographer and displayed a better-modulated instrumental aggression judged by Western standards. Kardiner says he finds evidence that Fantan received better parental care than did most of the others, but this assertion does not really hold up if Fantan's autobiography is carefully scrutinized. The parental care Fantan received, while in a number of respects unique, is not appreciably "different" or "better" in the sense the analyst imagines it. Fantan's behavior is just more understandable to Kardiner in Western terms.

While Kardiner creates a seemingly convincing pattern by manipulating the data to fit his theoretical structure, he frequently jumps without justification from his clinical terms and categories to popular jargon to characterize the Alorese in their life histories as "vicious," "greedy," "incapable," and the like. These vulgar Western terms describe stereotyped motives and emotions in a way that reflects adversely on the moral wholesomeness of the person or group they are applied to. How do these value judgments get us anywhere in our efforts to understand the lives of people as different from us in so many respects as these Alorese? We argue that they can accomplish no such purpose in any authentic way. These descriptive terms, as we shall see, are merely convenient labels that Kardiner uses to communicate Western notions of motivation and character structure to his Western audience at the simplest gut level, which incidentally also helps dramatize the picture of neurotic adaptation he has already explained in clinical language.

To understand Kardiner's miscalculated operations we must look more closely at the individual life histories themselves. They may have a different story to tell. First, we shall consider some general characteristics of the Alorese life histories, that Kardiner overlooks but that are important to our understanding of them. Second, we shall examine the relevance of Kardiner's analysis in describing and elucidating the texture, details, and inner coherence of specific lives.

It seems clear to us in surveying the spectrum of experience recounted in these eight Alorese life histories that the Alorese do not have our particular kind of strong, introspective, soul-searching bent or interest in reading between the lines. Perhaps we should say they do not have a strong interest, which we would recognize, in sharing their deep, private feelings with others. We are not, however, making any kind of value judgment about this. It is our impression that the Alorese live spontaneously in the givenness of their cultural life world, one very important aspect of which seems to be that actual behavior and experience seen in typified terms, not the hidden or repressed motivation behind the behavior itself, provide the authentic meanings of social life.

In the autobiographies, for example, it is difficult to find any expressed evidence of a strong resentment or hatred of parental treatment, which Kardiner assumes to be present but repressed and which in his mind has awesome significance for the course of healthy ego development. Contrary to Kardiner's assertion, the Alorese accept the treatment they received as natural in light of previous sedimented experience, and there is little soul searching or second guessing to figure out whether this treatment was right or wrong, or whether the parent was justified or acted out of some malicious or cruel motive. The effects on basic personality that Kardiner derives from poor maternal care, it seems to us, are plausible only when this treatment has demonstrably negative meaning for the person who has been exposed to it. The organized meanings of experience available to a person determine by and large his strategies and adaptations to life. If life, for example, becomes "threatening" or "meaningless" in a way he can understand, it then becomes his existential reality and can effectively curtail his options and undermine his resources (such as his self-confidence).

In their autobiographies these Alorese subjects say they were sometimes beaten, sometimes rewarded, sometimes taken care of by the parent. But these experiences are not as incomprehensible to them in their self-reports as they appear to Kardiner. How do they react to punishment or frustration? They express anger or resentment occasionally; they shrug it off; or they run away, a culturally constituted safety valve. We do not deny that Alorese children get angry at their parents. What we cannot see is how a certain amount of understandable frustration and anger accumulates to the point of becoming the permanent basis of resentment and hatred for the parent and, by extension (as Kardiner alleges), for society, too. The Alorese simply learn to cope with the existential realities of their situation in certain institutionalized ways, which they come to accept as natural. These patterns form the basis of subjective understandings and ego adaptations that are perfectly appropriate in that cultural setting.

There is, therefore, a vast difference between the arrangements of social life as they are "objectively" described in Alor by the external observer and the subjective meanings they have for the individual Alorese. That the Alorese do not describe their reactions to seemingly "frustrating" events in the manner that a Westerner would does not mean they are incapable of organizing a "proper" reaction or that the original meaning is "repressed"; it simply means that the event has another meaning whose implications are not necessarily evident unless the subject verbalizes them or they become apparent in the organization of his subsequent behavior. The familiar Western meaning implied by a state of "maternal frustration" or the ramified significance of a "low affective salience of death" does not define any integrative subjective reality for the Alorese; rather, these events take their descriptive and analytical significance through Kardiner's manipulation of them to fit the predetermined semantic formulas of an already coherent pattern that is constituted in the investigator's own theoretical preunderstandings.

Kardiner not only assumes that he has found the clue to the meaning of events in these subjects' autobiographies; he claims that he has found the defensive compensations at the heart of Alorese psychological adaptation that these negative experiences generate. These culturally organized defenses protect the individual from his hatred, from his low self-esteem, and allow him substitute means of overcoming these unacceptable feelings and images by giving him the illusory sensation of validating his self-worth. Being the obedient child of supernaturals, engaging in financial dealings, excelling in cross-sex tasks, boasting, and overasserting independence are some of the culturally established techniques, according to Kardiner, that are available to an Alorese to escape coming to grips with his impoverished emotional and sexual life or with his inability, because of weak ego resources, to gain status through more meaningful, culturally sanctioned alternatives.

Why, however, must these cultural alternatives for behavior be seen as defensive compensation for something theoretically purer and better, as though if the Alorese were better people with stronger character structures, they would be oriented or focused on different cultural goals? The culturally constituted defenses in which, says Kardiner, the fragile ego of the Alorese takes refuge are actually the very taken-for-granted fabric of social life in Alor and the experiential reality in which the people live and behave spontaneously. Every Alorese who reveals himself in his autobiography has found a culturally defined niche for himself and a series of roles that he has fashioned out of his thought, energy, determination, and interests. It is through these typified interests, attitudes, and understandings that he has become understandable to himself and, perhaps, meaningfully fulfilled (we could say through these typifications, as they are subjectively apprehended, the individual recovers himself self-reflexively). Does it then necessarily follow that this orientation must be some substitute or sublimation for failures encountered in some higher, more valuable sphere? That is, does such activity represent a turning away from a greater value and the settling for a lesser one?

It is culture that sets priorities of interests and values. Thus, by their own societal standards, some Alorese are obviously more successful than others. Nevertheless, most if not all Alorese make their choices from an acceptable range of cultural alternatives, some of which are simply more desirable than others in the context of Alorese values. For Kardiner even financial success, which is highly valued in Alor, is by implication nothing more than a defensive compensation for men, who want but lack a nurturant mother, while anything less than financial success becomes a defensive compensation for failure in *this* critical area. The Alorese end up the losers on all counts. A simpler explanation is that variations in temperament and interest in Alor determine occupational and life choices in a positive, creative, and reinforcing sense. We need not evoke such exotic explanatory factors as weak ego and defensive compensation.

"Incapacity," "disorganization," "failure," words that are used extensively to describe the Alorese lack of ego mastery, have only theoretical meaning in Kardiner's paradigm. Taken out of that context, they mean very little. In the autobiographies themselves the individual is conscious of doing things only for the reasons he states, which reflect in more or less distorted form reasons somebody else once gave him. Forever to seek the true "meaning" behind the individual's behavior through repressed traumatic events deriving from infancy is puerile if only we stop to consider how powerfully the individual at any point in life marshals forth personally sedimented meanings, which are in part cultural and in part idiosyncratically worked over in consciousness, to define his ongoing reality and the choices he must make. We think that Allport is right. In the course of its development, as it takes on conscious existential significance, behavior becomes functionally autonomous, that is, dynamically detached from its past and its original motivating circumstances. People live in the unfolding reality of their behavioral situation, and from this matrix they make choices that to a large extent maximize conscious values, interests, and orientations.

We might well ask for example, whether Fantan's decision to become DuBois's translator was really motivated by unconscious feelings of inadequacy that could be undone by the ethnographer's attention or by his repressed desire for a generous mother substitute owing to the frustrating maternal care he received as a child. This kind of in-terpretation would be consistent with Kardiner's general view of Alor-ese psychodynamics. If, however, we look at the present life situation Fantan describes in his life history, several more likely causes closer to Fantan's existential reality become apparent.

First and foremost, Fantan was interested in the money and financial stability it would bring: he was economically vulnerable, had recently been involved in bitter financial litigation, and was expecting the birth of a child, an additional expense. Second, the relationship would give him obvious prestige in his own eyes. Fantan clearly recognized the Western ethnographer's economic and political power, a factor related to Fantan's education and acculturational experience and his accep-tance of certain Western values (Fantan even saw the ethnographer's house as a heaven-sent sanctuary in which he could hide wealth and power objects to protect them from jealous relatives and creditors). If we had more information about DuBois's relationship with Fantan, we would be better equipped to understand the specific reasons for the value he placed on his association with her, as well as the reasons for the way he represents himself to her as he does.

We can now proceed one step further. Instead of reviewing Kardi-ner's interpretation in light of common characteristics abstracted from individual lives, we can consider the adequacy of the theory from the standpoint of the phenomenal texture of the individual life itself. While this subjective texture is the very stuff of the life history, we shall see that it takes us to a domain far removed from the universe of constructs Kardiner imposes on the autobiographies to explain charac-ter formation. As an example, we shall take Mangma, who is of cru-cial interest because in Kardiner's view he is the closest in his neurotic adaptation to the Alorese basic personality structure, and yet he mani-fests this adaptation in "extreme" form.

There are great difficulties in understanding this man and what he says about himself without knowing something of the larger context of his relationship with the ethnographer. This issue, unfortunately, goes unexamined or at least unreported save for a few offhand comments inserted into the text by the ethnographer. Kardiner may be correct in his assertion that Mangma wants attention and mothering from DuBois but feels he will not get any and thus entertains fantasies of robbing her, but substantiation for this claim is based only on Kardiner's inter-pretation of one dream. An assertion of this order could only be established with some certitude if we knew things about the subject and his relationship to the ethnographer that neither he nor DuBois reports.

In making this very critical interpretation of Mangma's character, Kardiner is simply working from his theory back to the data, in the process finding that the data can be made to form a plausible pattern in that framework. The analyst is making a deductive statement and offering it as proof of fact. Having reconstructed to his satisfaction the abstract basic personality structure of the Alorese from socialization data, and having discovered the general conditions that suggest Mangma approximates this hypothetical type, Kardiner proceeds to find specific evidence of the existence of the detailed psychodynamics that constitute the structure. In this case the evidence is Mangma's repressed need for mothering and his indirect and inadmissible fantasy of having to steal from the ethnographer when he perceives that his needs are being frustrated. The dream in which Mangma steals squash from the enclosed garden of his grandmother (DuBois was the only one in the village who had squash in her garden) is maneuvered to the forefront, since it can be worked into the interpretation, as proof positive that Mangma's repressed predatory adaptation and abandonment of direct striving in the face of maternal frustration constitute a fundamental reactive system in his character.

By the same token, Kardiner does not cite a shred of evidence for this presumed character dynamic except that Mangma's parents sometimes hit him and did not feed him, and that he took to gardening in a "protest of self-sufficiency." But these are really alleged causes of the psychological complex in Kardiner's model, not the character dynamics themselves. There are in fact no examples in the analysis of recurrent statements by Mangma himself about maternal frustrations and their supposed negative effects on his thinking or feeling that bear any resemblance to Mangma's description of his own experiential reality. Even if, as Kardiner would claim, repression rules out any such direct subjective awareness of conflict, there should at least be some compelling indirect indications (e.g., some feeling of anger at the way *other* children were treated by *their* parents). Kardiner's theory imposes a particular ordering of the data, but it is not the natural ordering of the data that validates his model.

What is this man really like, at least insofar as he reveals himself to us in the brief autobiographical account? Although we have only a very minute specimen of the subject's existential reality, elicited under rather artificial conditions, the life history of Mangma evokes a rich, all-encompassing cultural context, one in which many of the complex meanings that organize his actions and the events of his life are revealed to us. Without a doubt, Mangma has at least in part deliberately edited the events of his life for DuBois's benefit. We would like to know exactly why and how he has done this. However, the subject could misrepresent himself only so much, even if he chose to do so. There still remains, in spite of possible falsifications in the data, a basic inventory of personal experience that Mangma unselfconsciously relates in a natural, taken-for-granted way. Thus, whatever events he conceals, suppresses, or distorts for a particular audience, they still continue to take their distinctive meanings from a larger but stable subjective pattern whose characteristics can be identified.

Mangma begins his story by recalling a disaster (an earthquake) and hardships (hunger especially) that are highly charged events in this culture, regardless of how he represents them as pertaining to his own experience. From here Mangma goes on to relate an incident in which he shot somebody's dog and was punished for it, receiving both a beating and an admonition. After dwelling on the difficulties of life, Mangma introduces what will become a recurrent theme in his life history: his interest in gardening (ordinarily a female task in this culture), which seems to go back to childhood. He tells us he tended a field when he was very young, thus presumably asserting his mastery, but he was told by his mother that the field and its products belonged to her. He was rightfully angry and, in protest, he ran away. However, despite such frustrations he continued gardening. Kardiner interprets this pattern as a compensation for parental deprivation, a defense against the anxiety of feeling helpless ("I can do it myself: I don't need you"). But this interpretation may be quite spurious if we remember that the direct and practical rewards for mastery in gardening are obvious enough in this culture for women and men alike, to judge from the kinds of typified meanings Mangma assigns to nutrition, security, and status. The mere fact that adult powers and values were associated with gardening in Mangma's experience provides sufficient reason for the adoption and subsequent elaboration of this particular focus.

For a man with such an allegedly precarious ego structure and low self-esteem (vide Kardiner), Mangma surprisingly stressed goal-oriented coping behavior of an adult sort, even though such striving did not always result in his objectives. The weak ego he is supposed to have is not nearly so evident in Mangma's own account of his behavior as it is in Kardiner's constructs for explaining him.

As a child, Mangma lived in the fields off and on and was pretty much on his own for considerable periods of time. In our scheme of values this situation would indicate rejection of the parent and neurotic adaptation, but in Alorese culture it is merely a culturally recognized pattern available to children for developing social and economic skills on their own; it is quite consistent, moreover, with the general cultural picture of residential mobility and shifting social alliances on Alor. In any case, Mangma managed to work with others in gardening and hunting, which shows a capacity for cooperation rather than anomie or a disorganized ego. In his gardening he grew rice and other crops to sell for the purpose of buying *mokos* (metal kettledrums) and other wealth objects used for making marriage payments. Some of the harvest he gave voluntarily to his parents (which shows altruism); the rest of the share he sold for a *moko* (which shows enterprise). Subsequently, when some people learned he had a *moko*, they tried to pressure him to marry a girl so that he would be obliged to give them the hard-earned *moko* as a bride payment. They even accused him of sleeping with her. But Mangma fended off this false accusation, aggressively asserted that he was innocent, and agreed to undergo a trial by ordeal (sticking his hand in boiling millet) to prove it. He later exposed himself to the ordeal successfully, thereby forestalling an unwanted marriage and avoiding greedy claims on his property. Mangma's account continues in much the same vein, emphasizing his ability to overcome conflict and his gardening skills. If the narrative is true or even largely accurate, it is inconsistent with Kardiner's claim that this man had an underdeveloped ego.

In his analysis Kardiner assumes that Mangma is just lying about events or at least seriously misrepresenting himself because he wants to appear competent and successful in the eyes of his audience (DuBois and Fantan). In his heart of hearts Mangma is supposed to be extremely insecure and sensitive, craving uncritical love but convinced that his desires will not be fulfilled and that he has to make exaggerated claims to be worthy of this love. The presence of Fantan, the critical translator, stultifies Mangma's whole account of his life, according to Kardiner. But all of this makes sense only if the framework of Kardiner's analysis is accepted.

Even if Mangma had wanted to present himself in a favorable light, and even if he had wanted something from the ethnographer, the presence of insecurity or a feeble ego does not necessarily follow, as Kardiner alleges. A strategy of ingratiation and impression management would be perfectly reasonable as an existential choice alone, given the prestige and powers of whites for the Alorese. Indeed, quite to the contrary, the desire to present a favorable picture of himself can be interpreted as indicative of good self-esteem. If any Alorese whose life history was taken approximates ego disorganization and lack of self-worth, it is Lonmani, not Mangma. Lonmani presents a rather barren, unsuccessful life devoid of any hope of convincing others that she is worth anything; her own true experiential ordering corresponds to the weak ego hypothesis of Kardiner and probably even approximates Alorese conceptions of inadequate character.

Kardiner says that because Mangma is eager to impress DuBois and Fantan, he tells the least objectionable part of his life story. He is, in short, bluffing to "hide his inadequacies," which we learn "in his inarticulate way he is quite well aware of." In phrases such as these the design of a man's life as he sees it is reduced to a monolithic defensive maneuver. Kardiner seems unaware that what Mangma is relating constitutes in large measure the naively accepted reality in which he lives, not just an artful misrepresentation he is trying to foist on DuBois for reasons known only to Kardiner. Granted, this is a reality a Westerner like Kardiner with his biases could probably not readily understand or accept. Nevertheless, it *is* Mangma's subjective reality, Mangma's life, and he is doing the talking. As he talks he articulates the concerns that spontaneously resound in his Alorese experience. It is these concerns that form a pattern that defines his interests and orientations. Nothing about this pattern is so unusual as to be bizarre in Alorese terms or so incapacitating as to render him incapable of functioning in his society.

Mangma, in fact, seems to be typical in his attitudes and adaptations to institutionalized experience, as Kardiner also takes pains to point out in other contexts. He seems to be neither a remarkably successful nor a particularly maladaptive or deviant person. We prefer to see Mangma as simply one individual operating in a special culturally constituted but exotic experiential context. Although we have gained a partial knowledge of the cultural context of Alor, the meanings of his acts are sometimes hard to comprehend, as are the relationships between the events he describes. But this difficulty is due to the inadequacies of our interpretive framework to fathom everything in this alien setting, and in this particular man's existence, not to deficiencies in Mangma's character as such.

Mangma's typicality, we learn from Kardiner, is that he shares with other Alorese certain neurotic adaptations that arise out of encounters with institutionalized parental frustrations, abuses, and misrepresentations that rule out successful coping and organized, effective defensive maneuvers. Kardiner tells us that Mangma, like other Alorese, hated his mother and refused to obey; in this particular case, Mangma removed a deficit in parental care by learning to garden. This is a meager but culturally available defensive mode of compensation in Kardiner's opinion, as we have seen. Mangma's low self-esteem, shallow affectivity, and a lack of resourcefulness all derive from this original constellation of experience. Because of the all but incapacitating effects of such experience on ego development, only the most massively neurotic defensive adaptations become possible; these adaptations are channeled into culturally recognized forms such as pride, lying, avarice, boasting about trivialities, and envy, among others.

This very negative and demeaning picture of the man is quite unwarranted from Mangma's innocent description of himself. Such terms as "lying," "avarice," and "boasting of trivialities" imply not only a state of ego development but a moral unwholesomeness as well, at least to the kind of audience Kardiner is addressing. In perusing Mangma's narrative, we look in vain for any behavioral indicators of these presumed neurotic and unwholesome adaptations. If we juxtapose the terms "pride," "lying," and "boasting about trivialities" with the phenomenal subjective data of this man's life, and then divest them of the awesome significance they have in Kardiner's model, they dissolve into so many meaningless platitudes. They describe nothing of any analytic or real significance.

"Pride": whose pride is this? Is it a prideful response in Alorese terms to a truly wasted life, or merely a label that describes Kardiner's ethnocentric suspicion that the subject's accomplishments are not up to the claims he makes and the concern he shows for himself before the ethnographer? "Lying": Can it be established that the events Mangma describes are gross fabrications designed to conceal the ignominious and humiliating truth? There is no cross-checking with other experience to go by. Besides, there is a difference between telling a lie (or lies) and lying as a general adaptive strategy; Kardiner implies that Mangma lies as a strategy. But a person may tell a lie without using lying as an adaptation to life. Moreover, we must not forget that lying has a particular significance in Western thought and usually involves the notion of some deliberate alteration of an intersubjectively verifiable experience, which is the standard of what is real, what is truth. We suspect that in Alorese society the subjective alteration or distortion of experience may have an entirely different basis. For example, extraordinary states of mind might be more likely to be regarded as "real" in Alor because they are believed to happen rather than because they have been objectively verified to happen.

And what of "boasting about trivialities"? Is Mangma really boasting? He talks a good deal about his gardening, which Kardiner takes as an indication of defensive boastfulness that helps Mangma prop up his weak self-esteem. But gardening in Alorese culture is more of a female task and is not nearly so prestigious as financial activity. In view of the prevailing value system, would Mangma be boasting about this skill in the sense that we ordinarily understand boasting? We suggest that gardening is for Mangma a preoccupation in the sense that a businessman or an anthropologist in our culture might find it hard not to talk about business or anthropology.

The use of the word "triviality" suggests a strictly ethnocentric way of evaluating Alorese experience. Gardening and financial litigation may be trivial preoccupations of a people who are ill equipped to do anything better for Kardiner, but not for the Alorese themselves. These matters are the stuff and substance of their very existence.

At the level of Alorese sociocultural evolution, large-scale productive efforts, formal political organization, and advanced technological specialization would be ruled out, but there is no justification for equating techo-cultural level with level of ego organization and adequacy of sublimations, as though there were a simple isomorphism between the two of the kind suggested by Freud in *Civilization and Its Discontents* (1962). The Alorese have found all kinds of creative and destructive outlets for ordering their experience, which involve planning, organization, and coordination—in fact, all the attributes of a secure ego the Alorese allegedly lack. They have simply focused on pursuits different from those of the West and other societies at their technological level.

Kardiner's theory does not really get us very far if we are interested in understanding the unique individual, in context, who relates his life in its rich subjective complexity, rather than in proving to ourselves that a life history can be interpreted by translating it into the categories of a model embedded in the thought and assumptions of our own Western experience.

Conclusions

If the human mind in another culture does not respond to experience in a predictable, closed fashion that could be accounted for by our Western theories, then it is we who are lacking the tools to interpret behavior and generalize about it in its contextually defined richness and complexity. Our science, it seems, comes to grips with alien experience only by robbing it of its unique richness and translating it into abstract meanings. To understand the individual in his human fullness we must therefore suspend total commitment to our scientific preconceptions and enter a dialogue with the life history. By asking questions not bound to a closed, predetermined system of explanations, like personality theory, we establish a dialectic exchange and open up the possibilities of questions and answers that reveal human experience in a significantly changed context more closely approximating the original one in which the life history as a subjective activity unfolds before us.

Kardiner's theoretical pronouncements about personality—to cite one example among several (e.g., Devereux and Sachs) we have examined—are devoid of any insight either into the nature of Alorese culture or into the matter of how Alorese subjective experience interacts with it, which raises the basic issue of how personality theory violates the integrity of subjective narratives. His interpretation has analytical as opposed to merely theoretical interest only to those already convinced that basic personality structure describes and predicts a sociopsychological reality and needs not be rigorously evaluated. (We agree that the model has theoretical or at least speculative interest, but it requires testing or evaluation different from what Kardiner advocates.)

Our aim in criticizing Kardiner is not to portray the Alorese as models of mental health or human adjustment, or to ridicule any possibility of establishing universal standards of mental health. We have no fixed notions at all of what the Alorese should or should not be. We merely wish to free the Alorese from what we believe is an arbitrary, ethnocentric, artificial, and perhaps unproductive way of understanding them.

Had Kardiner focused more on the unique and special texture of individual lives, and had he paid closer attention to the stream of events as the subject related them, some picture of character structure with demonstrable correspondence to the subject's true experiential condition might have emerged. The subconscious may well exist and may importantly motivate behavior, but when its presumed ramifying effects are manipulated with the liberties Kardiner takes, and with so little available data, we have a right to be suspicious of his conclusions. Yet the little we have does at least represent a specimen of the subject's personal world. If we go back to the subjectively organized events of the autobiography and see them in the cultural and interpersonal context that generated the meanings through which they were intended, we are then working more effectively at understanding the text of the life history as an individual and unique product.

Chapter 5
The Study of the Individual-Culture Relationship

One of the most popular uses of the life history in anthropology and social scientific research is the investigation of the nature, dynamic characteristics, and parameters of the individual-culture or individual-social system relationship. Research has generally focused on the following areas: (1) how the sociocultural system affects the individual's role behavior, self-concept, and values; (2) how the individual, as he reveals himself in the life history, affects his community and society, sometimes acting as a source of significant culture change; and (3) the cybernetic interplay between the psychological order embodied by the individual and the sociocultural order represented in the patterned organization of family, community, and society.

Several fundamental and largely unquestioned assumptions about the nature of people and society undergird whatever specific form this sort of research takes. In these life history analyses the data are preordered according to a dialectically defined functional model that assumes that there is an inherent or at least potential conflict between the interests of the individual and the interests of the social order, and that culture operating through socialization purposively orients individual lives in certain ways so that individuals learn to want to do (motivation) what they have to do (role, demand, duty). The analyses recognize that individuals respond variously to socialization, depending on their social, cultural, and psychological situation, and that problems of deficient communication account for deviancy and imperfect fit. The life history in its detailed self-reporting of individual experience can throw light, it is thought, on the specific mechanics of this process and thus makes it possible to derive and test hypotheses of a more general order.

Such studies invariably make heavy use of role theory as it has developed in the social sciences. By using the role concept so essential to social system theory, social researchers almost inevitably commit themselves to an attitude of sociogenic determinism in regard to individual behavior. They contend that the individual learns through positive and negative feedback from experience that his best interests are served through conformity to social arrangements, specifically, to the requirements of the social roles he must perform. The creative input the individual provides in altering his life design, his standing up to the system in however modest a fashion, is played down by comparison.

It is possible to state some of the implications of these assumptions in the formulation of the social and individual spheres of this model:

1. Social. (a) Society operates as a social system in equilibrium consisting of statuses whose specifications must be met by individuals if the system is to continue in its normal functioning. (b) Society is best understood in its normative dimensions. (c) Socialization is designed to provide individuals with the motivations, attitudes, and knowledge to operate in the various roles that constitute their social system.

2. Individual. (a) Individuals are plastic and hence readily susceptible to the socializing influences of the society into which they are born. (b) Individuals are conformists in the conclusions they draw from their socialization experience and in the adaptive choices they make in social life. (c) Individuals lack creativity and are rarely able to work over their socialized experience in any meaningfully novel way or to draw conclusions not provided by socialization. (d) Individuals are instinctively selfish and are in basic conflict with society unless they are effectively socialized.

Applying these assumptions generates a fully articulated functional model, which in whole or in part forms the basis of specific research strategies (see figure 1). Functionally oriented research in the life history usually takes several variables from this model and explores their relationship. Six basic kinds of relationships may be identified in a functional model linking the individual to society: (1) The *socializer-socialization relationship* focuses on who provides socialization and the relationship between the role and/or personality of the socializer and his socialization strategy. (2) The *socializer-environment (system) relationship* emphasizes how the socializer uses the system as a basis of feedback in making socialization choices. (3) The *socialization-system relationship* is concerned with the relationship between socialization in its normative and behavioral aspects and the requirements of the sociocultural system or some part of it. (4) The *socialization-personality relationship* deals with the relationship between intended and

Figure 1:
A Model of System-Socialization Interaction

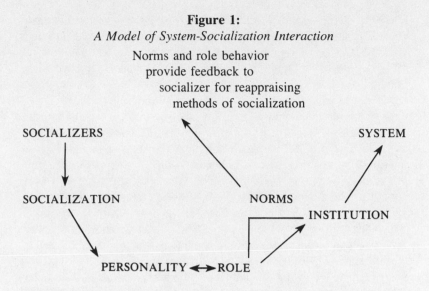

Norms and role behavior
provide feedback to
socializer for reappraising
methods of socialization

SOCIALIZERS   SYSTEM

SOCIALIZATION   NORMS
                                                    INSTITUTION

PERSONALITY ◄►ROLE

unintended aspects of socialization and personality consequences. (5)
The *personality-role relationship* focuses on the relationship between
personality characteristics and the requirements of role performance,
on the effects of personality on role, and on the question of whether
social roles satisfy individual personality needs. (6) The *personality-
system relationship* has to do with the relationship of character traits to
functional requirements of larger institutional settings.

Basic Approaches

In practice, actual life history research usually explores some aspect of
either social role or socialization or the interface between the two, using the individual as some kind of case test. Role-oriented studies
(studies of personality-role and role-system relations) may use life histories to understand how social action is embodied in the individual
through the social role that links him to the system and how psychological processes influence formally defined social behavior. Where
the focus is on sociocultural change, the study of the individual may
be directed to determining problems of psychological adaptation and
modes of adaptation to changing role demands. Where the focus is on

relatively stable systems, and roles are constant, the researcher may emphasize how nonadaptive individual variations are brought into line with the normative requirement of roles. Works by Hughes (1965, 1974), Aberle (1967), and Spradley (1969) are all essentially role-oriented studies.

Since it usually gives a great deal of insight into the texture and detail of the individual-culture interplay, the life history is an extraordinarily sensitive source of information for testing hypotheses about the dynamics and processes of social organization, most particularly at a microlevel of analysis. If the life history is that of a person in a highly placed position, his accounting of his development over time tells us a good deal about decision making, about how it operates in crucial sociocultural contexts and how it affects real people.

Socialization-oriented studies (studies of socialization-personality and socialization-role and/or system relations) include those that use the life history to understand how socialization affects personality development and how the socialization process articulates with social role and the social system through the individual. How, such studies ask, are socialization messages interpreted and subsequently internalized or rejected, and how does this process affect the mode of the socialized individual's participation in various social roles? Studies in this area include Watson (1970) and Hughes (1974).

In addition to these two dominant research orientations, there are several residual categories. Life histories and other personal documents may be used to study personal deviancy in social context from various perspectives other than a strictly sociogenic one. Deviance certainly has important implications for the ongoing functioning of the system. We might wish to investigate the subjective experience of deviancy or the psychological concomitants of deviancy revealed in the autobiographical account. In the process we might become interested in how the individual becomes deviant, without necessarily following a unicausal sociogenic model, paying proper attention to the individual's own interpretation of what might have led to self- and social definitions of deviancy. We might also be interested in the consequences of a person's deviancy on his social style and personal interaction, comparing this with other examples of deviancy in other life history accounts. In any event, this kind of approach, even when it eschews any deliberate functional commitment, obviously falls under the purview of studies of the social-individual nexus, because such studies usually implicitly follow an interactional perspective involving social and psychological variables. Oscar Lewis, for one, has shown an interest in deviant individuals in the context of the culture of poverty.

Finally, there is the potential use of the life history to understand the personality of the deviant, but in terms of the creative or innovative force of people of unusual character in transforming their societies, whether this be negative or positive by our standards (cf. Wallace 1969, Langer 1972).

However, we should not mistakenly assume that a sociological model of the life history overdetermines the results of research or skews our eventual understanding any less than does a psychological one. The sociogenic approach is in fact burdened by many preunderstandings. Most critically, it assumes that a specific social reality, existing in a particular way for the individual and definable in terms of the author's categories, can predictably affect the individual's behavior and vice versa. One problem is that this social reality is defined apart from individual thought or intention but is nevertheless made to be an integral part of the individual's intrapsychic processes and makeup. In other words, things of different orders and meanings (individual-psychological versus culturally shared, superpersonal) can be artfully constructed or manipulated to form a completely plausible pattern. But do these plausible patterns really have any meaning within the actual subjective framework of a given life history? In such a situation we see what the investigator has put together for us, a model, constructed in varying degrees of elegance and explicitness, for understanding that person. Yet what we in fact understand is the way the investigator makes sense of the person in social context by assimilating aspects of his behavior and their interrelation into typified, common-object and common-sense properties. This process of course involves an a priori judgment in which the investigator assigns reported subjective experiences to certain categories after he has measured or determined their significance against standards for inclusion in these categories. Indeed, this classification is what enables him to form a plausible pattern, for the model already possesses a more or less closely reasoned logic or common-sense coherence, even if it has not been thoroughly "tested" or "verified."

As an example, we could examine the strategy of testing the relationship of socialization to kinds of role performance, using the life history as a source of detailed data to elucidate this process. Several basic, unstated assumptions, however, underlie such a research orientation. (1) It is assumed that the role is a discrete, bounded, social action entity that corresponds to a similarly bounded cognitive-motivational structure in the performer's mind that in some way activates the behavior in question. (2) It is assumed that the socialization process creates the cognitive-motivational structure that is tied to or demanded by the role. (3) The hypothesis or model is confirmed if measurable aspects of socialized behavior can be bounded, identified, and given a value that corresponds to the value representing the intrapsychic structure.

But there is no reason, really, to assume that this set of assumptions does any more than reflect the anthropologist's description of the world as one ordered into discrete parts that have predictable and causally understandable relations with one another. The unity of experience as the individual knows it is not necessarily sorted into these categories or rules by these relations unless he ceases living spontaneously in his everyday thought and begins to use scientific constructs to explain the world (we suspect that even social scientists fall short of this analytical approach, for that matter). In other words, this kind of role theorizing is several orders removed from direct experiential involvement in the world with its everyday, taken-for-granted, trivial concerns. Surely the individual rarely sees any need to resolve logical contradictions or eliminate inconsistencies of the kind scientific theory seeks to expunge or assimilate into a larger synthesis. Moreover, he is not usually aware in assigning reasons to his own decisions that he "obeys" scientific principles in ordering his life.

In the following pages we examine several studies that either use the life history to examine and test notions, theories, and assumptions about role, socialization, and society, or else use these constructs as a way of better understanding the life history itself. Again, following Ricoeur's lead, we confront these interpretations, which are based on sociological models and functional theory, with our own phenomenological hermeneutics, just as we did with the psychoanalytic approach to personality in the previous chapter. We intend to bring into the open the subjectivity and uniqueness of the life history text, which is concealed or distorted in the sociological approach, to underline the absence of dialogical engagement in this interpretive enterprise, and to raise questions about how the text has been constructed as part of the negotiated encounter, a matter that is usually treated as irrelevant to the sociological understanding of the life history.

Socialization and Role

Role, Identity, and Socialization

In *Eskimo Boyhood: An Autobiography in Psychosocial Perspective*, Charles C. Hughes seeks to mediate the concepts of role and socialization, on the one hand, with such concepts as identity formation and adaptation, on the other, thus specifying the nature of the interaction of society and the individual. The significant emphasis on intrapsychic processes and on learning (socialization) differentiates this study from others we shall consider later in the chapter.

While the dominant conceptual determinants of Hughes's analysis of his Eskimo subject's life is the role of classic sociological formulation, the author has attempted to reconcile role theory with socialization and identity perspectives. Drawing on Spiro (1961) and Talcott Parsons (1964), Hughes sees the role as the link between the personality and the social system, or as the meeting ground of choices and action in which individual need is reconciled with social demand. Hughes's view is that socialization provides the individual with the organized motivation for performing socially defined, appropriate roles, so that the performance of these roles conversely becomes the source for basic kinds of need satisfaction. At the same time, the successful performance of roles maintains the social system within certain limits in a state of equilibrium with its environment.

Hughes asserts that this model, when applied to the life history, allows us to understand how Nathan Kakaniak, an Eskimo boy, becomes a fully individualized person who has developed certain needs and attitudes in relation to his experience, and who is at the same time fully Eskimo and able to operate within Eskimo society and meet his needs in terms of culturally defined social transactions. Hughes is saying that the role approach allows us to understand the development of a particular life in its sociocultural context without violating the integrity of the individual either as a psychologically unique private person, or as a component of society.

Hughes is not content to operate exclusively in this constricting role framework. He attempts to expand his model to take into account the actor's subjective frame of reference to some extent. He does this by assimilating the subject's behavior as an actor in social roles into his self-identity, which can be defined as an "image or set of images, conscious or unconscious, which the individual has of himself" (Wallace 1968:46). In his analysis of the life history Hughes shows clearly and convincingly that Nathan is aware of his need to maintain a viable, acceptable image of himself and of the difficulties of doing so as he grapples with the demands, frustrations, and contradictions of certain transactions with his environment (e.g., going to school, learning to hunt), which for analytical purposes can be organized into different role categories. In other words, role becomes part of Nathan's subjective reality, with all the stresses and strains this involves.

This interpretive strategy allows the author to remain true (at least in theory) to the subjective veracity of the life history, thus minimizing some of the distortion that enters the analysis when one attempts exclusively to infer "meaning" through categories and models external to the subject's reality. Hughes's approach is much closer to the immediate data than are the analyses of life histories we have seen so far, and he is less severely bound by theoretical judgments and preconceptions in the hermeneutical sense.

Once this course of interpretation is attempted, there is no guarantee that the differences between scientific categories and the subject's frame of reference will be adequately bridged or that a dialectically produced resolution or synthesis will be achieved. Does Hughes emerge successfully in his interpretive endeavors? We feel that he does only to the extent that he is aware of the problem and sufficiently concerned to take it into account. As we shall see, Hughes is only marginally involved with this problem; essentially, he is committed to his analytical preunderstandings.

The richness of the life history material cannot easily be reduced to the dimensions of the analytical task that Hughes sets for himself. Nathan's stream-of-consciousness narrative coheres in complex, multifaceted statements about the self and subjective awareness that cannot be translated into the tidy, discrete boundaries of this or that role, like hunter or schoolboy, whose existence Hughes has established a priori in his preconceived analytical framework.

Nathan's report of his own growing up, recorded in his youth, is a deeply felt effort to render retrospectively, in selective fashion, the things that were once (and may still be) part of an involved total experience. The world of a boy growing up in Saint Lawrence Eskimo culture has an overall tone and feeling very different from the interpretive units of the ethnographer. Hughes, for example, treats the roles Nathan played as apprentice hunter and son as though they were separate, meaningful categories into which his life could be arranged and understood. But in doing so, Hughes violates the experiential unity of events, feelings, attitudes, and ideas through which Nathan comes to terms with his life as a particular person in a particular, subjectively bounded existential reality. Adopting our own hermeneutics, we feel that we can truly understand the full meaning of one dimension of experience in its detailed, subjectively articulated texture only in relationship to other dimensions or aspects that impinge on it and give it, ultimately, its special value.

It is quite obvious in the autobiographical account that Nathan was never able to disentangle his experiences of becoming a hunter from his awareness of the concrete details of his particular relationship to his father, who was also his teacher. Learning to be a hunter, as he saw it, was part of that relationship, and the extent to which he mastered the skills his father taught him was a measure of his adequacy as a son. Failure to perform on the hunt at the level of his own expectations was not just a failure in the economic sense—a lapse of competence having certain economic consequences—it was a self-defined disappointment to his father as his teacher and, to a certain degree, to other members of the family as well. Nathan's total concept of himself as an individual in a complex network of sentiments, duties, and feelings to others was directly engaged and brought into play in his sense of himself as an apprentice hunter.

At one point, after Nathan is criticized by his father for being squeamish about killing little birds and sleeping on the job, he feels chagrined, humiliated, and abjectly unworthy in failing to meet his father's demanding but reasonable expectations. Part of the hunter's job is making the journey back home after a hard day, when he is cold and exhausted and the way is uncertain and filled with dangers. Nathan is terrified of having to go back by way of the cemetery for he is frightened of ghosts. He would prefer returning by a shorter but more treacherous route. But by now he has learned a lesson of sorts about the hunter's responsibilities, and, while dreading the ordeal, he masters his fears and assumes the determination, stamina, and nonchalance of a hunter in order to make amends to his father and convince him that he is the kind of son his father would be proud of. To talk about this behavior as appropriate to the apprentice hunter or to the son is beside the point, for Nathan's actual definition of this problem and his solutions to it embrace interlocking dimensions of experience that meet at the resolution point of his own self-consciousness of being a particular person in the process of rehearsing and becoming certain possibilities to himself. This holistic rendering is tellingly revealed in the following passage about this situation:

> *The next thing Dad said was, "Let's go home." At the sound of going home, a thought of which way we would take shot into my mind. I asked right away, "Which way are we going, Dad?"*
>
> *He pointed to the way we came, saying, "That way. The way that goes toward the lake and follows the edge of the lake toward the village."*
>
> *Oh! No! Not in the dark. I felt very creepy, and wasn't even by the graves. I tried to avoid that way by saying to Dad, "Why do we go that long way? Why don't we make a short cut this way, straight to the village?"*
>
> *His answer gave me the shivers: "That way is short but it is not easy to walk carrying a heavy load. It is gravel almost all the way. But this long way is easier to walk on and we can save time, even though we have to walk in a curved way." Jeepers! But I had to go with him.*
>
> *Aw! The scary place. I wished we didn't have to go through that place, but we were going to. My other unpleasant thoughts were replaced with scares.*
>
> *I was not so happy. But I was keeping that to myself. I wouldn't let my father know it. So when he asked me why I wanted to make a short cut to the village, I said, "Oh, I just wondered."*
>
> *Then we went for some way. I didn't feel good. My legs were a bit wobbly but they went all right. It was my turn to carry the long pole. I held it up on my back. We walked without saying a word, like we always did. I couldn't look around now. I kept my eyes on the ground just ahead of my feet. I seemed to hear voices. Strange noises. I thought I saw some ghostly figures with the corner of my eyes. Once I almost scared myself right out of my skin, when I bumped into my father. He had held up his step for a short moment to adjust the bag he was carrying to make it more comfortable. I didn't see him because I had my eyes fixed down. I knocked him hard and nearly made him fall forward. I just stood still and waited for what I was going to get.*
>
> *I got what I expected. Right away he looked at me and asked, "What is the matter? Were you asleep? Didn't you see me?"*

*I couldn't tell him the truth, because I knew he would say that
I was silly. So I just made up my answer: "Oh, oh, I was looking the other way. I couldn't see you." —and other excuses, the
best I could think of.* (Hughes 1974: 136–137)

Hughes himself, in trying to interpret the life history, recognizes the
difficulties of treating the hunting role separately, apart from the context of the father-son relationship in Eskimo society. His awareness
that the two are bound together, however, is an awareness of the limitations of his approach; it is not a basic starting point in the way he
conducts his analysis. We argue that the role concept compromises the
integrity of phenomenal consciousness, no matter how useful it is as a
model or analytical tool, and detracts from our understanding of the
unitary properties of a subjective account of a life. Contrary to what
Hughes actually implies, the role simply does not bear a one-to-one
correspondence with significant points of self-reference and self-appraisal in the life history. The arenas of social experience cross-cut,
intersect, and become confounded to some extent in the thoughts and
feelings of the individual, who is obviously not predisposed to evaluate his experience with reference to these delimiting constructs, reasons, and categories.

If we assume that society impinges on the individual in any particular sense to socialize or equip him for some future state, we are adopting the position that society must work on the individual in certain
ways for its own good. Assumptions of this kind are drawn from abstractions based on modal tendencies derived from a body of data that
has already been organized in such a way that certain frequencies of
behavior take on critical saliency. Such assumptions, however, cannot
be made to bear any demonstrable relationship to the experiences of
any particular individual. In reality, the individual's true horizons of
consciousness consist of emergent concrete possibilities, and subjective experience takes the form of particular figures, events, and situations—not abstract possibilities or modes. Thus, Nathan as apprentice
hunter is learning both specific skills to be used in definite situations
and a more general cognitive orientation. But he is learning all this for
reasons of his own, from his father, a particular man, who interposes
his own subjectivity into the learning process. These pertinent concrete facts project themselves in consciousness as abstract possibilities
for the future. But at any point, abstract possibilities become definite
events in the real choices or nonchoices of the subject and lose their

deterministic efficacy. Choices are always subjectively ordered and arise out of a complex process of compromise with perceived environmental demands. As such, clearly, what the individual makes of himself or causes to happen to himself may bear only a tenuous relationship to the analyst's model of what or how it "should" have happened.

What makes it especially difficult to interpret this Eskimo life history is the absence of information about the present life of the subject and the omission of significant details about the context in which the autobiography was set down. Unlike some of the life histories we have examined so far, this one reveals very little about the relationship of the ethnographer to the subject and the incentives of the subject in cooperating in this venture. We must always keep in mind that the life history occupies no privileged position as an objective entity, for it is the retrospective re-creation of experience of a particular person for his own purposes at a definite point of his life.

It is puzzling that Hughes tells us next to nothing about his personal relationship to Nathan. We do not even know how he met the young man in the first place. Did he meet him before his hospitalization or in the hospital? Did he know Nathan's family? If so, how well did he know them? It would be important to know if Hughes knew something about Nathan's life from the time the autobiography ends (at the time Nathan was fourteen) to the time Nathan set down his life history. He himself wrote it over a period of time (unspecified) in his late teens and early twenties. Some knowledge of these intervening years, particularly those in the hospital, would help put the life history in better perspective and elucidate motivation.

Hughes speculates at several points about Nathan's reasons for wanting to write down his life history. Was it to compensate for being in the hospital by recalling an earlier and happier time of freedom and learning? Was it a challenge? Was it to please the anthropologist? If we knew more about the context of Nathan's subsequent life and his relationship to Hughes, to the hospital, and to his own tuberculosis, we could ask reasonable questions about the hidden and elusive meanings of events in Nathan's life that would open up the dimensions of inquiry. We could then see the unfolding events in light of underlying covert intentions and choices. However, without such information, we must either content ourselves with trying out role analyses of the kind Hughes proposes or else indulge in guesswork and indirect inferences about the complexities of Nathan's mind.

We suspect that the experience of having tuberculosis must have played a large role in Nathan's motivation for agreeing to write his autobiography and the manner in which he selectively fashioned an edifice out of the elements of his earlier life. Significantly, Nathan puts as much temporal distance as possible between himself and the life he is recollecting. Nothing in the life history really points to the subsequent deterioration of his health; if anything, the autobiography resounds with images of hard, healthy physical activity in which the subject tests his body against the harsh demands made on it by his society and environment. Perhaps Nathan is using the experience of relating his life to resolve symbolically the conflict of being sick and incapacitated with tuberculosis. The narrative often mentions overcoming sickness and bodily fatigue in the constant necessity of physical exertion and struggle for survival. That quality of immediate feeling and experience so powerfully conveyed in the life history, as Nathan directly confronts himself in nature with his full awareness, may in part reflect the particular vantage point of events recollected from a sickbed. If so, imagination may have reworked events at conscious and unconscious levels into forms that Nathan could deal with in his present situation.

Hughes treats the events of Nathan's life history, as we all tend to treat data, as though they were empirically real and hence a laboratory for testing concepts and theories. But these events make sense to a large extent only as a function of Nathan's present interests, fantasies, anxieties, and defenses. Of course, any attempt to understand Nathan's present subjective condition, and hence the way he recollects his past, without knowing something of antecedent events must perforce be an exercise in speculation. As a case in point, Hughes refers several times to Nathan's timidity in social relations and suggests that this shyness may be due to the isolated life he led until he was five or six and the subsequent shock of dealing with a larger, more complex world. And yet other Eskimos were similarly isolated, experienced very much the same kind of disruption, and did not evidence this trait. Perhaps Nathan is here merely reinterpreting the meaning of earlier events in the light of anxieties about himself and his experience that have developed since the end of the life history. His subsequent history of sickness and a growing incapacity to manage normal life situations might well have cast any earlier certainty about life in some kind of fundamental doubt. If so, Nathan could read negative meaning into experience and see uncertainty and misgivings when there were originally more positive feelings and values.

Like so many who attempt to analyze life histories, Hughes assumes the psychological and social events described by the individual lead a life of their own *apart from* the individual. In fact, however, none of this life history exists apart from the subjective mind that is continuously re-creating it self-reflexively out of an exceedingly complex psychological and interpersonal matrix.

When we rigidly adhere to a predefined framework, elegant though its application may be (as in Hughes's admirable application of the functional and role models), we are no longer open to asking questions that can throw light on relationships and connections (for example, the full implications of subjective intentionality) that fall outside our pregiven dimensions of inquiry. Through Hughes's analysis we learn that roles, in the way he defines them, can appear to satisfy certain needs; that roles may be in "conflict" with each other and cause psychological strain; and that these processes can be analyzed and described. However, "psychological strain" and "needs" as experiential entities in a subjective product like the life history are phenomenally valid only in the total structure of subjective consciousness and its unique inner articulation. When these states are translated out of unique consciousness into the scientist's descriptive units, they lose their intrinsic meaning and become self-descriptive of a predefined theoretical order.

It may seem strange that in this life history we know much less of the immediate aspects of the subject-investigator relationship than in some of the other studies, and yet Hughes's treatment adheres more closely in many ways to the immediate properties of subjectively defined events, and his interpretive approach interferes much less with the subject's authentic narrative, than does Devereux's or Sachs's analysis. And yet, perhaps this is so precisely *because* Hughes does stay in the background to such a marked degree and refrains from imposing his personality on his analysis of the material.

Hughes's attempt to use identity theory in his role analyses enables him to maintain at least the vestiges of a dialectically tenable relationship between the subjective events he is interpreting and the external constructs he is using to make sense of it. It is hard to say if this dialectic has produced any novel insights not accounted for by the author's model (preunderstanding). It is evident in the analysis itself, however, that there are serious discrepancies between the interpretation and the demands of the subjective data.

The problem of reconciling Nathan's complex self-imagery of involvements with his father as guide and teacher with the analytical separation of hunter and son roles is a case in point. From our stand-point, this problem suggests the analytic limitation of our own unex-amined Western bias to think of economic events as occupying an ob-jective, impersonal sphere of activity functionally differentiable from the individual's meaningful sphere of close interpersonal behavior. Es-kimo culture would certainly suggest that such a distinction may be unimportant for us to make.

In sum, we know from our studies of "primitive" societies that the economic, social, political, religious, and educative spheres (to men-tion just a few) are inextricably bound together so that the actor cannot separate them in his own thinking. Hermeneutics reminds us that re-gardless of subject matter, our recognition of the unity of experience is essential in any interpretive quest where the questions asked are truly open.

Studying Role, Society, and Culture

The two life histories discussed below focus on behavioral adaptation interacting more or less directly with the demands of society, and un-like Hughes's study, both minimize the application of mediating psy-chological variables.

Role, Adaptation, and Culture Change

Guests Never Leave Hungry: The Autobiography of James Sewid, a Kwakiutl Indian, edited by James Spradley, represents a significant attempt to use both role and identity models to understand culture change and conflict as perceived by an individual in his life history. Essentially, this book is the story of a man who has successfully man-aged to adapt himself to both white and Kwakiutl culture. Intelligent and enterprising, he was able to get ahead in the white world while at the same time he fulfilled the destiny of his tribal socialization, be-coming the chief and spokesman for his people in their relationship with the larger, white-dominated society.

Spradley's analysis is interesting and occasionally even convincing, but, like so many such attempts at interpretation, his contains an un-questioning acceptance of the interpretive or analytical context that is created and a total disregard for the operations of the ethnographer and his informant that have brought this context into being.

In his analysis Spradley acts as though the material in the life his-tory and test results reflect, via his theoretical framework, the realities and the empirical bases of essential features in his model, such as "culture conflict" situations and the personality and identity components of the subject, which are presumed to be tied to these external events. Spradley contends that James Sewid has achieved what he calls a "bi-cultural" adaptation to conflicting external demands; that is, the subject has managed to conform to values and has performed roles in both the Western and Kwakiutl worlds without suffering the crippling effects of cultural marginality, identity disorganization, alienation, and role stress. But the very phenomenology of the life history itself shows that the narrative consists of the claims of one man who wishes to be taken for a certain kind of person. It is, after all, James Sewid who is doing the rendering for his own reasons.

The life history clearly reveals that Sewid is engaging in an ongoing act of projecting himself to his audience (he expected the life history to be published) as a self-reliant, responsible, virtuous leader of his people. We do not, however, see him exhibiting these traits in any intersubjectively verifiable way, although it may well be that others would agree with these claims if we could talk to them. Spradley treats these assertions, in any event, as though they reflected real, not merely idealized, behavior and identity. In the absence of any clarification, Sewid's assertions about himself are simply subjectively claimed identities. We might perhaps say that James Sewid in the context of recollecting his life is subjectively and retrospectively re-creating a personal relationship to his environment that corresponds to his self-perceived desire to be taken as having certain orientations, interests, skills, and accomplishments. His rendition of himself from the outset reflects his image of self. The events of his life compellingly reflect what he means them to be rather than what Spradley would choose to call them under the rubric of social or psychological reality.

By looking at the way the subject lives in his experience rather than evaluating him through constructs of social or theoretical relevance, we see a man who thinks and seemingly acts largely in the forms of culturally typified experience that has to do with collective acts and shared categories of behavior. It is rare to see a person who is so thoroughly a public figure in the image he claims for himself. And while Sewid undoubtedly had some very personal feelings and thoughts about the nature of his own activities, he chose to repress them in his self-rendition for the public record. Thus, the autobiography has a certain one-sidedness. The strong desire to be taken as a public, virtuous man concerned with the well-being of his people edited the flow of recollected experience to the point where the narrative must be taken as only an approximation of the many-leveled complexities of Sewid's subjective awareness of himself.

This life history contains no self-questioning of his motivation, no anguished self-conflict. All is as if preordained. Sewid's very thoughts about the typified events of his life are themselves in the nature of typified or rationalized explanations and justifications. Even the experience of grief at the death of somebody close to him is cast in these terms. At one point he regrets the passing of his old friend, Simon Beans; but his regret is that Simon could no longer help Sewid with the work he had chosen to do for his people. Any feeling for the individuality of this man and appreciation of him as a unique being has been suppressed, perhaps unconsciously so.

This life history is in certain respects, we believe, a managed concoction, where events are put together so as to suggest Sewid's favored image; but, at the same time, parts of the narrative seem to represent a spontaneous, relatively unselfconscious expression of natural states of mind. Sewid's responses to crises, for instance, reveal a man seemingly incapable of looking at people or things in any way other than their typified significance for him as a leader.

One of the most problematic aspects of Spradley's evaluation of the life history is his assertion that Sewid lived equally in both white and Kwakiutl worlds and successfully performed roles in both contexts, as though he had managed to balance life elements that were in profound conflict with one another. This claim, however, arises out of the categorization process, that is, the theoretical bias of seeing a twofold structure consisting of opposed entities in potential dialectical conflict (e.g., White versus Kwakiutl). Spradley interprets "Sewid," "father," and "Vice-President of the Native Brotherhood" as social identities belonging to the native category, while "boat owner," "rector's warden," and "net man" belong to white culture.

When we use roles a priori to describe entities or components in a preexisting social system, it is simple enough to place answers to preformulated questions like "Who am I?" into one or another of the categories of the model (this process by the way, removes any ambiguity attached to these aspects of self-reference). Contrary to the claims of the analysis, however, Sewid tended to see and think of his self-identifications in unitary fashion, as being structured around dominant interests and life goals (e.g., leadership) that spanned both cultures and characterized his whole mode of psychosocial adaptation. These roles, forming the basis of Sewid's self-identity, both white and Indian, were in reality hopelessly confounded as a consequence of continuously being assimilated into what was already a larger and more meaningful context of change and adaptation.

What this implies is that change had already moved the Kwakiutl society of which Sewid was a part strongly in the direction of accommodation if not assimilation with the white system. Sewid, for example, was a devout Anglican Christian even though he continued to participate in potlatches and traditional ceremonies like the Himatsa initiations. But these traditional events and ceremonies had become so divested of any religious significance that they did not engage any religious commitment at variance with deeply held Christian beliefs. It was easy enough, without doing massive violation to the self, to be a good Christian and at the same time participate in these ceremonies out of whatever motivations made these events salient. Indeed, there is virtually no self-perceived conflict in the life history in the religious sphere of activity, even though there are indications of potential conflict. For Sewid, Kwakiutl ceremonies could be maintained alongside his Christian faith as features of his social and recreational life and used to meet status needs for personal prestige and validation of his chiefly role (for example, he organized the ceremonies for the tourist trade to bring additional income to the people).

Instead of saying his unique character enabled him to make a positive adaptation and bridge potential conflicts of being in both Kwakiutl and white worlds, it would perhaps be more correct to maintain that he simply adapted himself to a state of affairs in which an accommodation to white society already existed. Outside the obvious conflict between saving (a white value) and generosity (still an important traditional value), very little conflict and agonizing are reported in the book except for an occasional reference to the anger Sewid felt that Indians were held in such low esteem, even though he knew they were in reality as good as whites. Sewid's awareness, as it emerges in his recollected life history, is of being in a situation where mastery of the environment and assimilation into the white world were inevitable, if only certain obvious rules of behavior were followed, such as exercising responsibility and self-discipline.

Furthermore, Sewid's self-perceived role as leader in a white world was itself a choice for, and an affirmation of, modulated change in an already changing cultural situation that demanded certain kinds of performance from anybody who represented the collective interests of

Kwakiutl society, as he did. We are suggesting, then, that the subject saw his role as implementing the direction of change that he knew Kwakiutl society was taking; he did not see himself as some sort of political broker mediating changes to a people who were caught in a severe culture conflict and had to compromise their sacred beliefs and institutions.

Knowing in some detail the relationship of the ethnographer to the subject and the interactional setting would give us an idea of the socially mediated dimensions of this life history, which is, after all, the product of human activity played out in a particular social context. Unfortunately, the reader has little to go on, a situation we have found to be common in published life histories. If we had only a little insight into the relationship that led up to the telling of the life history, we could more easily address some of the issues that have been raised. For example, the extent to which James Sewid was fundamentally a public rather than a private man, as we maintained he might be, could tell us more of Sewid's motives and give us some idea of how his rendition of self was adapted to specific behavioral settings. It is possible that Sewid had strongly idiosyncratic emotions and private feelings that he chose purposefully to suppress in relating his life history because he identified the life history as a forum in which to establish his socially relevant credentials.

Moreover, we do not know to what extent the author himself may have set Sewid requirements for telling his life story. Are we to assume that the life history was a totally spontaneous outpouring on Sewid's part? It is more than likely that some guidelines were set through mutual agreement, that some questions were asked in the process of eliciting the material, that the anthropologist's mental states influenced the editing of the story. It is interesting that Spradley recorded the life history knowing that the subject would read it and pass judgment on it. The whole thing, in fact, sometimes seems as if it were managed by both parties to ensure that Sewid came out looking good. There is certainly little or no evidence of human frailty or self-doubt in the life history. Does this mean that Sewid truly believed himself to be an exemplary man? Or does it mean that less flattering episodes in the subject's life were deliberately or implicitly ignored by either or both men in accordance with certain requirements that had been established in the data-collecting setting of "what the life history should look like."

Significantly enough, Sewid virtually never talked about his family.

In the whole life history only a few pages are devoted to his wife and children (there is practically no counterpart for this omission in any other published life history from a non-Western subject). Why? Is it because his consciousness of himself was dominated by specialized and typified concerns, or does it represent a wish to remove his private life from public scrutiny? Does it possibly reveal a lack of interest in his family? Surely Spradley could have provided some assistance to the reader in explaining these seemingly strange omissions.

In summary, three problems of interpretation in Spradley's approach emerge in light of our understanding of the autobiography and its larger social and psychological context.

1. If we look at the phenomenological significance of the actor's point of view, the autobiography must be seen as a subjective claim to be what it describes rather than any empirical truth to which fixed validity can be attached for testing or theory construction. Apart from its subjective intentionality, the document has nothing unequivocal to yield. The problem of getting intersubjective consensus for events described in the life history is an extremely difficult one.

2. If the first point is meaningful, the presumed culture conflict and bicultural adaptation are totally artificial, contrary to the consistent subjective definitions that emerge in the life history. Sewid throughout his life history emphasizes what he regards as the perfectly manageable task of adapting to already changing roles and interests.

3. It is difficult to take the life history very far interpretively without knowing the interpersonal influences that structured the data-gathering situation. We can, of course, still comment on the properties of subjective consciousness embodied in Sewid's report. But if we knew more of the whys and hows of the interpersonal setting, we would be somewhat better able to find the hidden forces that organized experience into its published form. For example, what is a purposeful claim designed to elicit a particular reaction from the audience, and what is a relatively unselfconscious living in the spontaneous recreation of experience? A greater knowledge of Spradley's relationship with his informant and the larger context of this research might help to disentangle problems of this sort.

The Individual, Society, and Cultural Constraints

Sun Chief: The Autobiography of a Hopi Indian (1942), edited by Leo Simmons, is the famous autobiography of Don Talayesva, a Hopi man. Though it has been the object of several different attempts at interpretation, here we shall be concerned with the one done by Aberle (1967). Aberle's analysis represents yet another example of using the life history to shed light on the nature of the culture-individual/personality relationship. Unlike many of the other analysts we have so far looked at (except for Kardiner), Aberle did not collect the life history he attempts to explain, nor did he know the subject personally, as far as we are aware. The autobiography was collected by Simmons from interview data and from a diary that the informant kept at Simmons's request and subsequently made available to him. Thus Aberle, like Kardiner, is approaching the document as an outsider to the immediate interpersonal situation that brought it into being. Although Aberle did not know Don Talayesva personally, he obviously did extensive reading in the Hopi literature and, as an expert on the neighboring Navaho, may have had some firsthand contact with the group.

The analysis is dominated by structural-functional assumptions and does not pretend to be very interested in Don Talyesva as a unique life. The basic approach is to differentiate the system and the individual as distinct though interrelated components, with the system having by far the greater dynamic force and influence. Aberle says we must first understand the workings of the system and its parameters, including built-in strains of the system and the recurrent problems posed by the system for individual psychological adaptation. (In other words, the nature of the individual-culture relationship is essentially determined by the nature of the social system.) It is then possible to use the life history, in conjunction with other data, to establish the range of individual responses to recurrent life situations permitted by the system functioning within its normal parameters. Don's life history may represent an atypical specimen for Hopi culture but, Aberle argues, it nevertheless falls within an acceptable as well as predictable range if the system and individual variations are already known and understood.

Perhaps the most insidious assumption embodied in this approach is the investigator's belief that he can understand the life history by working from the system down to the individual, as if society set situations to which the individual had to adapt within a certain range of possible responses. This assumption means that culture sets certain limits on individual adaptation that can be formulated from ethnographic data and tested against life history material. But the reality this formulation bypasses, a reality strongly brought out in the life history itself, is that the *individual*, living in a subjective world, creates his problems out of his dynamic interaction with his environment and develops his own existential solutions, which he identifies for us in the process of recollecting his life. This kind of utmost personal meaning may not be reflected in the crude matrix of "ranges of variation" generated by the model.

The subject is not talking about some abstract system whose functional demands he totally comprehends; he is talking about how he thinks he behaves, feels, and values, and how he actively projects himself on his environment—that is, about his subjectively dynamic experience as it is worked over idiosyncratically and assimilated into typified cultural rationalizations. In his autobiography Don is a dynamic agent who makes people respond to him as an individual, thus establishing a qualitatively unique series of interpersonal situations that is not accounted for by the constructs of the social system Aberle derives. This uniqueness is what makes it difficult to reduce his world to abstracted categories. While many of Don's actions, thoughts, and feelings are typically Hopi, the way in which he articulates them (e.g., his special emphasis on his spirit guide and its influence in the way he conducts his life), and the way they are expressed as a unified style of adaptation have a forceful uniqueness all their own.

It is one-sided to view society as one objectified entity acting on another objectified entity, the individual. This view makes it necessary to "explain" relationships, to concoct some sort of particular theoretical effect they must have on each other. For the functionalist such a model is closed; all that remains is for the right data to be put in the proper slots. For the investigator interested in a specific subjectively experienced life, experience itself is open and filled with myriad possibilities, some of which have become concrete subjective realities for that person. We are not saying that the functionalist approach is wrong; we are merely saying it deflects attention away from the particular problems and solutions that a unique individual, upon reflection, has found to be a valid description of his unfolding life situation.

Aberle uses his functional model to make sense of identifiable personality traits, and he takes a sociogenic viewpoint to order the life history data. Don is assumed to be suspicious and distrustful, which is probably true. Indeed, Don himself describes a number of childhood events in which he feels he was lied to and deceived by family members. Aberle takes this description to reflect objectively the existence of typical social strains and socialization themes affecting individual behavior.

In reality, however, all we can say is that Don, in the act of relating his life, is searching his past for some plausible explanation for his current distrust, and he hits upon a subjectively charged sequence of encounters as convincing to himself. But, in fact, he may merely be reading into early childhood events meanings that were actually not present and hence had nothing to do with the true initial effects of socialization, whatever they might be. The empirical status of such statements by Don must be questioned. Don's subjective account has its own internal phenomenal coherence, of course, but, strictly speaking, only from the point at which he relates his life. And the integration of his life as a subjective act in this sense is of a different order than the integration of events as they have been put in a causal or functional configuration devised by the external observer.

In his eagerness to show how even Don's deviancy can be understood in the larger Hopi context, Aberle misrepresents or at least erroneously describes certain aspects of Don's character. For example, Aberle describes him as hungry for prestige. The data, however, contain little to suggest that he is very concerned with his own prestige or his perception of others' opinions about him. In fact, by his own admission he seems to be rather lazy, fun loving, and in some respects unambitious. Aberle cites Don's cultivation of whites as a means of gaining prestige when more traditional avenues fail. This seeking out of foreigners, however, could just as easily be explained as part of Don's rather obvious curiosity, his consistent interest in adventure and expanding experiential boundaries. He became friendly with Navahos, too, a decidedly unusual characteristic for a Hopi. Cooperating with whites also gave Don an easy source of income and made it possible for him to indulge himself and be a little lazy. Moreover, he seems to have enjoyed the stimulating intellectual exchanges with white anthropologists. He comes across in his life history as an intelligent, intellectually curious person despite elements of distrustfulness and insecurity in his character.

His aggressiveness, too, appears to be overstated in the analysis. Given his own subjective definitions of his life situation, Don's behavior was entirely reasonable. We suspect that many Hopis in the community saw it that way, too. Why would he be selected as sun chief of his clan if he were overly and disturbingly aggressive in the eyes of his kinfolk? There is certainly no indication in the life history that he intimidated them in order to further his political ambitions. Without necessarily being aggressive in any overtly hostile way, Don is clearly outspoken and not afraid to stand up for himself, which is illustrated in the autobiography at several points. He tells old Reverend Voth and other Christian missionaries just what he thinks of them and their "stupid, harmful religion," and he directly confronts Nathaniel, who was suspected of being a witch and who, in Hopi belief, could have destroyed Don for his presumptuousness.

Aberle focuses throughout his analysis on the typical aspects of Don's experience in his cultural setting, and his extreme but nevertheless *typically* extreme pattern of deviancy (or, we might say, his very unusual but culturally understood adjustments, defensive maneuvers, and patterns of compensation). At the same time, Aberle provides very little information about the subjective texture of the life history, since the interpretation focuses on abstract analytical categories. While the kind of functional analysis Aberle advocates is honorable and may ultimately prove to have its own vindication, the approach obscures, confuses, or excludes from consideration certain kinds of understanding and a range of issues.

The analyst who comes to a document like a life history with preconceived notions about the society and insists on using the life history as a testing ground for his ideas will inevitably selectively reduce the autobiographical material to the dimensions of his preunderstandings. In doing so, two things happen: (1) alternative points of view either are not considered or are evaluated within the general framework of the model, which reduces their effectiveness as avenues to understanding; and (2) the unique richness of the phenomenon in its integrated but detailed subjective complexity may be lost.

Why do we so often avoid the potentialities of a hermeneutical dialogue between our models, which should be open and provisional enough so that we can pose new or alternative questions to them, and the unique and awesome totality of a document or item of behavior, which should indeed help us to pose those very questions for our theories and methods? Aberle's approach reminds us once again of the limitations of a model-oriented anthropology where the ethnologist is not rigorously self-critical of the assumptions of his analytical scheme and his own operations in using it.

Conclusions

The intention of these sociological (or sociogenic) approaches to the life history, with their emphasis on role, socialization, adaptation, constraint, social system, and so forth, is to illuminate and explain issues other than the understanding of the individual life itself. By focusing our analytical and critical interest on an abstract connection, transaction, or process, we avoid the individual who in speaking to us is trying to make sense of himself.

Why do we make something other than the individual the starting point in approaching the life history? Perhaps because our minds are inescapably bound to theory. By inclination, social scientists tend to approach the particular through the general. But why can we not use the individual to understand the individual and build from there to understand the general characteristics of the individual-culture relationship? This procedure is certainly a more justifiable approach to the life history from an epistemological standpoint. In the radical alteration of our methodology to meet the challenge of the individual's self-report, we must suspend rigid commitment to constructs such as society, role, and adaptation, which carry with them assumptions about the nature of human experience that can easily congeal into rigid prejudices when they are maintained inflexibly and unquestioningly through the authority of tradition. The very nature of prejudice in the hermeneutical view is to obstruct understanding in a changed context of awareness. And what is the life history but a phenomenon embedded in a temporal and/or spatio-cultural context different from our own?

The models used in these analyses make us aware that in a sense the analysts by their insistence on operating in typified modes of classification and synthesis, are reaffirming in these particular life histories what they knew already about the structure and process of the social world as a recurrent, predictable affair legitimated by already established procedures. In other words, Hughes, Spradley, Aberle, and others are merely making a case for a preconceived notion of how to use the life history to illustrate a "problem" in social science; their entry categories are scarcely modified in the actual act of analysis, for there is little dialogue with the life history text in the form of new questions that would open up novel vistas or insights. These approaches take us ever further from the actual human texture elucidated in the life history document itself and what it conveys about being a subjectively experiencing person in society.

Probably the most significant hidden assumption in these studies of the life history is that the social system and the individual are conceptually distinguishable for investigative purposes. This assumption creates an epistemological problem, for the life history is an act in which the individual relates his life and by that act subjectively constitutes his social-experiential environment. The environment of the life history, to put it another way, has been assimilated into subjective experience and takes its only meaningful form in that sense. If the focus were on the individual as the center of his context of experience and inseparable from it—instead of falsely opposing him to his pseudo-objective experience—we could ask how the individual as ultimate agent manages his self-defined transactions with reality and how he comes to terms with his subjective understanding of the demands and events of *his* world. These questions would allow us to glimpse the texture of being another person in the world as a phenomenally real thing and not as a construct imposed from outside.

Chapter 6
Women's Life Histories

So far, with the exception of Blanca's narrative, we have discussed only male life histories. Moreover, the studies that we have critiqued, which follow an interpretive path different from our own, have all dealt *only* with men. This is not an oversight on our part. We purposefully kept the life histories of women apart because they reflect some of the difficulties associated with the study of women in general (Watson-Franke 1972). In this chapter we will explore to what extent and in what ways female life histories differ from male life histories in regard to the circumstances of their collection, their content and style, and their interpretation. As we shall see, the female life history raises specific problems of interpretation because of a strongly developed male bias in the social sciences.

The Woman's Point of View

The special meaning of women's lives and the problems it raises is an old one, as the following example makes clear. In the first half of the eleventh century a Japanese woman whom we know only as Lady Sarashina or Takasue's daughter recorded her life history (Sarashina 1971). The narrative is not a diary. Lady Sarashina obviously wrote it later in her life and it covers almost her whole life from girlhood to old age. Lady Sarashina focuses her account on events that illuminate her development as a self. She writes about her frequent pilgrimages to shrines and temples, about death, and about dreams. While she mentions having experienced conflicts in her relationship with her mother and having felt very close to her father, the life history is concerned for the most part with female siblings and friends. Only a few sparse comments refer to a husband and the birth of children. However, she does describe the type of relationship she would like to have had with a man: a distant, dreamlike bond, in which the man was a romantic visitor who did not interfere with her life in general. Obviously

Lady Sarashina did not reject male companionship in principle, but she did want an existence of her own apart from men.

This message has not met with the approval of her readers. Her life is of special interest to our discussion because it has been commented upon by various scholars through the centuries. While Lady Sarashina emphasizes her relationship to nature and the spiritual world— accepted topics in male autobiographies—a scholar of the eighteenth century comments: "this book is nothing but a vague, rambling account of her life and it has no central point" (Sarashina 1971:32).

What the *central point* is supposed to be is spelled out in a comment by a present-day scholar: "She has deliberately illuminated certain facets of this life, such as travels and deaths and dreams, while leaving in complete darkness such *central events* as her marriage and the birth of her children, which could hardly be omitted from a journal" (ibid.: 23; italics ours).

Lady Sarashina did not *omit* these events. She does mention them, but only briefly. She directs her attention instead to experiences, thoughts, and places that were of obvious interest and fascination *to her*. In a male autobiography short mention of marriage and children would suffice, but in a woman's life they become "central events" and society expects a woman to remember and emphasize them.

Our point in beginning our discussion of female life histories with an autobiographical account of a literate woman of eleventh-century Japan is that Lady Sarashina's case can serve as a reminder to anthropologists that it may be important to grasp their informant's subjective view instead of simply imposing their own on the data. Since Lady Sarashina was literate, she had the opportunity to record directly her most private thoughts and feelings. The comments that scholars have made about her book reveal that women's attempts to make sense of the world, apart from simply re-creating and maintaining their lives as wives and mothers, are not taken seriously by traditions and preunderstandings that view the male experience as the exemplary model. Anthropologists have a tremendous responsibility to reverse this pattern. Theoretically, at least, anthropologists are aware of their own arbitrary cultural orientation in structuring the data-collecting situation, and if they use this insight they may be able to elicit a life history that takes account of the informant's point of view, however foreign or incomprehensible it may seem at first glance.

Lady Sarashina's account shows that societal norms define the importance of certain events in a person's life. In a woman's life the important events ordinarily mean her existence as wife and mother, for it is these roles that interest men. This very same attitude is expressed in *The People of Alor*. In analyzing the life history of one of the female informants, Kardiner states his surprise and disapproval of the content of this woman's recollections: "It must also be noted that in a woman of forty who has five children *it is very strange* indeed that the most vivid memories and those that are the most highly tinged affectively pertain to her childhood" (DuBois 1944:437; italics ours). This informant remembered childhood events during specific discussions initiated by the anthropologist on nurturance, child care, and Alorese attitudes toward such matters. Is it so strange really that, under these circumstances, a woman would think back to the days of childhood, when she was taken care of by others? In the Freudian frame of reference that Kardiner employs, obviously, a woman can have no real life of her own. She is expected to see her life in reference to others, as a resource and servant, and to deny that she, too, is a self.

This view of women, so typical for the social scientist trained in the Western tradition, makes it hard to obtain female life histories that describe women as autonomous personalities, as selves in their own right. The problem is more severe for the life history than for the self-initiated autobiographical account, for the life history as an anthropological document is usually of interest to at least two people, the person who recalls his life and the person who initiates the narrative, listens, and takes down the record. Thus the woman who remembers and recalls must have sufficient self-esteem and a feeling of self-worth to wish her own individual life recorded, and, equally important, the recording partner must share this sense of importance and respect. Nevertheless, as Paulme (1963:1–2) has pointed out so aptly, anthropologists, like other social scientists, have been trained to listen to men first, and to see men as the more interesting and knowledgeable members of society.

Collecting Women's Life Histories

Although the first life history of an American Indian published was that of a woman (Anderson 1825), this work was soon followed by a plethora of male life histories (cf. Kluckhohn 1945:102–103). If in fact there has been such a lack of interest in women as persons, why have a considerable number of female life histories been collected at all? It is difficult to find in-depth information to answer this question, and we must content ourselves with sparse remarks that appear in prefaces and footnotes. Yet these data sometimes give us some insight into the relationship between informant and anthropologist.

Langness (1965:12) aptly points out that female life histories have usually been collected in order to present the "women's view." This attitude is consistent with the peculiar function of women in much anthropological research of providing supplementary information and/or giving insight into the "deviant" (female) aspects of a culture. Some female life histories (e.g., of the Alorese [DuBois 1944]; of Mountain Wolf woman [Lurie 1961]; and of Menomini women [Spindler 1962]) clearly have been collected to supplement male life histories that were already available. This attitude expresses the typical Western doubt that the female experience could ever explain the whole culture or even a central aspect of it as well as the male life history might. In other words, women unlike men, are not seen as true representatives of their societies.

Some female life histories have been collected to gain additional data about the culture in general, in which case the account then becomes part of a larger research project. Baba of Karo (Mary Smith 1964) is the classic "supplementary" woman. Though Baba's story fills a whole book, her account is really only a side-product in the context of the ethnographer's central intention. Collecting Baba's life history was part of a larger study of the social organization and economy of a number of Hausa villages carried out by Michael G. Smith on behalf of the Colonial Social Science Research Council. But since the Islamic tradition of the Hausa prevented a male from studying domestic units because of purdah marriage and the exclusion of men from the compounds, Smith had to rely on his wife, who recorded Baba's history from November 1949 to January 1950. Baba was chosen "because of her advanced age, intelligence, forthrightness, and faith in the Smiths' good intentions" (M. G. Smith 1964:11).

Baba also provided the deviant aspect according to Michael Smith, whose comments expose his strong male ethnocentrism: "Baba might be regarded as deviant, in that she bore no children, *but this is not uncommon among Hausa women* (ibid.:12; italics ours). Does Smith mean to imply that many Hausa women are deviant, inasmuch as childlessness is not uncommon? By whose standards, then, is Baba deviant? We do not know. Baba is also criticized in other contexts for not living up to British standards: "Baba's inaccuracy about the sequence of political events, which is characteristic of Hausa women, leaves room for error and doubt" (ibid.13). Thus, because the Smiths have difficulty assigning dates to the major events of her life, they try, for example, to date Baba's marriage with respect to the British occupation. But was it important to Baba herself whether her marriage took place before or after this event? The Smiths may have found it especially hard to understand Baba's sense of time, since in other respects Baba frequently plays up to them, giving them positive evaluations of British influence in her culture.

While most female life histories seem to have been collected by women, some accounts have been recorded by men. The anthropologist's interest, sensitivity, exactitude, and/or simple respect for the informant may be more important variables than his or her sex per se. The life history recorded by Frank Linderman (1972) of Pretty Shield, medicine woman of the Crow, is an example. Pretty Shield's story gives us a better feeling for the informant's participation and the anthropologist's operations than does Baba's, because Linderman often records his own comments and questions, clearly indicated as such, or these queries become indirectly but clearly known through Pretty Shield's replies. Pretty Shield, significantly enough, also volunteered to tell her life story to Linderman because she was deeply impressed with his interest, sincerity, and knowledge of Crow culture. We have here, then, one of those rare cases where the informant more than the anthropologist is the initiator of the dialogue. Linderman states that Pretty Shield would have been his choice for a subject in any case, because of her age (she knew her people when they still lived their traditional life on the Plains), because of her keen mentality and her willingness to talk without restraint, and because she was a "Wise-One," a medicine woman.

But even in this obviously good relationship between informant and anthropologist, characterized by trust and interest on both sides, difficulties were unavoidable. Linderman, interested in the female experience in Crow culture, had instructed Pretty Shield to discuss only events involving women. He became aware that his rigid request prevented her from relating incidents that she found interesting: "I began to fear that my repeated admonition to tell only a woman's story had

prevented Pretty Shield from telling many of her adventures" (ibid.:
55). A remark by Pretty Shield proves that Linderman was correct in
his assumption:

> You have asked me for only a woman's story, and I have found
> one. It is about a woman I used to know, a woman and a mouse;
> and even the mouse was a woman-mouse, so I will tell you the
> story. (Ibid.:118–119)

Pretty Shield's attitude also expresses a desire that is often at the
root of an informant's decision to allow his life story to be recorded,
that being the nostalgic wish once again to revive the past. Pretty
Shield's situation was especially tense and sad, for Crow life as she
had lived it as a young woman was gone forever; she was now old and
the Crow had irrevocably lost their traditional existence. Indeed, with
the exception of a few isolated, bitter references to whites, Pretty
Shield never discussed the upsetting changes that had taken place in
her culture.

One of the more detailed accounts of the circumstances of collecting female life histories is Colson's *Autobiographies of Three Pomo
Women* (1974) (the life histories were originally recorded between
1939 and 1941). As a member of the Social Science Field Laboratory
of the University of California, Colson was asked to collect a short life
history as part of her training in research methods. This was a typical
case where the anthropologist's needs and interests defined the research topic and data-collecting situation. Colson, however, was so in-
trigued with her study that she returned the following two years to collect more life histories, and she concentrated on women because she
was aware of the lack of data about them in this respect: "Lengthy personal accounts from women are all too few, and it is rare indeed to
find the accounts from women who are of the same culture and approximately the same age. These three life histories combined to a
great degree to give insight into the life of Pomo women of a particular generation" (ibid.:1).

A recent collection of life histories of four Yaqui women was likewise motivated by the lack of data on women's lives. "Women were
chosen as informants because information obtained from or about
women is underrepresented in Yaqui ethnographic sources, just as it is
in the broader field of life history literature" (Kelley 1978:6). However, this account of Yaqui women, like many other female life histo-

ries, has a male predecessor, in this case *A Yaqui Life: The Personal Chronicle of a Yaqui Indian* (Moises, Kelley, and Holden 1971).

At times female informants are chosen to tell their life histories because of their extraordinary personalities or eventful lives. Such seems to have been the case with Anauta (Washburne and Anauta 1940), an Eskimo woman whose life was shaped to a large extent by the unusual circumstances surrounding her birth. During the night Anauta was born, a courageous young hunter died out in a storm. Anauta was named after him, which meant that she would be brought up by the dead hunter's mother. In this way the dead man's spirit could enter the child's body and thus be born again.

Anauta subsequently experienced a male-oriented childhood but grew up to become a woman, married, and became a mother in traditional fashion. The conflicts this situation must have presented to Anauta open many questions that are not answered, nor even asked, in this account. How did Anauta feel about her identity? She was called "my son" by the hunter's mother, for in the belief of her people she had become the person for whom she was named. Throughout her childhood she was constantly reminded of her former existence as a hunter. One day when she failed to accomplish a task and was about to give up, she was told:

> *Anauta would not cry. You did this when you were here before. You can do it again. Try once more.* (Ibid.:14).

The life history does not make clear whether Anauta's knowledge about her predecessor made it harder or perhaps easier for her to grow up. The male identity, judging from her account, was obviously seen as working to her advantage. When she was compared with her two female friends, it is said that

> *having been brought up alone with O. [the hunter's mother, who is now Anauta's], and with the pattern of Anauta-the-man constantly before her, she was more mature and self-reliant for her age than the other two.* (Ibid.:16)

There are places where one would like to know more of Anauta's thoughts and reactions. The construction of an igloo is explained at one point, and it is known that men and women have their well-defined spaces in an igloo. Which instructions was Anauta given and how did she react toward them, considering the changes in her life over a long span of time? On another occasion, when Anauta's mother uses a woman's knife for a particular task, we wonder which instruments Anauta used and how she felt about it. And if she used exclusively male instruments in her youth, she must have changed to female tools later on. How did this affect her sense of identity? This life history could have provided significant answers to the issues of sexual identity, but instead emphasis is placed throughout on Anauta being a good "boy" and later a good "woman." The only conflict that is emphasized in her account is that between the traditional world of the Eskimo and the white outside world.

Anauta elicited considerable curiosity, and she was asked by several people to write down the story of her life, but she felt that she could not do it:

> *I can't write well enough myself, and I haven't found anyone yet who was a writer who understood me and my early life well enough to write this book for me.* (Ibid.:xiv)

She finally found this person in Heluiz Chandler Washburne, who together with Anauta reconstructed this extraordinary woman's life. Unfortunately, however, the account conforms in many ways to the established picture of women in anthropological treatises as male-defined beings. W. T. Grenfell, who knew Anauta personally and who wrote a preface to the book, introduced Anauta to the reader in the following words: "Anauta, subject and co-author of this book, is well known to me. *Her father* came to my help as a herder when I was introducing a reindeer herd to our coast. Among *his* chief characteristics were courage, resourcefulness, and a smile that never came off. And withal *he* was a quiet, gentle man" (ibid.:v; italics ours). Grenfell's introduction contains no more "information" about Anauta.

One of the most explicit and interesting explanations of why women would agree to give their life histories is provided by Laurentin, who, as an anthropologist and physician, worked among the Nzakara of Central Africa. While her older informants were motivated by the wish "to recall the past," the time before the whites, the young women who came to her volunteered their stories because they all shared the problem of being childless: "They came to me asking me, a doctor, to cure them. Feeling that the inability to bear children, from which all of them were suffering, was the result of previous happenings, they were anxious to tell me about their lives as accurately as possible so as to insure recovery" (Laurentin 1963:121–122).

These examples suggest that there is more than one motive for collecting a female life history and more than one bias that interferes with collecting such data—although our Western taken-for-granted images of women certainly play a major role in this process. In these cases there seems to have been much more interest in the "facts" (i.e., the normative aspects of the culture) than in the subjective, personal experiences of the informant (her opinions, feelings, and reflections). In a number of instances, for example, the life history data provided by the informant were supplemented and, indeed, were confounded by information given by other informants or other sources (see Washburne and Anauta 1940; Laurentin 1963; Colson 1974). Where this is so, it becomes impossible to judge accurately an individual's own true range of interests, knowledge, and responsibilities. We should not be too surprised by all this, however, for it is consistent with the usual research motive in anthropology of describing a larger cultural context rather than making sense out of an individual's personal experience.

The female life history becomes a virtual paradox in anthropology: while women are not seen as models, as people who lead exemplary lives, the normative aspects of their accounts are nevertheless emphasized. But this paradox may be easier to understand when we remember the nature of woman in the intellectual tradition of the West. According to our own taken-for-granted assumptions, the woman is the resource in the material sense and yet she does not herself initiate explanation. We are familiar with this picture from ancient Greek philosophy, where the female is *materia*, but the *demiurg* is male.

The anthropologists who recorded these life histories saw their female informants pretty much in this light. They saw them as subjects who could provide a rich body of data out of which the anthropologists, in their "wisdom," might create an order—for example, by providing the "correct" time sequences or by focusing on "important" events as compared with trivial experiences. They made little attempt to interpretively develop the subjective meanings these women themselves gave to their world. Moreover, these same ethnographers seemed to think it unnecessary to link these women's experiences and their meaning to the meaning of the world in general, an issue that leads us to the wider problem of interpretation. The particular role of the female life history and the specific problems associated with it in anthropology become more clearly visible when we consider this crucial issue.

Interpreting Women's Life Histories

In general, "life histories are often used to portray some aspect of either culture or anthropology, or both, that otherwise is believed to have been neglected" (Langness 1965:14). This is especially true for the female life history. While ethnographies give the general overview, that is, the public, male-oriented version of the culture, the life history is used to provide the "women's view." As Langness points out, "it is primarily for this reason that life histories of women have increased in number during the past twenty years" (ibid.).

But does this necessarily imply that the "woman's view" has gained in significance? The supplementary character of many female life histories already suggests that this is not the case. These accounts give insight into the female component of culture, but they are not seen as an example of human struggle, or as an attempt of making sense of the world in general. The critique of Lady Sarashina's life history is a case in point.

Like most male life histories, female life histories have been presented to the reader as self-explanatory. But while a number of male accounts have been subjected to elaborate psychological or sociological interpretation, only a very few systematic attempts at interpreting female life histories in nonliterate cultures are on record. The most outstanding of these is undoubtedly Kardiner's analysis of the autobiographical Alorese materials collected by DuBois (1944) (see chapter 4). Why is this so? Must the reason be sought in the inherent "dullness" of women's existence? Or does it lie in the cultural tradition of those who recorded these lives down on paper and chose not to analyze them? We can understand this problem better once we have taken a closer look at the Alorese case.

When DuBois did her extensive fieldwork on Alor, she collected a vast body of ethnographic data, including eight life histories, four male and four female. Thus, a golden opportunity existed for making sense of Alorese experience through the eyes of both men *and* women, but even a superficial look suffices to make us skeptical that DuBois and Kardiner were equally interested in both sexes. While the lives of the four male subjects take up 177 pages, those of the four women take up only 136 pages. The discrepancy becomes more striking with respect to the interpretations carried out by Kardiner; the interpretations of the male life histories average about 6 pages, whereas only one of the woman's life histories is given as much space. Interpretations of the other three female life histories average only 3 pages apiece (and one woman is not even worth the trouble of having her psychodynamics diagrammed!).

This treatment corresponds with Kardiner's general remarks that portray Alorese women as less interesting people. In a classic instance, Kardiner comments on the life of Lonmani: "She has only a limited range of indifferent subjects about which she can talk" (DuBois 1944:468). But Lonmani's life history brings to light dramatic and sometimes tragic events. As a child she was frightened by an assumed encounter with a notorious killer; thieves stole the corn that her relatives had grown, leaving the family in difficult straits; the village anticipated the arrival of a messianic Good Being, enunciated by the prophet Malelaka; Lonmani suffered the early losses of her father and mother; when the villagers did not pay their taxes, they were dragged off to government camps by soldiers but were subsequently rescued; an influenza epidemic decimated the local population; Lonmani left her husband and child at great emotional cost, for she kept visiting the child almost daily.

To call this "a limited range of indifferent subjects" does not do justice to the experiences and sufferings endured by this woman. True enough, such experiences seem to have made Lonmani into a person who is insecure and fearful of involvement. Though her report is full of tragedy and pain, her rendition is often less interesting to read than the accounts of some of the other Alorese informants. However, all this is a matter more of style than of content, a difference that Kardiner apparently does not take into consideration. He apparently lets his lack of interest in his reconstruction of Lonmani's character dynamics interfere with his judgment of her autobiographical account.

A more interesting subject, in Kardiner's opinion, is Tilapada, who "seems to be a well-adjusted person insofar as this society permits." The clue to Kardiner's interest in this woman may be Tilapada's wish to "participate in masculine activities," which is "the most dominant trend in her life" (ibid.:434–435). Kardiner then qualifies his approval: he criticizes Tilapada's "resentment" toward the female role. Since she displays some traits that are typically male for that culture, Kardiner sees something positive in her, something he understands and is therefore able to discuss, where otherwise he is quite helpless in coping with these women's individual or female-defined reactions to their environment. For example, when another woman, Kolangkalieta, decides to sleep alone and go away because her husband beat her up when she came home late from the fields, Kardiner comments that Kolangkalieta "seems throughout her life to have been quick to take offense" (ibid.:499). This statement is hardly sympathetic to the woman's point of view.

Kardiner's obvious lack of interest in the female life histories becomes acutely visible in his concluding remarks when he discusses basic Alorese personality and how the collective life history materials fit into this scheme. While he finds all four male accounts helpful in this task, he omits three of the four accounts of the women: "We can use most profitably the autobiographies of four men and one woman for comparison with the basic personality structure" (ibid.:548). Significantly, no reason is given for ignoring the other women. And while Kardiner does not state explicitly the reason for singling out Tilapada, the only female representative worthy of discussion in the context of Alorese basic personality, her pursuit of masculine ideals seems to make her a more desirable person and more complex psychologically than, for example, either Lonmani or Kolangkalieta, in neither of whom are "masculine strivings" present (ibid.: 549). Toward the end of his discussion Kardiner refers exclusively to the male records: "There is much more to learn from a comparison of the four men" (ibid).

This approach is a disturbing one. By implicitly taking the male as the model, Kardiner examines only the male attributes of each woman in reference to the basic personality structure, and he is at a loss to explain a woman's life when these characteristics are lacking. An absence of masculine characteristics seems to indicate for Kardiner a corresponding absence of personality and personhood!

How can women's experiences disappear like this, becoming unimportant and without meaning? Kardiner, by relying on Freudian theory as the basis of his interpretation, can fall back on only a very limited view of women for making sense of these life histories. And yet women are not totally absent, for Kardiner focuses on women's maternal role, a point consistent with the Freudian theory of personality formation. The mothers of all four men are discussed at some time or another and in some detail. Ultimately, maternal care is made responsible for the success or failure in these men's lives. Thus the woman is an agent in relation to men, not a being in her own right, and in her maternal role she remains, for better or for worse, in the background, as a resource, catalyst, or supplement to men's activities.

Kardiner's picture of women's role is a most impressive illustration of Freud's claim that women's goals are passive in nature. Women offer continuously, asking nothing in return, not even to be recognized as people. What alone counts is the effect that women have on the lives of men. Outside this sphere their existence does not seem worthy of much detailed reflection. Because of his strongly developed male-oriented bias, Kardiner cannot perceive these female informants as subjects whose experiences have intrinsic meaning, whose lives can provide models and manifest the essense of experience in Alorese terms as forcefully as the lives of men. To admit this possibility would mean for Kardiner to concede that women have, indeed, something to say.

It seems clear that the basic personality as it appears in a particular society—and as Kardiner defines it—must combine male as well as female characteristics as they are understood in that cultural setting. This issue brings us to the very basic question of the meaning of human experience in general, and the meaning of the female experience in particular.

The Meaning of Experience

As the previous discussion indicates, different people have different ideas as to what constitutes a meaningful experience as compared with a trivial happening. This philosophical and cultural problem has far-reaching proportions: "However paradoxical it may seem the concept of experience seems to me one of the most obscure we have" (Gadamer 1975:310). Science attempts to objectify experiences by making possible their repetition through others; experience then changes from being an idiosyncratic, individual act to being a normative, repeatable event that is thus shared and therefore understood by all members of a given culture. If we apply this idea to the anthropological setting, we can more easily recognize the anthropologist's interest in reporting experiences that have been lived through not only by one person but by many, not by an outsidier who defies the cultural norms but by an accepted and accepting member of society. In a world of male-oriented values this interest poses a problem for the female informant and the anthropologist who works with women. In order to be acceptable and thus credible to men, the female informant can act in two different ways. (1) She can act out, within certain limits, accepted experiences that follow the general, male model available to her. In other words, she can act like a man and under certain circumstances she may be rewarded for her performance, although she also runs the risk of criticism. Kardiner's evaluation of Tilapada and other female Alorese informants is a typical example of this position. (2) She may focus instead on experiences that are known as specifically female in her culture and thus risk being ignored or denigrated.

Why is this male-limited way of looking at female experience so? One very simple, but very serious, possibility is that various significant female experiences cannot be objectified by male scientists in the way of personal reenactment since these experiences depend on the physiological makeup of the female. The situation is significantly complicated by the fact that it is not only physiological limits that keep one sex from reenacting certain experiences of the other. In all cultures that we know of, a sex-specific division of experience places restraints on men and women in respect to the radius of other expressiveness and actions. In our own culture, for example, men will refuse to repeat certain experiences thought to be female-specific (housework) and will prohibit women from reenacting experiences that are thought of as male-specific (Catholic priesthood).

Since most scientists have been male for centuries in Western culture, it is the men who have defined the standards of objectifying experience. This fact has left its mark on theories that explain human action and interaction: woman and her experience are declared either a mystery that cannot be explained or an unimportant issue that needs no explaining at all. The frequent helplessness of those social scientists who attempt to explain female experience makes this effect quite obvious. Kardiner's inability to cope with the experiences of the women from Alor is a good example, as is Freud's remark that "woman's psychology is a dark continent."

This issue is important if we want to evaluate the significance of male and female life histories in understanding a culture in general. The life history, if seen as a comprehensive cultural presentation from an individual perspective, cannot gain a wider cultural meaning in this type of intellectual climate if a female informant is involved. If only male experience is worth repeating and has become for us the only objectifiable experience, women are then isolated, haphazard beings who lack direction and goals. We end up with only a partial picture of the whole.

The anthropologist, however, faces the extra difficulty of cultural relativity, of confronting the fact that experience has different meanings in different cultural settings. Not only do the experiences of men and women differ in different societies, the attitudes toward perceiving and evaluating these experiences are likewise dissimilar. While men in our culture find it hard, if not impossible, to objectify female experience, men in other societies may not necessarily have such difficulties. Among the matrilineal Guajiro, for example, where women function as shamans and political negotiators, men are accustomed to listen to women's opinions and to accept the positive validation of female experience (Watson-Franke 1975, 1976b).

What is involved here is a process of learning: to have an experience means to learn something one did not know before. To repeat another person's experience means that one can potentially learn what the other person has already learned. Gadamer (1975:317) calls this process the "dialectical experience," an activity in which a former position is changed, new knowledge is won, and a new position is ultimately gained at the cost of rejecting the former. This process becomes possible, though, only if the person keeps an openness toward having experiences. It is precisely here that we see the dilemma of women in our own culture, for can it not be truly said that men in our culture lack the openness to learn from women? And are women open to learning from other women, for that matter? Are men and women prepared to correct former views by equally reenacting male *and* female experience?

It becomes clear that the concept of dialectical experience must operate within our society in a strongly male-oriented and male-directed framework that scarcely leaves space for female expression. Female experience, in sum, can only be taken as seriously as men's when women and their expressions are represented in the value structure of society as *agents* and *sources of ideas*, that is, when in the world of science female experience is objectifiable.

In the following pages we will attempt an interpretation of a female life history from the point of view (hermeneutically justified, we think) that she is a woman and enacts experience from that perspective. We will take the female experience as the dialectical experience through which we understand the culture as a whole and the conflicts between men and women in particular. The example we have chosen is Ruth Underhill's *Autobiography of a Papago Woman* (1936). The author collected and published this life history with the intention of making Papago culture in general understandable to non-Papagos through the experiences of her subject, Chona. Chona's life, however, can only create the climate in which dialectical experience can take place if the reader is *open* to what she has to tell us.

Chona: A Woman-Oriented Interpretation

Over a period of several years (October 1931–November 1935) Ruth Underhill collected the life history of Chona, a Papago woman, who was about ninety years old at that time. Underhill had respect for and interest in Chona and her people. Her objective—to make whites familiar with the Papago through Chona's story—makes this book one of the rare cases where a woman's account is intended to represent the culture in general. This motive had a certain impact on Underhill's evaluation of Chona's personality, as we shall see later.

Like all published life histories, Chona's account underwent certain editing to make it more readable to the Westerner: "There . . . remain, in representing an Indian autobiography, important questions of technique. Indian narrative style involves a repetition and a dwelling on *unimportant* details which confuse the White reader and make it hard for him to follow the story" (Underhill 1936:3; italics ours). This statement is congruent with the stated purpose of the account. However, it makes us aware that we have lost significant information, for why should Chona dwell on something *she* found unimporant? Is Underhill talking about something that is unimportant to the reader, to Underhill, or to Chona herself?

This issue represents one of the basic conflicts of presenting and interpreting data in anthropology; it is a matter not only of technique and methodology but also of understanding how others look at and make sense of the world in different ways. Underhill chose to make her report understandable to and meaningful to the non-Papago: "as a result the story has elaborations and emphasis at some points where Chona would not have placed them, and it stops short where she would have found repetition comfortable" (ibid.:4).

Every time the life history is used, as it is here, to give the reader insight into a culture as a whole, the anthropologist feels pressure to explain and validate the credibility of the informant. Perhaps it is mainly for this reason that Underhill stresses Chona's acceptance of her life. In this way Chona does not come across as a deviant person: "Chona accepted her culture completely. . . . She accepted her status without stress or rancor. . . . She submitted and found compensation in her life of child bearing and hard work (ibid.). Through such assertions of normalcy anthropologists render their informants' accounts reliable, typical cultural specimens. If Chona "accepts" her culture, she consequently demonstrates her belief in the system, thus bearing witness to the credibility of her own testimony. Chona, in other words, must be made to appear a normal person who does not make up strange tales for the anthropologist.

However, despite Underhill's reassurance of Chona's easy acceptance of Papago culture, we glean from her life story that her life was often filled with conflict and anxiety. There are indications that at times she attempted to rebel. Underhill, in fact, even goes so far as to concede that Chona is not the ideal Papago female type because Chona is "inclined to be independent and executive" and "has some urge to accomplish" (ibid.). Such commentary would perhaps not be necessary in the case of a male subject, where independence, executive potential, and the desire to accomplish would be highly valued.

In many ways Chona took her father as a role model, and for almost all of her life she was surrounded by men in important positions. Her father was a chief; one of her brothers became a curer; and both of her husbands held important ritual positions. Chona talks more often and in more positive terms of her father than of her mother. The first time she talks at some length about her mother she describes a situation that is conflict- and anxiety-ridden for Papago women: the men of the village prepare for war and Chona's mother is afraid that by having her menstrual period at the wrong time she will interfere with her husband's war activities, because the Papago believe that a husband cannot go to war when his wife is menstruating. Chona feels the anxiety of her mother. When she goes out to bring food to the hut where her mother has isolated herself, she asks her mother if the blood has come.

The topic of menstruation comes up several times in Chona's report and recurrently carries with it a whole host of negative connotations. Chona, for instance, talks about the danger it poses for the whole village and the limitations it imposes on the lives of women. Of course, men cannot reenact this experience as individuals or objectify as scientists, but it does have direct and far-reaching meaning for the female of this society.

In recalling her life, Chona also discusses the restraints placed on women's lives because of the warlike activities of the men. She emphasizes that women must interrupt their work when their husbands have killed an enemy. She recalls the resentment of a woman who had to interrupt her weaving and enter the purification rituals because her husband had returned as a killer. In Chona's memories these events are not glorious triumphs where the women exulted in the accomplishments of their husbands; instead these happenings represent hardships and seriousness. Some women, she says, did not want their husbands to become killers so that the women could continue with their work, and she remembers the wife of a killer who ignored the powerful taboos surrounding a killer and his family. This woman, who continued weaving in spite of the prohibitions, was punished for her lack of obedience by never being able to menstruate again.

Chona perceives very clearly the different worlds in which women and men live in Papago society. She and her sisters work hard while the brother goes out to the desert to seek visions because he will become a curer. Chona expresses her desire to go seek visions, too, when she says:

> *I could not go into the desert like my brother. I had no time; I had to work.* (Ibid.:24)

But Chona does not give up. She begins making up songs, an activity that brings prestige and influence to men (ibid.:4; Underhill 1938). Underhill refers to this seemingly important incident in Chona's life as a "minor maladjustment soon overcome" (1936:4). Chona also has visions, and finally she discovers that she has crystals inside her. This is a momentous discovery since the Papago believe that shamans who have their own crystals are especially powerful. Chona says at one point:

> *Some medicine men dream where to find [crystals] and they go out in the bare mountains and see them lying there. . . . But some men never have to find them. Their crystals grow inside them. . . . Those are the men who have great power.* (Ibid.:20)

But women do not make songs, they do not have visions, and they do not have crystals.

Chona, who sees her brother develop his full potential as a future curer, finally submits to an operation to have her own crystals removed. The shaman treating her tells her that these crystals will grow inside her again, but in her case this is not a promise of power but only a message of conflict, for she knows that she is not allowed to use them. Regrettably, we do not know what Chona felt and thought during this operation. Underhill always emphasizes Chona's acceptance of the female role and her negation of her potential as a self. Later, however, Chona speaks often about her power and her abilities, and at various times she refers to her crystals. Chona even manages to feel good about her accomplishments:

> *I learn well. I learn everything that the men sing. . . . [My grandfather] said when he was dying that none of his children would dream as he had but that his grandchildren would. And they did.* Yes, I, too. (Ibid.:17–19; italics ours)

Singing, essentially a male privilege, is important to Chona:

> *I know those songs . . . some women are thinking only of baskets and they do not remember such things. But I remember.* (Ibid.:21)

She dreamed a lot and heard music, which she interpreted as a sign that her crystals were growing again. Chona kept insisting that she had knowledge even though her crystals had been taken out:

> *I am one who knows things, because, even though they took my crystals out, there was always something in me.* (Ibid.:49)

She recalls her puberty ritual, during which the girls are given a medicine that is only known to shamans:

> *But I know, because my brother was a medicine man and because I myself have seen things.* (Ibid.:35)

As she grew older, she came to be more aware of the fact that women could not do the things that men did and resigned herself to it. When she finds a crystal in the desert, she gives it to her brother because

> *I had no use for a crystal then, I could not keep it. I, a woman, who was not meeting any spirit.* (Ibid.:52)

But later she indeed has various meetings with coyote, a spirit, in the desert.

When she finally starts curing, she again finds a crystal. And again she gives it up:

> *I did not know if a woman should have a crystal, and I gave it to my husband.* (Ibid.:58)

The loss of the crystals is mentioned prominently in still another context after she has another encounter with coyote, who tells her to cure if she wants to but to abstain from it if she cannot do it:

> *So always I sit back if I cannot cure. But I could have cured if I had not given away my crystals. Yes, I could have done much.* (Ibid.:61)

Chona at this point does not voice open rebellion. The message she conveys is that she gave away her power rather than risk having it stripped from her by others. This attitude probably made it easier for her to accept the loss, which obviously preoccupied her for most of her life.

As we commented earlier, Chona became aware of the tensions and conflicts between male and female experiences, and so it is little wonder that she exhibited feelings of doubt and worry concerning her own future as a married woman. As a girl, she says,

> *I used to think while I was sitting under the shelter with my basketry, about whether I would get a good man and whether I would like being married.* (Ibid.:27)

Much of what she heard around her could hardly have turned her mind toward marriage. Since her father was a chief, people brought their grievances to him, including such problems as marital conflicts involving wife beating. One incident stands out as especially frightening in Chona's mind. One day her father heard the case of a young woman who had been beaten because she resented her husband. Hearing this, Chona was so upset she mentioned it to her mother, whose reply certainly did not help to alleviate her fears:

> *It's all right to be afraid of men. All good girls are.* (Ibid.:28)

When her own marriage was finally arranged and she went to her husband's house, she was not happy. She describes seeing her mother leave, in tears, and she recalls her initial fear of her husband. But with time she gained confidence, made friends in the new family, and found out that she was lucky:

> *I hoped I would get a man who would take me to the dances and I did. Always we went and always together.* (Ibid.:40).

After many years of marriage, Chona's husband, who was a shaman, took a second wife. Chona did not accept this change, although it was common for Papago shamans to have more than one wife. Chona went home to her natal family hoping that he would send the other wife away and return to her. But this hope did not materialize. Instead her brother married her off to an older relative. Chona describes her second husband as a good-natured companion, but she was unhappy:

> *I did not love that old man. I was not fond of him. I used to go in the washes and lie flat under the greasewood and cry.* (Ibid.:55)

She was obviously still attached to her first husband, and when she heard about his death she was upset for a long time.

After the death of her second husband, Chona decided, at last, to live life her own way. When she was courted again she rejected her suitor:

> *I was tired. I said: "No, I am too old. I cannot cook for you." So I stay now with my grandchildren. Don't you think my baskets are good? I make them all day long, and the young women do the cooking. . . . I like to work at my daughter's house. . . . I can eat when I live there, and every year I go with her to the drinking ceremony. They want me, for I can sing.* (Ibid.:64)

Chona's description of her old age demonstrates that she has not lost her sense of independence, her longing to achieve, or her wish to make use of her special abilities.

Chona's frequent references to her father are a most interesting feature of her life history. Chona identified strongly with him, and through this identification she probably could deal with some of the conflicts she experienced being a strong-willed woman in a culture that gave men more options and opportunities. At the end of her puberty seclusion, for example, she was given a bath and remarked proudly that "they gave me a bath just as they did my father" (when he was a killer) (ibid.:33). She learned songs from her father, and it was

her father who explained to her that she would have to stay in an isolated hut after she gave birth. Chona felt that she had received a great
deal of knowledge from her father, and she felt abandoned after his
death when her brother married her off to an older man:

> *My father would not have allowed me to be offered to him for we
> do not marry relatives . . . I cried.* (Ibid.:54)

Ironically, it was male authority again that imposed this new marriage upon her. Chona did not speak up because

> *no woman has a right to speak against her brother, even if he is
> younger . . . and my mother had no right either, against the
> men.* (Ibid.)

With her father's death and the loss of her first husband she seemed to
have lost her allies in the male world.

Chona's reactions to these impositions on her did not disrupt the life
of her family or her community. She is proud of having been a good
Papago woman, although by her own admission it was not always
easy for her:

> *I was a good housekeeper. I did all the cooking and I fetched the
> water and ground the corn. I could catch the horses too and
> saddle them for my brothers. But I could not go out alone on the
> desert as they did. Why should I want to? That is a man's work
> and no woman with a right heart wants to be a man. But I was
> excitable. My heart was not cool. When I had finished my work I
> always wanted to race, and I was a good racer, the fastest of all
> the girls.* (Ibid.:29)

Despite all the indications pointing to Chona's subjective dis-
content, Underhill continues to stress Chona's acceptance of her culture. We would argue, however, that it is Chona's rebellion, however
muted, that is the more authentic aspect of her life history and gives us
the deeper insight into her character and the texture of what it is like to
be a woman in the male-dominated Papago society. Underhill chose to
see her subject in terms of her own Western preunderstandings when
she accentuated the accepting, submissive side of Chona.

Chona's life history, finally, is also a vivid reminder that Papago
society has been similarly unable to evaluate female experience on
equal terms with male experience. While the crystals were a sure sign
of special knowledge and power in a man, Chona had to have them re-

moved. Cultural norms forbade that others learn the explanation for such important matters from a woman. This incident reveals not only the Papago belief that women are potentially powerful, but also the strength of the male system to suppress the development of strong female forces within the male frame of reference.

The Papago themselves saw in Chona at least a potential rebel who had to be restrained in order to insure her cooperation for the good of all. Her operation was successful in that Chona did not become a shaman like her brother and challenge the established order; she even gave crystals away when she found them in the later years of her life. Still, the people around Chona could not claim total victory, for she seems to have believed to the end of her days that she was a strong woman, gifted with special knowledge and power. Chona, somehow, had confidence in the female experience.

Conclusions

The female experience in society as documented through the life history has been generally underplayed and underestimated because of the following attitudes and evaluative operations: (1) we perceive such experience as a supplementary product or as a document of deviancy; (2) we focus on the "accepting" woman who "fits" the conventional norms of society; and (3) we emphasize data that support a male-oriented view of women and ignore contrary data that support divergent attitudes and orientations. The result of these procedures is that a woman's life emerges only in reference to men and the full subjectivity of her self is lost.

It would be simple enough to explain all of this as nothing more than the result of Western ethnocentrism and sexism, which would make the anthropologist and his tradition the sole culprits. However, the matter is not that clear-cut. We must always bear in mind the informant's setting and take her special circumstances and experiences into consideration. Throughout this study we have placed special importance on the necessity to grasp the informant's views of the world, that is, to record an emic account. A reading of ethnographic records makes it clear that our own tradition is not the only one that displays a strong male bias. Chona's life is testimony to a pronounced male orientation in Papago culture, where only men are allowed to provide the essential explanations and thus give ultimate meaning to existence,

however exceptional a woman and her potential contribution to society. Strathern (1972), in her study of women in the New Guinea
Highlands, describes eloquently the verbal awkwardness of Ma Enga
women when they function in public, a result of their having been
discouraged for generations from speaking up in front of others.
The views held by women and men in the informant's culture, together with similar views in the anthropologist's tradition, ultimately
determine in their dialectical resolution the content and style of
a life history.

Since anthropologists have only recently begun systematically to
study the female point of view, our knowledge of the female emics is
still quite limited. It seems therefore more practical to start with ourselves, to examine our own biases in this respect and make an effort to
initiate changes so that we can achieve the openness that is necessary,
according to hermeneutics, if we wish to be able to experience at all.
Our own intellectual tradition has not entirely ignored the female experience, to be sure. Biographical and autobiographical material on
women has appeared especially in the psychological literature, but for
the most part it portrays the unhappy or deviant woman who is unable
to reconcile her own personal meaning in life with societal definitions
of her role. This emphasis seems to be the case no matter how sympathetic and finely textured the analysis (e.g., Binswanger 1958; Freud
1963; Allport 1965).

An outsider's readings of these documents and their interpretation
would no doubt result in a distorted impression of female experience
in our society. These studies do not suggest the countless successful
efforts of women to be competent and successful in creating meaning
in a world defined by men. Recent studies by feminist scholars (e.g.,
Shostak 1981) give more balanced and complete accounts of female
experiences because they include the struggles *and* victories women
achieve in the face of adversity. They show women as complete human beings who are capable and prepared to make their own statements on life.

Chapter 7
Prospects and Conclusions

Throughout the preceding chapters we have addressed in various ways the hermeneutical problem of bridging the gap between etic constructs and emic meanings. We might phrase this problem as a question: how do we get in touch with the life history as a unique subjective product embedded in what is to us an alien cultural context, when our minds seem inescapably to force us to impose on the life history the kind of organization by which we naturally or spontaneously, but sometimes artificially, make sense of experience?

Traditional life history analysis has almost totally ignored this problem. Researchers are willing to settle for the comfortable "understandings" that are generated by interpreting the data through the models, constructs, and common-sense categories of our familiar experience. We must confess that our own emphasis on returning to the phenomena themselves, on describing subjective modes of intentionality, and the like also has a rather one-sided quality. We believe, however, that our emphasis on interpretation has at least served the necessary function of raising important issues and directing attention to valid alternative approaches. It is undeniable that emics, phenomenology, and hermeneutics have to do with analyzing and bringing out the inner meaning of a *particular* life, a *particular* person, a *particular* text. The "scientific" advantages of such an approach remain uncertain.

If our etic constructs or categories are to have functional equivalence cross-culturally—that is, if they are to mean approximately the same thing to different individuals in their different subjective frames of reference—we must be prepared to correct our categories hermeneutically by projecting them into a dialectical relationship with the object of interpretation. To do so we must use our constructs to ask questions that are appropriate to the context of our data. Theoretically, this process should enable us to change our context of analysis and bring it into touch with our data, but in such a manner that our framework describes something of the essential meaning of the data without completely sacrificing its original abstract properties. The resulting, dialectically produced alteration in the framework could then be applied to another life history, corrected for the peculiarities of that case, and checked again against the original life history data to determine whether enough of a comparative structure that would have emic equivalence in the two sets of subjective data still remained.

It is indeed hard to imagine correcting or changing our theories, models, paradigms, and constructs in such a radical manner. If we did so, would they not cease to be finite ordering devices? Yet we know that our theories are really only provisional explanatory statements. Operating hermeneutically is not much different from testing a theory and altering it in light of the evidence, except that in the hermeneutical and phenomenological orientation we are trying to understand the particular case instead of attempting to refine our model so that it takes on greater predictive power. But there is no fundamental reason why these two approaches cannot be dialectically reconciled to some extent. If they were, we could understand in *both* senses at the same time: by understanding things through their common denominators, we would also understand their individualities, for the modified entry category or model would be characterized in terms of meanings appropriate to each and all the separate instances.

Let us take the example of role, for instance. The usual definition of role is a pattern of activity attached to certain social positions (statuses). As an entry category for cross-cultural comparison this definition is fine, but these abstract (and culture-bound) specifications may not describe the way a specific actor in a certain culture setting sees or interprets his own socially relevant behavior, nor does this construct have any necessary standardized meaning in that culture setting. Hence, describing his life history in terms of such role behavior may violate his subjective reality of "doing" in a complex configuration of feeling and thinking that may spill over the conventional notion of positions and particular patterns.

This problem requires us to redefine the entry category of role to take account of the subjective richness of individual experience. To some extent, perhaps, this can be done by defining role as the individual's conception of himself as engaging in certain activities that he believes have socially defined and delimited properties and consequences. By asking him and others to name the activity of self-reference in the native language, we can establish the correspondence between personally and socially meaningful boundaries of activity. Ultimately, by designating this activity (role) as an actor-societally shared definition of behavior having certain boundaries, we can apply it as an entry category for describing role in the life history of an individual from another culture, with some hope that this category might hold up or require only minimal modification or correction to be useful for comparative purposes.

The approach described above has been proposed by a number of psychologists interested in the cross-cultural study of cognition, among them Berry (1969), Triandis (1972), and Price-Williams (1975). These writers are advocating the correction of etic entry categories against emic (native) ones in the format of the graduated-steps experiment, where stimulus materials are varied in the experimental situation so that it becomes possible to determine the extent and circumstances under which our constructs describe true functional equivalences in native thought.

In life history research, however, where the emphasis is on the use of the life history for comparative or theoretical purposes, we must work with published texts that are fixed in final form. We have no control over the operations of the original data-collecting and editing process. In fact, we may be entirely ignorant of them. Thus, we cannot modify or vary stimulus materials as in an experiment dealing with delimited cognitive tasks. But we can, nonetheless, enter into a hermeneutical dialogue by projecting our entry categories and constructs as questions appropriate to the context of the text we hope to understand and by correcting them in light of answers we get back.

Some models, constructs, and categories lend themselves more readily to assimilating the native or subjective view than do others. The extent to which we alter or phrase the model to specify subjective dimensions or the viewpoint of the other, or at least take these conditions into account, determines to a large extent the degree to which it becomes responsive or sensitive to the emics of the situation we are investigating. For this reason self-identity theory would be closer to the emic view than psychoanalytic or behavioristic theories, with their strong etic foundations, and would require fewer modifications to bridge the gap separating it from descriptive relevancy for emic phenomena.

It is worth the effort of attempting to set up a model that would hold up as emically descriptive and still retain enough of a general framework to be comparatively useful. What we have in mind is a construct we call the "ideal self," which consists of a series of interrelated statements about the bases, structure, and functional implications of self-appraisal. This construct has already been described and applied to the analysis of one life history (Watson 1970), though the larger problem of interpretation and understanding was not addressed.

The notion of the ideal self assumes that in any given society a set of normative statements about ideal or proper behavior (personality functioning) is built into a wide range of diverse statuses. We are not talking about status prescriptions per se, nor the jural dimension of social action. Measuring up to the standards of the ideal self becomes a vital component in the way role behavior is articulated or phrased in meeting the demands of interpersonal situations. In Guajiro society, for example, certain rights and duties attach to the role of sororal nephew; they involve economic responsibilities to the maternal uncle as well as physical protection in various dangerous and threatening contexts. At the same time the nephew must phrase these responsibilities in a respectful, compliant, and unaggressive modality that we have identified as components or attributes of the Guajiro ideal self. Guajiros, in fact, reappraise significant role behavior in which they engage according to these self-standards and use the reactions of others, who judge them by these same standards, as a form of corrective feedback in modifying role performance. Discharging family responsibilities without doing so in the manner prescribed by the ideal self would be meaningless for a Guajiro, as well as socially disruptive in its consequences.

The model of the ideal self is one kind of explanation for behavior that arises out of our own tradition of scientific theorizing. To employ it as an explanation for behavior in an alien society is to impose it as a construct for understanding a particular set of data. Thus the ideal self is *etic* (i.e., an external construct) in relationship to the foreign body of data, and it is also an *entry category* for using the data as the model describes.

One advantage of using the ideal self is that it contains emic-type statements about native thought in its normative aspects along with etic-type or behavioral ones in the social action dimensions. In operationalizing the model, we actually proceed systematically from the purely emic to constructs that are principally etic. We begin with the ideal self, which consists of normative statements by native informants about proper behavior embodied in role performance. The anthropologist, ideally, is not making inferences in these operations; he is merely trying to describe a set of meanings or values appropriate to the subjective and cultural contexts he is working with. There is no reason to suppose that two different societies would have the same set of norms defining ideal personality; yet, from native statements, it may be reasonable to propose that different ideal selves in two different culture settings may be functionally equivalent in the sense that they are recognized by the people to constitute the basis for the individual's self-appraisal of his own socially relevant behavior. This aspect of the model might be referred to as the *normative*. Thus, it is relatively emic in its content and perhaps also in its understood functions.

We must then consider the cognitive dimension, or the psychological process of self-appraisal by which the individual, in a way meaningful to himself, draws upon the standards of the ideal self to evaluate his own behavior so that he can change it in more personally relevant, socially acceptable directions. This process too would seem to be fundamentally an emic phenomenon, although perhaps one more difficult to identify than the first because the individual is not always fully aware of his own thinking. Careful, systematic probing or analysis might uncover in the text of the life history statements regarding the extent to which the subject felt he was aware of the ideal self in appraising his behavior and how he thought he modified his behavior as a consequence. This dimension of our model might be called the *cognitive* dimension.

Finally, to what extent does the above-mentioned process impinge meaningfully on the sphere of social action or socially relevant behavior we call role (or role performance)? This operation might be described as the dynamic aspect of the normative and one that is cognitively mediated. Our notions of social action, which are embodied in such concepts as institutions and roles, are etic constructs by which we order alien sociocultural data, but they may not necessarily make sense to the actor, who may see and categorize the consequences of his activity very differently. However, since behavior is defined in terms of ideal expectations, perhaps we are not that far off in approaching the issue through the normative or, for that matter, through the ideal self.

If the social action consequences of the kind of self-appraisal we have talked about are meaningful to the actor in his categories of experience, and if they approximate the areas we have identified as roles, then it is possible to say provisionally that the model describes what it is intended to describe. The problematic element of this undertaking is to demonstrate that our constructs of social behavior (the various roles affected by the ideal self) cover the same units of experience in social context that the actor himself understands. For comparative and theoretical purposes, the exact roles emically meaningful to actors in different societies do not have to coincide (they may be different in number and quality); it is sufficient only that they (1) cover relevant actor-named and actor-identified social dimensions of experience, and (2) correspond to our significant role inventories for the different societies under study. This dimension of the model can be called the *behavioral*. Its comparative usefulness hinges on correcting the role entry categories by working them out against the cultural context until they assume equivalent emic significance.

The model of the ideal self can thus be diagramed into the orders of analysis and levels of operation shown in figure 2. The test of any method, of course, is whether or not it works. To find out if our formulations have any theoretical and methodological utility, we shall use the ideal self as an entry category in a brief comparative study of two life histories from two different cultures. We want to discover if the entry construct can be applied or worked out so that it demonstrates or explains the intended phenomena in a way that is culturally and subjectively meaningful to the subjects of the two life histories. If it does, we can take this as indicating that the construct represents a provisional synthesis of etic and emic features, that it is sensitive to the subjective features of individual lives in culture context but at the same time has enough of a framework to generate categories for meaningful cross-cultural comparisons.

Figure 2:
Model of the Ideal Self

Operations	Order	Mode
1. Statements about ideal self	Normative	Emic
2. Reported processes of self-appraisal against ideal	Cognitive	Emic
3. Modification of role entry categories against emically meaningful social activity units	Behavioral	Etic-Emic

The Ideal Self in Two Life Histories

To examine the ideal self we shall take the life history of Pedro Gonzalez (Watson 1970), a Guajiro Indian, and compare it with that of Don Talayesva (Simmons 1942), a Hopi Indian, from the standpoint of our construct, following the three steps of the model we have outlined above. We obviously cannot deal exhaustively with either 'life history in this exercise. All we can hope to do is to suggest the possibility of reconciling to some extent etic and emic approaches, the ideal self being one of perhaps many starting points.

The Normative Dimension

Pedro Gonzalez. The subject is an eighty-year-old Guajiro who related his life history on various occasions over a four-month period. He had once been rich and respected but at the time of the study was living out his final years as an unwanted hanger-on in his daughter's household. His life history account lends itself especially well to an understanding of the normative basis of Guajiro behavior because of the heavy emphasis he placed on rules and standards, and the manner in which he and others learned or did not learn how to pattern their behavior after the ideal. As a matter of fact, the concept of the ideal self, as we are using it here, grew directly out of the empirical investigation of this subject's own (emic) definitions of behavior.

His account is interspersed through and through with statements defining the kinds of proper behavior that are necessary, as he sees it, for adequate social performance. From an analysis of the subject's continuous reiteration of normative standards, we have identified certain behavioral modes that seem to constitute something of an ideal configuration against which behavior in a wide range of settings ought to be measured. This interlocking set of attributes most prominently features the qualities of respectfulness, compliance, responsibility, and unaggressiveness. The very translation of Pedro's thought into our own linguistic categories, of course, alters the original flavor of what he intended, and we must always bear this significant limitation in mind when an analyst claims to have "gotten into the other person's mind."

In talking about respect, Pedro evokes the strong and dominating image of his mother—a figure of great authority in this matrilineal society (see chapter 3). He tells us that he must respect his mother by not doing the things that would offend her, such as having sex in the same room with her or getting drunk in her presence. Showing respect also involves another component of the ideal self: compliance. By complying with his mother's rightful demands, he shows respect for her standards and her right to impose these standards on his behavior. In fact, he mentions obedience specifically in connection with not engaging in improper sexual behavior that would be disrespectful to his mother:

> *She never told me to make love to girls and I never did it in her presence.* (Watson 1970:29)

He stresses the importance of responsibility in contrasting his own behavior with that of his lazy, irresponsible brother. Assigned herding responsibilites in his youth, Pedro tried to follow orders systematically and assumed charge of watering and pasturing the animals while his father was away, which were demanding and time-consuming tasks. As Pedro comments:

> *A well brought-up boy offers to help his brother with herding. He is diligent, takes no notice of competitive enticements and knows what he is doing. He is interested only in his animals.* (Ibid.:21)

The brother refused to help and would run away and hide when he was faced with work. As it subsequently turned out, his brother's aberrant behavior was due to a supernaturally induced illness that altered his ability to think clearly and act sensibly and responsibly on the advice and counsel of others (ibid.:24–25).

The importance of unaggressiveness in the ideal self comes through in many different contexts. On one hand, it appears in the form of dutiful rationalizations for the idealized behavior in question. On the other hand, the subject evokes the feelings of horror inspired by the awareness of negative role models who behaved aggressively and thereby threatened the peace of society. At one point, as an example of how unaggressiveness was rationalized, Pedro states:

> *My mother did not like me quarreling or fighting with the children of other clans, and I was careful never to abuse the boys with whom I played. But there are many boys who are wicked, who play and who also fight. The reason why my mother prohibited me from fighting with other boys was because fighting cre-*

*ates conflict between the family of one and the family of another.
If somebody gets hurt then a damage suit is presented and there
is ill-feeling between the castas [lineages].* (Ibid.:44)

Pedro makes clear at several points that he was always peaceful and
unaggressive and desired only to be the friend of all.

Pedro cites one particularly terrifying picture of the unreasoningly
aggressive man, one of his powerful uncles, as a negative example:

*I remember that this uncle liked to make war with the other
castas. My uncle was a most terrible and violent person, who
was infamous for these qualities even among his kinsmen. Whenever he killed some innocent person, which was quite common,
his kinfolk admonished him for this dreadful act against society.
He would become angry at his kinfolk when he heard these
words of criticism.* (Ibid.:39–40)

After detailing some of his uncle's "crimes," Pedro recounts how he
left his uncle's household in fear after the uncle skinned a baby calf
alive in anger for nursing and taking the cow's milk:

*This experience made me so frightened I ran back home to my
mother and father. I did not understand why my uncle could do
such a terrible thing, taking the skin off a baby animal while it
was still alive.* (Ibid.:42)

These are just a few examples of normative statements that occur
again and again in the life history. They are not atypical examples.
They refer to rules whose complex implications define a significant
part of Pedro's recollected life experience.

Don Talayesva. This man is a Hopi Indian who was about fifty
when he related his life history to Leo Simmons. Although a man of
some apparent standing in his community, Don is nevertheless presented as a rather tortured person, deeply suspicious, and at odds with
many of the Hopi in his village of Oraibi.

Don's autobiography suggests convincingly that he accepted an
ideal self against which he consistently attempted to measure himself.
This ideal self was culturally embodied in the notion of following the
Hopi Sun Trail, the life path whose course reaffirmed the values of being Hopi, which was equivalent to being a good person. This Hopi
ideal self, although adumbrated in Don's earlier experiences, was first
communicated to him by his spirit guide when he "died" of pneumonia

and visited the Land of the Dead so that he might "know the right way
to live" (Simmons 1942:121). This event had great emotional impact
in his life.

A person who follows the Sun Trail, that is, one who reaffirms his
Hopi identity in thought and deed and who therefore cannot be *kahopi*
(un-Hopi) or a "two-heart" (witch), consistently exhibits behavior that
reflects three basic qualities. These standards of self-reference in
the Hopi Sun Trail are: (1) an attitude of carefulness, maintaining
an orderly relationship with the social, natural, and supernatural
worlds expressed in an idiom of respect and caution; (2) having "good
thoughts," which means assuming an attitude of cheerful optimism in
daily affairs and striving to screen out "bad thoughts" that would in-
jure the physical and spiritual well-being of others; and (3) peaceful-
ness and cooperation, which in a sense is the inevitable outgrowth of
living up to the first two rules. These traits, while they have their internalized expression in individuals, are functionally articulated with
prevailing ideas in Hopi culture—set in an uncertain environment
where successful sociocultural adaptation is an extremely precarious
affair—about the importance of ritually maintaining balance and a
state of inner purity toward nature and the supernatural.

As Don remembers it, his grandfather articulated some aspects of
the Hopi ideal to him when he was a child:

> *I was my grandfather's favorite. As soon as I was old enough to
> take advice, he taught me that it was a great disgrace to be
> called "kahopi" (not Hopi, not peaceable). He said, "My
> grandson, old people are important. They know a lot and don't
> lie. Listen to them, obey your parents, work hard, treat every-
> one right. Then people will say, 'That boy Chuka is a good
> child. Let's be kind to him.' If you do these things, you will live
> to be an old man yourself and pass away in sleep without pain.
> This is the trail that every good Hopi follows. Children who ig-
> nore these teachings don't live long." He told me that I was a
> boy after his own heart and could look into my life and see that I
> would be an important man, perhaps a leader of the people. . . .
> He advised me to keep bad thoughts out of my mind, to face the
> east, look to the bright side of life, and learn to show a shining
> face, even when unhappy. (Ibid.:51)*

Very early in life Don learned the significance of carefulness in connection with handling important resources such as water:

I also learned that water is as precious as food. Everybody appeared happy after a rain. We small boys rolled about naked in the mud puddles, doused each other with water, and built little irrigated gardens. In this way we used too much water from the little pond on the west side of the village where the women went to wash clothes and the men to water their stock. Our parents scolded us for wasting water and once my mother spanked me on account of my dirty shirt. During droughts we had strict rules for the use of water. Even small children were taught to be careful. (Ibid.:56)

These ideals, truly, run like strands throughout Don's lengthy narrative. And while the Hopi ideal self, as it emerges, is very different in content from Guajiro ideal behavior in some respects, in both cases the construct appears to have the same powerful normative importance for structuring the course of an individual's life.

The Cognitive Dimension

Pedro Gonzalez. We are interested here in whether the subject utilizes the ideal self in his life history as a subjectively defined basis of self-appraisal, that is, whether he measures personal failure as well as the failures of others against the standards inherent in the image of ideal behavior in order to correct his own shortcomings and the lapses of others. This process is essentially a dynamic and cognitive operation in which the subject judges and evaluates information according to sets of normative standards he has internalized into his thinking.

The narrative Pedro gives us is full of such acts of self-appraisal, which are cast in the form of either general conclusions about the value of proper behavior or a specific self-evalution following a particular personal failure. At one point Pedro assesses the generally negative consequences of failure to act responsibly in handling economic (and specifically, herding) duties:

Whenever I found a stray animal in the bush, I took it for myself, for I was interested, above all, in having many, many animals. This is always the concern of a young man who wants to be rich. Such a boy really takes care of his mother's animals. Many a little lamb becomes lost because the owner was lazy and did not have enough interest to watch his flocks while they were grazing. This is why a lamb or two, here and there, become lost. The guilty ones are the herdboys who are supposed to be caring for the animals, but who instead turn to play and idle games, like bathing in the lagoon, playing tops or marbles, shooting birds, and other useless pursuits. While the herdboys are busy with their games, the sheep or goats go off seeking another path. Ultimately, several of the little lambs are lost in the brush even though the majority of the flock is recovered. This happens because of the negligence of the herdboys who preferred to play games rather than discharge their responsibilities. When one sheep is missing he [the herdboy] knows immediately which one it is. . . . Until the herdboy finds his little sheep he does not return home . . . If he does not find the missing ewe during the day, he stays out searching until nine o'clock and then finally comes home, but he goes not to the rancheria to take his meal, but rather to the corral where the sheep are kept. Here he sits down and broods about his misfortune. (Ibid.:21–22)

In regard to the unaggressive aspect of the ideal self, Pedro appraised its negative significance by listening to his mother describe the consequences of aggressive behavior in others:

The advice my mother gave me was to love my friends and never fight with them, because the child who fights abuses the whole world and soon everybody refers to that child as "bad" and "ugly." The well-behaved child, however, is spoken of in terms of praise and respect. Sometimes when a good child needs money people will give it to him; but when a bad, aggressive child wants something he will not get it and people are angry that he should dare ask. When a good child comes to the rancheria, the people ask after his health and offer him food. (Ibid.:44)

The ideal of respect is also a basis for personal self-appraisal. This becomes clear at several points in the narrative. Shortly after describing how his mother beat his brother for molesting a girl and showing a lack of respect that could get the family into legal difficulties, Pedro measured his own behavior against the ideals of respect and obedience contained in his mother's injunctions. He realized how bad it was to disobey the mother and to do disrespectful things that would come to her attention:

I never did these sexual things around my mother. My mother did not realize what I was up to because I was a boy who never offended her to her face. I really respected her. I obeyed her when she told me to do something, and she never told me to make love to a girl. I never played around with girls in front of my mother. I always did this in the bush when nobody was there to see me. (Ibid.:29)

Pedro, according to his own account rarely fails to live up to the ideal self except in his sexual escapades and an occasional lapse in discharging his economic responsibilities, and he reaffirms throughout the course of his life history the relevance of the ideal self as a proper basis for self-appraisal and behavioral control. This commitment to the ideal is the outgrowth of observing others who have failed to measure up to cultural norms and of listening to parental advice and drawing the proper conclusions about acceptable behavior. Pedro's life history has a highly abstract and impersonal quality, but it still reveals the kinds of cognitive processes that are relevant to the study of the ideal self.

Don Talayesva. Since Don admits to falling short of the ideal more often than does Pedro, his life history throws greater light on the dynamic nature of how specific acts of self-appraisal are related to specific events in the life history.

After his initiation into the Katcina cult and his severe beating at the hands of the Katcinas to correct his unruly behavior, Don takes stock, perhaps, for the first time in his young life. The Hopi ideal now more than ever before seems to have the force and significance to change behavior:

I thought of flogging and the initiation as an important turning point in my life, and I felt ready at last to listen to my elders and to live right. (Simmons 1942:87)

Later at Sherman School in California Don begins to slide into white ways. He begins to get "careless" about the Hopi way of life, even challenging the two-hearts to kill him, a dreadful breach of the rule that one must maintain good thoughts and keep a cheerful face to the world. His "death experience" ensues shortly thereafter, and his spirit guide takes him to the Land of the Dead to teach him to "appreciate others, to be careful, wise, fair, and good" (ibid.:128). If he does not show that he has learned the lessons of life in his future conduct, his spirit guide warns him that he will "drop" him (i.e., Don will die).

Sometime after the initial, shocking impact of the death experience registers and Don has the opportunity to work through it, he assesses the implications of the event with considerable assurance and measured tranquility:

> *It was important that I had learned how to get along with the White man and earn money by helping them. But my death experience had taught me that I had a Hopi spirit guide whom I must follow if I wanted to live. I wanted to become a real Hopi again, to sing the good old Katcina songs and to feel free to make love without fear of sin and rawhide.* (Ibid.:134)

Returning to Hopiland, he is initiated into the proper adult ceremonial societies and becomes an authentic Hopi. He realizes how important the gods and spirits are in holding up the world. A Hopi must be careful to do the proper things and to hold good thoughts to please the gods. After the performance of the Soyal ceremony, a sun-renewal ritual, in which he takes part, he recalls:

> *I had learned a great lesson and now knew that the ceremonies handed down by our fathers means life and I regret that I ever joined the YMCA and decided to set myself against Christ once and for all.* (Ibid.:178)

Periodically Don recognizes that by being angry and thinking angry thoughts, by being careless in his ritual duties, he departs from the Hopi Sun Trail and jeopardizes his very existence. Perhaps one of the most serious crises is when his last child dies in infancy and he cries out that he is not going to have any more children. This is a *kahopi* act, for it shows a careless disrespect for life and reveals unreasoning pessimism and heavy, tragic thoughts. Almost immediately after this incident, his spirit guide (perhaps we should say his conscience) appears in a dream and admonishes him, telling him he has strayed from the Hopi Sun Trail. He advises him to brace up and get back on the Hopi Trail. If Don does not, the spirit guide will return to judge him. He is told to be "good" and "wise." Don awakes happy and uplifted, knowing the course of action he must follow (ibid.:290).

In Don's account we can distinguish the element of personal self-appraisal from normative statements per se. Often Don discusses normative behavior in an entirely impersonal manner, as statements of fact or definition. In other contexts, however, it is evident that Don is thinking over these values and their implications for his own immediate behavior as well as for his larger life plan. We see this as a complex and dynamic psychological process of which the subject is consciously aware to a great extent.

Thus far, we have tried to keep our analytical categories out of the evaluation process as much as possible. True, we have labeled two differing normative complexes the "ideal self," but we have tried to convey the emic distinctiveness and individuality of each. Each does indeed appear in the form of genuine statements about correct or ideal behavior, at least so far as we can tell, as we operate in the limiting context of our own language and cultural tradition, which structures our interpretation. In talking about normatively based self-appraisal as a cognitive process, we have tried to show only that the individuals in both life histories use very different, culturally specific ideals in basically the same way to appraise, judge, and correct their own behavior or their ideas about behavior, citing the rewards attendant on measuring up to the ideal and the punishments and dangers experienced for failure to do so.

The Behavioral Dimension

The most difficult task in our analysis is to make emically valid comparative statements about the behavioral implications of the ideal self in the lives of our two subjects. This task constitutes the most valid possible test for the construct. When we use an analytical category like significant role behavior, do we in fact have any assurance that this category corresponds to the subject's (culturally derived) conceptions of the social outcomes of his decisions? Perhaps a way of approaching the problem is first to determine whether a subject perceives that social boundaries in experience are influenced by the type of thinking we have identified as the ideal self. If so, then by comparing his situation with another's, we may be able to establish whether these social boundaries and categories, although enclosing different behavioral contents in the two settings, have at least equivalent social and psychological significance. That is, do these social categories, as perceived, apply in both instances to a significant range of relevant social behavior and psychological adaptation? We hope here only to sketch the main outlines of the problem.

Pedro Gonzalez. Pedro's account provides considerable evidence to suggest that the kinds of complex cognitive operations involved in self-appraisal lead to behavior in various social and economic areas that is more efficient, desirable, and adaptive in its social consequences. In fact, Pedro himself appears to connect directly the measurement of his behavior against the ideal and the ways in which he has actually modified his own behavior. Thus, the linkage is a mental (or emic) one rather than an inferential one based on a presumed relationship suggested by theory.

Early in his life history Pedro recalls his responsibilities as a herdboy. He recreates the emotional and psychological situation that follows from an act of negligence in which the herdboy through carelessness permitted a lamb to become lost. The hypothetical herdboy (undoubtedly Pedro himself) suffers acutely from appraising his behavior against the ideal self of responsibility, for he realizes the dreadful personal and social implications of his failure:

> *After he has finished his meal he goes slowly to his hammock and lies there feeling sad and defeated because he has lost the ewe. There is no pleasant dreaming for this boy.* (Watson 1970:22)

But this painful self-assessment leads the herdboy to become ever more conscientious in his behavior:

> *Before it was three o'clock in the morning he rises and starts out in search of the lost ewe. He may have to travel long distances. Along the way he asks everybody about the animal. When he finally finds the ewe he is very glad because now the creature is back in the fold where it belongs. He then returns home and the mother joyfully gives him the morning meal.* (Ibid.)

Such self-evaluation not only modified what we would call Pedro's economic role behavior (herding); it drastically improved his standing with his mother and hence affected his familial role as son and provider, for in Guajiro society, as we saw earlier in the Eskimo example, we cannot make a neat distinction between economic and kinship behavior.

We have already referred to Pedro's self-appraisal that sexual behavior showed a lack of respect and compliance in his relationship to his mother. Sexual behavior is a psychological event and properly belongs to the previous category. But in evoking a departure from the ideal and assessing the situation, Pedro also indicated how this assessment affected his behavior around his mother and channeled conduct into the approved normative modes.

Unfortunately, Pedro's autobiographical account is weighted heavily on the normative aspects and therefore we have relatively few opportunities to explore the critical sequence of self-appraisal and behavior modification that we hypothesize operates in the ideal self. In spite of this, the narrative mentions enough recurrent situations to suggest that the process does operate and that the affected areas of behavior correspond in part at least to certain of our role categories. We can, however, go only so far in using our descriptive role terms to lineate the subject's reality, because the subject's conceptions involve complex interweavings of thought and action that would have to be reduced to discrete categories in our own thinking. Moreover, his world also explores areas of behavior that are not even adequately labeled in our language. For example, Pedro assumes supervisory functions toward his uncle at funerals and other public events when the older man is drinking and has to be protected from the dangers of drunken behavior. This behavior, in turn, is linked to Guajiro notions of authority, danger, collective responsibility, and the unsocialized self that alcohol activates and that threatens the group. In any event, the behavior that Pedro corrects in himself does appear relevant within the context of the larger concerns and orientations of Guajiro culture and is therefore socially functional.

Don Talayesva. Unlike Pedro, Don by his own admission frequently breaks the rules and thus fails to live up to the Hopi ideal. We have a greater chance in his account to observe the mechanics of self-appraisal in relation to actual behavioral change. That there should be such marked differences in the two life histories may be due to several possible factors: the personalities of the two men; different cultural values having to do with revealing the self to strangers; and the circumstances of the data-collecting situation and how it appeared to the two subjects.

In Don's life there are a number of critical turning points, periods of personal self-searching that have serious implications for his subsequent behavior, as he sees it. The first critical occasion is Don's initiation into the Katcina cult. After he realizes its significance and how it was meant to set him on the proper path, his behavior improves markedly. As Don himself observes:

*I began to pay more attention to the stories of the old people and
learned much about the world, gods, and spirits. . . . Whenever
my father talked to me I kept my ears open, looked straight into
his eyes and said, "Owi (yes)." One of the first rules is to rise
early, run to the east edge of the measa and pray to the Sun God
to make me strong and brave and wise.* (Simmons 1942:87)

Don changes not just a limited sector of role behavior but rather his
general attitude toward the many roles and responsibilities he must assume. The obligation to be a "true" Hopi, perhaps the most important
of these, calls for a proper mental outlook and the willingness to exercise care and respect through the performance of the proper rituals and
ceremonies so essential to the society's survival.

A second crisis is his first encounter with the spirit guide, already
briefly alluded to. As Don sees it, his death journey and his reawaken-
ing to Hopi values follow serious infraction of his Hopi ideal identity
under the competing influences of white culture. Shortly after his recovery and newfound peace of mind, he returns to Hopiland with the
desire to perform the ceremonies, work hard, and reaffirm his traditional identity:

*As I watched the dances, I wanted to be a Katcina again and to
sing the old songs.* (Ibid.:137)

He works diligently at planting and herding, accepts his ritual responsibilities with gusto, carefully observes the sexual taboos connected
with ceremonial participation, and finally indicates his desire to be initiated into the Wowochin, an adult ceremonial society. His sense of
being in tune with the Hopi ideal is continually validated in a number
of cultural areas by adaptive behavior that conforms to the specifications of the ideal self.

At regular intervals in his subsequent life account, Don reacts with
depression and anger to adversities (e.g., the death of his children, impotence, illness), and his mind fills with bad thoughts. At these critical
moments the spirit guide returns to remind him of what he must do to
be a good person and get back on the right track of life. After these
experiences Don redoubles his efforts to be positive, careful, and
peaceable in his dealings with other Hopis and the supernaturals, although despite the best intentions he frequently finds himself getting
sidetracked and forgetting his own resolutions.

Don's "role" behavior, like Pedro's, is heavily tied to a complex network of kinship obligations. It is less fruitful to think of his "son" or "uncle" role than to consider his attitudes and behavior to particular classes of kinfolk and to culturally defined and recurrent, though changing, contexts of social activity. His ritual roles are embedded in this larger context. If there is any difference between Don and Pedro, it is that Pedro modified his behavior as a result of self-appraisal to conform to the specifications of what we would call economic and political responsibilities, secular in orientation and divorced from supernatural considerations; while Don evaluated his conduct more in terms of its implications for ceremonial and ritual duties involving a clearly recognized relationship to the supernatural world. Each sphere of emically real social behavior comprehends a series of interlocking roles that are of more or less equivalent significance to the individual in each culture setting. We feel that the major outlines of the "ideal self" model may be supported by the study of these two life histories from different cultures.

We hope that this little excursion offers at least some evidence for our contention that the comparative study of behavior can be accomplished with constructs that are emically sensitive to the subjective authenticity of life histories. Whether or not this model of the ideal self would hold up with an expanded number of cultures and individuals remains to be determined by those who are interested in pursuing this line of research. We suspect that the dimension of behavior modification, especially, may have to be refined and redefined far beyond what we have suggested, as it is worked out against the unique categories of different cultures, before it has the kind of conceptual clarity and power that would make it useful in comparative research and theory testing.

Conclusions

It is not entirely clear to us why the life history has been so neglected in anthropological research. Undeniably, as social scientists we are interested in investigating large-scale social processes where individuals considered in their own terms seem to have a very limited role. But the fact remains that there is a good deal of intracultural variation at the level of the local community, the household, and, of course, the individual himself (Pelto and Pelto 1975). By recreating their immediate behavioral situation through "private culture," individuals may cumulatively affect the larger culture (e.g., family, community); their impact in a smaller, more homogeneous society, at least, may be of considerable importance. So it is not just to understand the idiosyncracies of individual experience that we are studying life histories; we may also find that life histories offer us precise documentation about how individuals, in the process of changing their lives for themselves, also alter the environment for others and thus act as significant agents of social change.

Apart from adapting theory and other constructs to understand the subjectivity of particular life histories in different cultures, we might well want to reverse the process and start with the life history as a basis for constructing theories about the role of individual behavior in culture change and culture transmission. If we look carefully at the life history as a subjective document, we can see the individual's self-perceived impact on his social environment. By corroborating his statements with other versions, as in the family autobiography approach, we get some feeling for the dimensions, scope, and intensity of individual influence radiating outward to the family and from the family to the neighborhood and even to the larger society. Just where we must draw the line defining the outer limits of the individual's impact on society surely remains to be empirically investigated and cannot be dismissed or given a pat answer based on stereotyped assumptions about the individual's alleged role in society.

We hope our essay has suggested some new lines of inquiry utilizing the life history that might be fruitfully pursued in addition to those that have traditionally been done. The basic life history research orientations, both traditional and experimental, that we have either critiqued or advocated include (1) the study of personality, including psychodynamic, self-identity, and cognitive dimensions; (2) the study of the individual-society relationship with emphasis on socialization, role, and the impact of the individual on existing institutional processes; (3) the study of the individual's role and impact in micro and macro processes of social change; (4) the phenomenological aspects of subjective consciousness; and (5) the hermeneutical problem of reconciling "objective" frameworks of analysis (that is, our anthropological preconceptions embodied in theories and models) with the subjective properties of the life history document.

The last issue, as we see it, is in some respects the most crucial. Our approach to hermeneutics is not merely to use it as a vehicle to study phenomenological problems; we are also concerned with developing a dialectic metalanguage for bridging the gap and reconciling the difference between seemingly incompatible orders: the subjective and culture-specific, on the one hand, and the theoretical and comparative, on the other.

If we understand our own interpretive activities in using scientific models and theories, we exert some measure of control over what they can be made to accomplish, and we can modify them in light of alternative strategies and operations, thereby expanding our framework of interpretation and our range of insights. If we go back to the phenomena themselves with our minds comparatively free of prejudices and preunderstandings, we become aware of the limitations of our models and we can then correct our analytical and interpretive tools to make them more sensitive to the complex meaning of events in other cultures. We share the opinion of Geertz (1973a:5) that the study of cultural data is not so much the experimental, scientific search for law as it is the interpretive search for meaning.

However, the hermeneutical view of a single life history, while extremely valuable, may not necessarily be sufficient in our search for ever-elusive regularities and meanings in the individual-culture transaction. For the investigation of certain problems we need some preformulated research strategy involving the collection of many life histories from a single culture and the comparison of life histories from several or many different cultures. The systematic comparison of life histories, whether the comparison occurs in a structured framework, on a strictly idiographic basis, or in an emically modified etic framework, may well yield patterns and new relationships that can be used to test old theories or to generate new ones to explain the many-faceted nature of individual experience.

In the epistemological position we have adopted, the "social world" that we have created as an object apart from individuals must ultimately be regarded as a construct derived from the complex articulation and interplay of many life histories at a hypothetical point in time. The study of institutions is really the story of many individual lives recurrently intersecting in socially constructed activity that has both shared and endlessly varied individual meanings. Hence, the institutional, while seemingly abstract, is the expression of life histories, although the individual in relating his life does not usually relate "institutional participation" in any simple fashion, since for him life is experienced in what phenomenologists call "inner time," as ongoing continuity, so that sectors of relevant social experience are bound together in many-stranded networks into a single interconnected stream.

If we can take all social categories and constructs back to subjective experiential phenomena (Berger and Luckmann 1966), which is the raw data of individual lives, it is hard to understand why the life history genre has been so neglected in studies concerned with the epistemological bases of the social construction of reality. Perhaps researchers feel that this issue can best be understood at an abstract level, as various typifications that intersect with subjective minds. They may feel that although sociality is ultimately maintained by individuals, its essential nature does not require the study of individuals to illuminate.

We argue the contrary, that if we can learn properly to suspend our preconceptions, and if we look at the way individuals in their life histories actually maintain the construct of social existence as phenomenal realities, we may indeed learn that the subjective process undergirding society may be qualitatively different from the "typical" processes we had hitherto imagined. Individual lives may or may not confirm our suspicions about "typical" process. But in any event, the efforts we have advocated allow us to elaborate and intensify our understanding of the individual experiential foundation.

Bibliography

Aberle, David F.
1967   "The Psychosocial Analysis of a Hopi Life History." In
        Personalities and Cultures, edited by Robert Hunt, pp.
        79–138. New York: Natural History Press.

Agar, Michael
1980   "Hermeneutics in Anthropology: A Review Essay."*Ethos*
        8:253–272.

Allport, Gordon W.
1942   *The Use of Personal Documents in Psychological Science.*
        Social Science Research Council Bulletin 49. New York:
        The Council.
1965   *Letters from Jenny.* New York: Harcourt, Brace and
        World.

Anderson, Rufus
1825   *Memoir of Catherine Brown, a Christian Indian of the
        Cherokee Nation.* 2d ed. Boston: Crocker and Brewster.

Angrosino, Michael V.
1976   "The Use of Autobiography as 'Life History': The Case of
        Albert Gomes." *Ethos* 4:133–154.

Barnouw, Victor
1963   *Culture and Personality.* Homewood, Ill.: Dorsey Press.

Bauman, Zygmunt
1978   *Hermeneutics and Social Science.* New York: Columbia
        University Press.

Becker, Howard S.
1966   "Introduction." In *The Jack-Roller: A Delinquent Boy's
        Own Story*, by Clifford R. Shaw, pp. v–xviii. Chicago:
        University of Chicago Press.

Berger, Peter L., and Thomas Luckmann
1966   *The Social Construction of Reality: A Treatise on the
        Sociology of Knowledge.* New York: Doubleday

Berry, James
  1969   "On Cross-Cultural Comparability." *International Journal
          of Psychology* 4:119–129.

Bertaux, Daniel
  1981   "From the Life History Approach to the Transformation of
          Sociological Practice." In *Biography and Society: The Life
          History Approach in the Social Sciences*, edited by Daniel
          Bertaux, pp. 29–45. Beverly Hills, Calif.: Sage
          Publications.

Betti, Emilio
  1962   *Die Hermeneutik als allgemeine Methodik der
          Geisteswissenschaften.* Philosophie und Gedichte Serie.
          Tübingen: Mohr.

Binswanger, Ludwig
  1958   "The Case of Ellen West." In *Existence: A New Dimension
          in Psychiatry and Psychology*, edited by Rollo May, Ernest
          Angell, and Henri F. Ellenberger, pp.237–364. New
          York: Simon and Schuster.

Blumer, Herbert
  1939   *An Appraisal of Thomas and Znaniecki's The Polish
          Peasant in Europe and America.* Critiques of Research in
          the Social Sciences. New York: Social Science Research
          Council.

Boehm, Gottfried
  1978   "Einleitung. Die Hermeneutik und die Wissenschaften. Zur
          Bestimmung des Verhältnisses." In *Seminar: Die
          Hermeneutik und die Wissenschaften*, edited by
          Hans-Georg Gadamer and Gottfried Boehm, pp. 7–60.
          Frankfurt: Suhrkamp.

Bowes, Pratima
  1971   *Consciousness and Freedom: Three Views.* London:
          Methuen.

Brandes, Stanley
  1982   "Ethnographic Autobiographies in American
          Anthropology." In *Crisis in Anthropology: Views from*

Spring Hill, 1980, edited by E.A.Hoebel, Richard Currier, and Susan Kaiser, pp. 187–202. New York: Garland Publishing Co.

Brislin, Richard W., Stephen Bochner, and Walter J. Lonner, eds.
1975   *Cross Cultural Perspectives on Learning*. New York: Halsted Press.

Cicourel, Aaron
1964   *Method and Measurement in Sociology*. New York: Free Press.
1974   *Cognitive Sociology: Language and Meaning in Social Interaction*. New York: Free Press.

Cioffi, Frank
1971   "Freud and the Idea of a Pseudo-Science." In *Explanation in the Behavioral Sciences*, edited by Robert Borger and Frank Cioffi, pp. 471–515. New York: Cambridge University Press.

Colson, Elizabeth
1974   *Autobiographies of Three Pomo Women*. Archeological Research Facility. Department of Anthropology, University of California, Berkeley.

Coreth, Emerich
1969   *Grundfragen der Hermeneutik: Ein philosophischer Beitrag*. Freiburg: Herder Verlag.

Crapanzano, Vincent
1977   "The Life History in Anthropological Fieldwork." *Anthropology and Humanism Quarterly* 2(2–3):3–7.
1980   *Tuhami: Portrait of a Moroccan*. Chicago: University of Chicago Press.
1981   "Text, Transference, and Indexicality." *Ethos* 9:122–148.

Devereux, George G.
1969   *Reality and Dream: Psychotherapy of a Plains Indian*. New York: Doubleday, Anchor Books.

Dollard, John
[1935]   *Criteria for the Life History, with Analysis of Six Notable*
1949   *Documents*. New York: P. Smith.

Douglas, Jack and Jon Johnson, eds.
1977   *Existential Sociology*. New York: Cambridge University
        Press.

DuBois, Cora
1937   "Some Psychological Objectives and Techniques in
        Ethnography." *Journal of Social Psychology* 8:285–301.
1944   *The People of Alor: The Social-Psychological Study of an
        East Indian Island*. Minneapolis: University of Minnesota
        Press.

Dyk, Walter
1938   *Son of Old Man Hat: A Navaho Autobiography*. Recorded
        by Walter Dyk. New York: Harcourt, Brace.

Dyk, Walter, and Ruth Dyk
1980   *Left Handed: A Navaho Autobiography*. New York:
        Columbia University Press.

Earle, William A.
1972   *The Autobiographical Consciousness*. Chicago: Quadrangle
        Books.

Eckhardt, Kenneth W., and Norman B. Schwartz
1983   "A Book of Books: Langness and Frank on Life Histories."
        Reviews in Anthropology 10(1):73–78.

Erikson, Erik
1958   *Young Man Luther: A Study of Psychoanalysis and
        History*. New York: Norton.
1969   *Gandhi's Truth: On the Origins of Militant Nonviolence*.
        New York: Norton.
1975   *Life History and the Historical Moment*. New York:
        Norton.

Frank, Gelya
1979   "Finding the Common Denominator: A Phenomenological
        Critique of Life History Method." *Ethos* 7:68–94.

Freeman, James M.
1979   *Untouchable: An Indian Life History*. Stanford: Stanford
        University Press.

Freud, Sigmund
  1962   *Civilization and Its Discontents.* New York: Norton.
  1963   *Dora: An Analysis of a Case of Hysteria* (1905). Vol. 4 of
          Collected Papers, New York: MacMillan, Collier Books.

Gadamer, Hans-Georg
  1967   "Die Universalität des hermeneutischen Problems." In
          Kleine Schriften I. Philosophie, by Hans-Georg Gadamer.
          Tübingen: Mohr.
  1971   "Replik." In *Hermeneutik und Ideologiekritik*, edited by
          Jürgen Habermas, Dietrich Heinrich, and Jacob Taubes,
          pp. 283–317. Frankfurt: Suhrkamp.
  1972   *Wahrheit und Methode. Grundzüge einer philosophisichen
          Hermeneutik.* 3d exp. ed. Tübingen: Mohr.
  1975   *Truth and Method.* Translated from the 2d ed. (1965).
          New York: Seabury Press.
  1976a   *Philosophical Hermeneutics.* Translated and edited by
          David Linge. Berkeley: University of California Press.
  1976b   "Semantics and Hermeneutics." In *Philosophical
          Hermeneutics*, by Hans-Georg Gadamer, translated and
          edited by David Linge, pp. 82–94. Berkeley: University
          of California Press.

Garfinkel, Harold
  1967   *Studies in Ethnomethodology.* New York: Prentice-Hall.

Geertz, Clifford
  1973a   *The Interpretation of Cultures.* New York: Basic Books.
  1973b   "Thick Description: Toward an Interpretive Theory of
          Culture." In *The Interpretation of Cultures*, by Clifford
          Geertz, pp. 3–30. New York: Basic Books.
  1976   "From the Natives' Point of View: On the Nature of
          Anthropological Understanding." In *Meaning in Culture*,
          edited by Keith H. Basso and Henry A. Selby, pp.
          221–237. Albuquerque: University of New Mexico Press.

Gottschalk, Louis, Clyde Kluckhohn, and Robert Angell, eds.
  1945   *The Use of Personal Documents in History, Anthropology,
          and Sociology.* Social Science Research Council Bulletin
          53. New York: The Council.

Gusdorf, Georges
 1980 "Conditions and Limits of Autobiography." In
  Autobiography: Essays Theoretical and Cultural, edited by
  James Olney, pp. 28–48. Princeton: Princeton University
  Press.

Gutierrez de Pineda, Virginia
 1950 "Organización Social en la Guajira." *Revista del
  Etnológico Nacional* (Bogota) 2:1–257.

Hallowell, A. Irving
 1955 "The Self and Its Behavioral Environment." In *Culture
  and Experience*, by A. Irving Hallowell, pp. 75–110.
  Philadelphia: University of Pennsylvania Press.

Heidegger, Martin
 1962 *Being and Time*. Translated by John Macquarrie and
  Edward Robinson. New York: Harper and Row.

Hirsch, Eric D.
 1967 *Validity in Interpretation*. New Haven: Yale University
  Press.

Hughes, Charles C.
 1965 "The Life History in Cross-Cultural Psychiatric Research."
  In *Approaches to Cross-Cultural Psychiatry*, edited by
  Jane M. Murphy and Alexander H. Leighton, pp.
  285–328. Ithaca: Cornell University Press.
 1974 *Eskimo Boyhood: An Autobiography in Psychosocial
  Perspective*. Lexington: University of Kentucky Press.

Husserl, Edmund
 1931 *Ideas: General Introduction to Pure Phenomenology*.
  Translated by W. R. Boyce Gibson. New York:
  Macmillan.
 1960 *Cartesian Meditations: An Introduction to Phenomenology*.
  Translated by Dorion Cairns. The Hague: Martinus
  Nijhoff.
 1970 *The Crisis of European Sciences and Transcendental
  Phenomenology: An Introduction to Phenomenological
  Philosophy*. Translated by David Carr. Evanston, Ill.:
  Northwestern University Press.

Kaiser, Gerhard
1978   "Nachruf auf die Interpretation?" In *Seminar: Die Hermeneutik und die Wissenschaften*, edited by Hans-Georg Gadamer and Gottfried Boehm, pp. 426–443. Frankfurt: Suhrkamp.

Kardiner, Abram
1939   *The Individual and His Society.* New York: Columbia University Press.
1945   *The Psychological Frontiers of Society.* New York: Columbia University Press.

Kelley, Jane H.
1978   *Yaqui Women: Contemporary Life Histories.* Lincoln, Nebr.: University of Nebraska Press.

Kluckhohn, Clyde
1939   "Theoretical Basis for an Empirical Method of Studying the Acquisition of Culture by Individuals." *Man* 39:98–103.
1943   "Review of *Sun Chief: The Autobiography of a Hopi Indian*, edited by Leo W. Simmons." *American Anthropologist* 45:267–270.
1945   "The Personal Document in Anthropological Science." In *The Use of Personal Documents in History, Anthropology, and Sociology*, edited by Louis Gottschalk, Clyde Kluckhohn, and Robert Angell, pp. 78–173. Social Science Research Council Bulletin 53. New York: The Council.
1949   "Needed Refinements in the Biographical Approach." In *Culture and Personality*, edited by S. Sargent and M. Smith, pp. 75–92. New York: The Viking Fund.

Kroeber, Alfred L.
1908   "Ethnology of the Gros Ventre: War Experiences of Individuals." *Anthropological Papers of the American Museum of Natural History* 1(4):196–222.
[1922] "Introduction." In *American Indian Life*, edited by Elsie
1967   Clews Parsons, pp. 5–16. Lincoln, Nebr.: University of Nebraska Press.

Landes, Ruth
[1938]   *The Ojibwa Woman.* New York: AMS Press.
1969

Lang, Hermann
1978   "Sprache: Das Medium psychoanalytischer Therapie." In
         Seminar: Die Hermeneutik und die Wissenschaften, edited
         by Hans-Georg Gadamer and Gottfried Boehm, pp.
         252–271. Frankfurt: Suhrkamp.

Langer, Walter C.
1972   *The Mind of Adolph Hitler.* New York: Basic Books.

Langness, L. L.
1965   *The Life History in Anthropological Science.* New York:
         Holt, Rinehart and Winston.

Langness, L. L., and Gelya Frank
1981   *Lives: An Anthropological Approach to Biography.*
         Novato, Calif.: Chandler and Sharp.

Laurentin, Anne
1963   "Nzakara Women." In *Women of Tropical Africa,* edited
         by Denise Paulme, pp. 121–178. Berkeley: University of
         California Press.

Leighton, Alexander H., and Dorothea Leighton
1949   *Gregorio the Hand Trembler: A Psychobiological
         Personality of a Navaho Indian.* Papers of the Peabody
         Museum of American Archaeology and Ethnology, 40.
         Cambridge, Mass.: Peabody Museum.

Lewis, Oscar
1959   *Five Families: Mexican Case Studies in the Culture of
         Poverty.* New York: Basic Books.
1961   *The Children of Sanchez: Autobiography of a Mexican
         Family.* New York: Random House.
1964   *Pedro Martinez: A Mexican Peasant and His Family.* New
         York: Random House.
1966   *La Vida: A Puerto Rican Family in the Culture of
         Poverty—San Juan and New York.* New York: Random
         House.
1970   "An Anthropological Approach to Family Studies." In

Anthropological Essays, by Oscar Lewis, pp. 81–89. New York: Random House.

Linderman, Frank B.
[1932] *Pretty Shield: Medicine Woman of the Crow*. Originally
1972   published as *Red Mother*. New York: John Day.

Little, Kenneth
1980   "Explanation and Individual Lives: A Reconsideration of Life Writing in Anthropology." *Dialectical Anthropology* 5:215–226.

Lurie, Nancy O.
1961   *Mountain Wolf Woman, Sister of Crashing Thunder: The Autobiography of a Winnebago Indian*. Ann Arbor: University of Michigan Press.

Mandelbaum, David H.
1973   "The Study of Life History: Gandhi." *Current Anthropology* 14:177–206.

Marett, R. R.
1934   Review of *The Method and Theory of Ethnology*, by Paul Radin. *American Anthropologist* 36:116–118.

Merleau-Ponty, Maurice
1962   *Phenomenology of Perception*. Translated by Colin Smith. London: Routledge and Kegan Paul.

Miller, Ann, and Peter Stephenson
1980   "Jakob Hutter: An Interpretation of the Individual Man and His People." *Ethos* 8:229–252.

Mintz, Sidney W.
1979   "The Anthropological Interview and the Life History." In *The Oral History Review 1979*, pp. 18–26. Oral History Association.

Moises, Rosalio, Jane Holden Kelley, and William C. Holden
1971   *A Yaqui Life: The Personal Chronicle of a Yaqui Indian*. Lincoln, Nebr.: University of Nebraska Press.

Myerhoff, Barbara
1978   *Number Our Days*. New York: Dutton.
1982   "Life History among the Elderly: Performance, Visibility,

and Re-Membering." In *A Crack in the Mirror: Reflexive Perspectives in Anthropology*, edited by Jay Ruby, pp. 99–117. Philadelphia: University of Pennsylvania Press.

Myerhoff, Barbara, and Jay Ruby
1982   "Introduction." In *A Crack in the Mirror: Reflexive Perspectives in Anthropology*, edited by Jay Ruby, pp. 1–35. Philadelphia: University of Pennsylvania Press.

Natanson, Maurice
1966   "Introduction." In *Essays in Phenomenology*, edited by Maurice Natanson, pp. 1–22. The Hague: Martinus Nijhoff.
1970   *The Journeying Self: A Study in Philosophy and Social Role*. Reading, Mass.: Addison-Wesley.
1973   *Edmund Husserl: Philosopher of Infinite Tasks*. Evanston, Ill.: Northwestern University Press.

Palmer, Richard
1969   *Hermeneutics: Interpretation Theory in Schleiermacher, Dilthey, Heidegger and Gadamer*. Evanston, Ill.: Northwestern University Press.

Parsons, Elsie Clews, ed.
[1922]   *American Indian Life*. Lincoln, Nebr.: University of
1967   Nebraska Press.

Parsons, Talcott
1964   *Social Structure and Personality*. New York: Free Press.

Paulme, Denise
1963   "Introduction." In *Women of Tropical Africa*, edited by Denise Paulme, pp. 1–16. Berkeley: University of California Press.

Pelto, Pertti, and Gretel Pelto
1975   "Intra-Cultural Diversity: Some Theoretical Issues." *American Ethnologist* 2:1–18.

Plummer, Ken
1983   *Documents of Life: An Introduction to the Problems and Literature of a Humanistic Method*. Contemporary Social Science Research Series. London: George Allen and Unwin.

Price-Williams, Douglass
1974 "Psychological Experiment and Anthropology: The Problem of Categories." *Ethos* 2:95–114.
1975 *Explorations in Cross-Cultural Psychology.* San Francisco: Chandler and Sharp.

Radin, Paul
1913 "Personal Reminiscences of a Winnebago Indian." *Journal of American Folklore* 26:293–318.
1920 "The Autobiography of a Winnebago Indian." *University of California Publications in American Archeology and Ethnology* 16:381–473.
1926 *Crashing Thunder: The Autobiography of an American Indian.* New York: Appleton.
1933 *The Method and Theory of Ethnology: An Essay in Criticism.* New York: McGraw-Hill.

Ricoeur, Paul
1970 *Freud and Philosophy: An Essay on Interpretation.* Translated by Denis Savage. New Haven: Yale University Press.
1974a *The Conflict of Interpretations: Essays in Hermeneutics.* Edited by Don Ihde. Evanston, Ill.: Northwestern University Press.
1974b "Existence and Hermeneutics." In *The Conflict of Interpretations*, by Paul Ricoeur, edited by Don Ihde, pp. 3–24. Evanston, Ill.: Northwestern University Press.
1974c "A Philosophical Interpretation of Freud." In *The Conflict of Interpretations*, by Paul Ricoeur, edited by Don Ihde, pp. 160–176. Evanston, Ill.: Northwestern University Press.
1974d "The Hermeneutics of Symbols and Philosophical Reflection: I." In *The Conflict of Interpretations*, by Paul Ricoeur, edited by Don Ihde, pp. 287–314. Evanston, Ill.: Northwestern University Press.
1979 "The Model of the Text: Meaningful Action Considered As a Text." In *Interpretive Social Science: A Reader*, edited by Paul Rabinow and William M. Sullivan, pp. 73–101. Berkeley: University of California Press.

Rogers, Carl
1951 *Client-Centered Therapy.* New York: Houghton-Mifflin.

Rosaldo, Renato
    1976   "The Story of Tukbaw: 'They Listen As He Orates.'" In
            The Biographical Process, edited by Frank Reynolds and
            Donald Capps, pp. 121–152. The Hague: Mouton.

Ruby, Jay, ed.
    1982   *A Crack in the Mirror: Reflexive Perspectives in
            Anthropology.* Philadelphia: University of Pennsylvania
            Press.

Runyan, William McKinley
    1982   *Life Histories and Psychobiography: Explorations in
            Theory and Method.* New York: Oxford University Press.

Sachs, Wulf
    1947   *Black Hamlet.* Boston: Little-Brown.

Sapir, Edward
    [1922] "Sayach'apis, a Nootka Trader." In *American Indian Life*,
    1967   edited by Elsie Clews Parsons, pp. 297–323. Lincoln,
            Nebr.: University of Nebraska Press.
    1932   "Cultural Anthropology and Psychiatry." *Journal of
            Abnormal and Social Psychology* 27:229–242.
    1934   "The Emergence of the Concept of Personality in a Study
            of Culture." *Journal of Social Psychology* 5:408–415.
    1938a   "Why Cultural Anthropology Needs the Psychiatrist."
            Psychiatry 1:7–12.
    1938b   "Introduction." In *Son of Old Man Hat: A Navaho
            Autobiography*, recorded by Walter Dyk, pp. v–x. New
            York: Harcourt, Brace.

Lady Sarashina (Sugarawa Takasue No Musume)
    1971   *As I Crossed a Bridge of Dreams: Recollections of a
            Woman in Eleventh Century Japan.* Translated by Ivan
            Morris. New York: Dial Press.

Sartre, Jean-Paul
    1947   *The Age of Reason.* New York: Alfred A. Knopf.
    1956   *Being and Nothingness.* Translated by Hazel Barnes. New
            York: Philosophical Library.

Schleiermacher, Friedrich
    1967   "Hermeneutik." In *Werke*, edited by Friedrich Lücke,

reprint of 1928 edition, edited by Otto Braun and Johannes
Bauer, 4:137–206. Aalen.

Schutz, Alfred
1967a *The Phenomenology of the Social World.* Translated by
George Walsh and Frederick Lehnert. Evanston, Ill.:
Northwestern University Press.
1967b *Collected Papers, 1: The Problem of Social Reality,* edited
by Maurice Natanson. The Hague: Martinus Nijhoff.
1970 *On Phenomenology and Social Relations.* Edited by
Helmut Wagner. Chicago: University of Chicago Press.

Schwartz, Norman B.
1977 *A Milpero of Petén, Guatemala: Autobiography and
Cultural Analysis.* University of Delaware Latin American
Studies Program. Occasional Papers and Monographs, no.
2.

Sexton, James, ed.
1981 *Son of Tecún Umán: A Maya Indian Tells His Life Story.*
Tucson: University of Arizona Press.

Shostak, Marjorie
1981 *Nisa: The Life and Words of a Kung Woman.* Cambridge:
Harvard University Press.

Simmons, Leo, ed.
1942 *Sun Chief: The Autobiography of a Hopi Indian.* New
Haven: Yale University Press.

Smith, Mary F.
1964 *Baba of Karo, a Woman of the Moslem Hausa.* New York:
Praeger.

Smith, M. G.
1964 "Introduction." In *Baba of Karo, a Woman of the Moslem
Hausa,* by Mary F. Smith, pp. 11–34. New York: Praeger.

Spindler, Louise S.
1962 *Menomini Women and Culture Change.* Memoirs of the
American Anthropological Association, no. 91. Menahasa,
Wis.: The Association.

Spiro, Melford E.
  1961   "Social Systems, Personality and Functional Analysis." In
          Studying Personality Cross-Culturally, edited by Bert
          Kaplan, pp. 93–128. New York: Harper and Row.

Spradley, James P., ed.
  1969   *Guests Never Leave Hungry: The Autobiography of James
          Sewid, A Kwakiutl Indian.* New Haven: Yale University
          Press.

Strathern, Marilyn
  1972   *Women in Between: Female Roles in a Male World: Mount
          Hagen, New Guinea.* New York: Seminar Press.

Thomas, Evan A.
  1978   "Herberg Blumer's Critique of *The Polish Peasant*: A Post-
          Mortem of the Life History Approach in Sociology."
          Journal of the History of the Behavioral Sciences
          14:124–131.

Thomas, William I., and Florian Znaniecki
  [1920] *The Polish Peasant in Europe and America.* 2 vols. New
  1927   York: Alfred A. Knopf.

Triandis, Harry C.
  1972   *The Analysis of Subjective Culture.* New York: John Wiley
          and Sons.

Underhill, Ruth M.
  1936   *The Autobiography of a Papago Woman.* Memoirs of the
          American Anthropological Association, no. 46. Menasha,
          Wis.: The Association.
  1938   *Singing for Power: The Song Magic of the Papago Indians
          of Southern Arizona.* Berkeley: University of California
          Press.

Wagner, Helmut R.
  1970   "Introduction." In *On Phenomenology and Social
          Relations: Essays by Alfred Schutz*, edited by Helmut R.
          Wagner, pp. 1–50. Chicago: University of Chicago Press.

Wallace, Anthony F. C.
  1968   "Anthropological Contributions to the Theory of
          Personality." In *The Study of Personality: An*

Interdisciplinary Appraisal, edited by Edward Norbeck, Douglass Price-Williams, and William McCord, pp. 41–53. New York: Holt, Rinehart and Winston.

1969   *The Death and Rebirth of the Seneca.* New York: Random House.

1970   *Culture and Personality.* 2d ed. New York: Random House.

Washburne, Heluiz Chandler, and Anauta
1940   *Land of the Good Shadows: The Life Story of Anauta, an Eskimo Woman.* New York: John Day.

Watson, Lawrence C.
1970   *Self and Ideal in a Guajiro Life History.* Acta Ethnologica et Linguistica no. 21, Series Americana no. 5. Vienna: Stiglmayr.

1974   "Defense Mechanisms in Guajiro Personality and Culture." *Journal of Anthropological Research* 30:17–34.

1976a   "Understanding a Life History As a Subjective Document: Hermeneutical and Phenomenological Perspectives." *Ethos* 4:95–131.

1976b   "The Education of the Cacique in Guajiro Society and Its Functional Implications." In *Enculturation in Latin America: An Anthology*, edited by Johannes Wilbert, pp. 289–302. Los Angeles: Latin American Center, University of California.

1978   "The Study of Personality and the Study of Individuals: Two Approaches, Two Types of Explanation." *Ethos* 6:3–21.

1982   *Conflicto e Identidad en una Familia Urbana Guajira.* Caracas: Universidad Catolica Andres Bello.

1983   "Second Thoughts on Oscar Lewis's Family Autobiography." *Anthropology and Humanism Quarterly* 8(1):2–7.

Watson-Franke, Maria-Barbara
1972   "Women's Studies." *Bulletin of the International Committee on Urgent Anthropological and Ethnological Research* 14:29–36.

1974   "A Woman's Profession in Guajiro Culture: Weaving." *Antropológica* 37:24–40.

1975   "Guajiro Schamanen (Kolumbien und Venezuela)."
          Anthropos 70:194–207.
1976a   "To Learn for Tomorrow: Enculturation of Girls and Its
          Social Importance among the Gaujiro of Venezuela." In
          Enculturation in Latin America: An Anthology, edited by
          Johannes Wilbert, pp. 191–211. Los Angeles: Latin
          American Center, University of California.
1976b   "Social Pawns or Social Powers? The Position of Guajiro
          Women." *Anthroplógica* 45:19–39.

Watson-Franke, Maria-Barbara, and Lawrence C. Watson
1975   "Understanding in Anthropology: A Philosophical
          Reminder." *Current Anthropology* 16:247–262.

White, Robert W.
1973   *Lives in Progress*. 3d ed. New York: Holt, Rinehart and
          Winston.

Winch, Peter
1964   "Understanding a Primitive Society." *American
          Philosophical Quarterly* 1:307–324.

Wittgenstein, Ludwig
1968   *Philosophical Investigations*. Translated by G. E. M.
          Anscombe. Oxford: Basil Blackwell.

Index

Aberle, David F., 155–158
Abui, 119
Adaptation, 99–100, 123; bicultural, 150–154; neurotic, 121–134
Agar, Michael, 13
Aggression, 192–193, 194, 196
Alaulaa, 70
Allport, Gordon W., 9, 30, 125
Alor, people of (life histories), 99–100, 118–134; cultural context, 122–134; life-history construction, 118–120; phenomenological attitude, 121, 123–124, 126, 128–134; preunderstanding of researcher, 120–122, 124–125, 127–134; relationship to ethnographer, 119–120, 125–128
Anauta (life history), 167–169
Angrosino, Michael V., 15
Author. *See* Ethnographer
Autobiography, 2, 45, 49n, 62, 163

Baba (life history), 164–165
Barnouw, Victor, 10
Bauman, Zygmunt, 43n
Becker, Howard S., 30
Behavioral dimension, 189–190, 199–203
Being-in-itself/being-for-itself, 36
Bertaux, Daniel, 12–13
Betti, Emilio, 39
Bicultural adaptation, 150–154
Biography, 3, 101, 112
Blumer, Herbert, 9
Brandes, Stanley, 15

Cacique, 70
Categories of interpretation, 59–65; choices, 64–65; cognition, 62–63; conflicts and doubts, 64; dialectical relationship, 61; individual-sociocultural relationship, 59–60; life-history construction, 60; phenomenological attitude, 60, 61–62; preunderstanding of researcher, 60–61; self-identity, 63–64; sociocultural context, 59
Chavafambira, John (life history), 112–117; cultural context, 114–116; dialectical relationship, 112–113, 115–117; life-history construction, 112–113; preunderstanding of researcher, 116–117; self-identity, 114–116
Choice. *See* Freedom and choice
Chona (life history), 176–184; conflicts, 177–183; male and female roles, 177–184; preunderstanding of researcher, 176, 182
Cioffi, Frank, 108, 111
Cognition, 62–63, 110–111
Cognitive dimension, 189, 195–199
Colson, Elizabeth: *Autobiographies of Three Pomo Women*, 166
Conflicts and doubts, 64, 88–89, 92–93, 177–183
Consciousness: existential, 36–38; unity of, 65, 142–145, 149, 151–152
Consciousness, philosophy of. *See* Phenomenology
Conversation, 41–43
Coreth, Emerich, 40n
Crapanzano, Vincent, 12, 101; *Tuhami: Portrait of a Moroccan*, 14, 50–57
Crow Indian culture, 165–166
Crystals, 178–180, 182–183
Cultural context, 59–60, 66–71, 80–81, 92, 108, 112–117, 122–134, 174–175
Culture conflict, 150–154